Identifying Marks

Identifying Marks

Race, Gender, and

the Marked Body

in Nineteenth-Century

America

JENNIFER PUTZI

The University of Georgia Press · Athens and London

© 2006 by the University of Georgia Press

Athens, Georgia 30602

All rights reserved

Set in Minion by Bookcomp, Inc.

Printed and bound by Thomson-Shore

The paper in this book meets the guidelines for

permanence and durability of the Committee on

Production Guidelines for Book Longevity of the

Council on Library Resources.

Printed in the United States of America

10   09   08   07   06   C   5   4   3   2   1

Library of Congress Cataloging-in-Publication Data

Putzi, Jennifer.

   Identifying marks : race, gender, and the
marked body in nineteenth-century America /
Jennifer Putzi.

      p.   cm.

   Includes bibliographical references and index.

   ISBN-13: 978-0-8203-2812-6 (alk. paper)

   ISBN-10: 0-8203-2812-x (alk. paper)

   1. American literature—19th century—History and
criticism.   2. Body, Human, in literature.
3. Branding (Punishment)—United States.
4. Tattooing—United States.   5. Sex role in
literature.   6. Race in literature.   I. Title.

PS217.B63P88 2006

810.9'3561—dc22   2005030335

British Library Cataloging-in-Publication Data available

For my mother, Judy Westerman

CONTENTS

ILLUSTRATIONS

ACKNOWLEDGMENTS

This book has been years in the making and a number of very special people have contributed to its growth—even if they weren't always aware of having done so. For their lifelong love and support in whatever I've chosen to do, I thank Kathy McKinnon, Ray Putzi, Debbie Tossas, Jeff Putzi, Stephanie Barnes, and Kate Kendrick. Although he isn't here to see this book, I owe Raymond Putzi my love and gratitude as well; if he hadn't been willing to sacrifice so much in order for his children to succeed, I never would have even imagined writing a book. I also want to thank the many professors who have taught and encouraged me in college and graduate school. At Augustana College, Nancy Huse and Roald Tweet nurtured (and humored) my love of nineteenth-century American literature. At the University of Nebraska–Lincoln, Bob Bergstrom and Maureen Honey did the same, pushing me to refine my thinking and writing about texts. I was incredibly fortunate at UNL to be a part of a cohort of graduate students who supported one another at every step of the long and arduous way—coursework, comps, dissertations, job market, and so on. For their friendship and advice, I thank Heidi Jacobs, Tami Davidson, Lydia Kualapai, Robin Miskolcze, Brett Barney, and James Cox. For suggestions and help here and there along the way, I am grateful to Margot Mifflin, Zabelle Stodola, Dawn Keetley, Melanie Dawson, and Liz Barnes. I would also like to thank Nancy Grayson, my editor at the University of Georgia Press, and the anonymous readers who gave me such valuable feedback on this manuscript.

For material support during the writing of this book, I thank the University of Nebraska and the Woodrow Wilson Foundation. Pieces of this book have been published in the following journals: part of chapter 1 in *Western American Literature*; part of chapter 3 in *Legacy: A Journal of American Women Writers* (published by the University of Nebraska Press); part of chapter 4 in *Studies in American Fiction*; and part of chapter 5 was published in *College Literature*. I thank the anonymous readers at these journals for their incredibly helpful suggestions for revision.

Three people deserve to be singled out for their contributions to this manuscript and to my life. Sharon M. Harris has been my mentor and friend for twelve years now, and I cannot thank her enough for all she has done for me. I am a better scholar, teacher, and person because of her. I can say the same of Simon Joyce, my partner in everything I do. He will be embarrassed when he reads this, but I can't think of a more appropriate place to tell him how much I love and appreciate him. His sharp intellect and endless patience have certainly made this a better book. Finally, Judy Westerman, my mother, has given me unconditional love and support for thirty-five years, and I hope I have given her some of the same for at least part of that time. She taught me to love books, for which I am eternally grateful, and showed me by example that it is possible to work hard in order to get what you want. She is a constant inspiration, and this book is dedicated to her.

Introduction

"Carved in Flesh"

Two of the most visually striking figures in nineteenth-century American literature are Nathaniel Hawthorne's Hester Prynne and Herman Melville's Queequeg. Both stand out primarily for their marked bodies, for the ways in which their personal and communal histories are, in one way or another, physically inscribed on them. The scarlet *A* on Hester's bosom, for example, signifies her transgression of the laws of the Puritan fathers and is intended to be a reminder of the wages of sin. Hester's marked body thus functions as her personal punishment yet also as a threat to others who may be tempted to follow her adulterous example; as such, the letter is part of a detailed system of corporeal discipline integral to the Puritan sense of order and community. Queequeg's tattoos are similar in that they are a reflection of the Polynesian society in which he was born and had lived prior to shipping out as a "harpooneer." As the narrator of *Moby-Dick* explains, they are "the work of a departed prophet and seer of his island, who, by those hieroglyphic marks, had written out on his body a complete theory of the heavens and the earth, and a mystical treatise on the art of attaining truth" (366). Despite the narrator's claim that Queequeg cannot read his tattoos "though his own live heart beat against them," they remain a most intimate link to his native culture (367). In spite of the notable differences between them, Hester and Queequeg can both be said to embody culturally located systems of values and beliefs regarding human behavior and the position of the individual within the larger community. They carry these marks with them whether they remain within that community or venture outside its geographical or ideological parameters.

Although Hester and Queequeg receive their marks within very different cultures, historically and geographically (respectively) distant from the nineteenth-century American society in which they were produced and initially (re)presented to the reading public, their marks function similarly to highlight the ways in which the bodies of these characters are always already marked by gender and race. It is possible, one might argue, to see the scarlet letter and the tattoo as superfluous, as mere reinforcements of the difference already inscribed onto the

1

gendered or racial body by either nature or culture. Yet as Peter Stallybrass and Allon White claim, "[t]he body is neither a purely natural given nor is it merely a textual metaphor, it is a privileged operator for the transcoding of these other areas" (192). The mark may be intended to reinforce difference, yet as I suggest throughout this book, it also calls the "naturalness" of difference into question, thereby reinforcing the importance of the kinds of social or cultural phenomena that I examine here: racism, domestic violence, slavery and captivity.[1] The mark clearly requires a reading, an interpretation of the "transcoding" work it has done.

In *Identifying Marks*, I use the marked body to theorize the borderline between the biological and the cultural (even, perhaps, to question the existence of such extremes) in nineteenth-century America, "transcoding" tattoos and scars within the larger paradigm suggested by Stallybrass and White. Theories of the grotesque that focus on excessive corporeal deviations from the norm are central to my approach. As Mikhail Bakhtin, Susan Stewart, Mary Russo, and others have pointed out, the grotesque body stands in opposition to the classical body. While the classical body is contained and closed off, the grotesque body is open to penetration, to violation, and, I would argue, to the mark. Theoretically, the grotesque body is subject to the "conquering gaze" of the unmarked; as Donna Haraway explains, "This is the gaze that mythically inscribes all the marked bodies, that makes the unmarked category claim the power to see and not be seen, to represent while escaping representation" (283). Yet I propose that the tattooed or scarred body marks the precise location at which the cultural status quo (or the classical body) can be called into question. Physically and ideologically, the tattoo and the scar both sustain *and* disrupt the "conquering gaze" of the classical male body. *Identifying Marks* focuses primarily on the bodies of men of color and women, both white and of color—bodies, in other words, that were not thought to signify personhood in the nineteenth century and were, therefore, by their very nature grotesque. Yet the underlying assumption of this study is that white male bodies are *not*, in fact, unmarked; rather, the white male attempts to escape or conceal his own marked body by marking another, by *making an other* out of a noncitizen, a nonperson. As I discuss in the following chapters, although the white male body functions culturally as the norm, not all writers accept that norm as their own. The kinds of marks considered here make manifest the body's "transcoding" of nature and culture, biology and the social, raising issues of agency and power that may otherwise be suppressed and ignored. The tattoo and the scar, I suggest, expose the inner workings of the status quo as well as the functioning of the grotesque.

[In the context of nineteenth-century American literature and culture, it is important to understand that the mark indicates an action, a situation in which the body is physically inscribed, usually through the agency of another individual. Queequeg, for example, is marked by a Polynesian tattoo artist. His *choice* to be marked is clearly important, as it is connected to his racial and tribal identity; his tattoos are an important link to the fictional Kokovoko, which he has left behind in order to satisfy his curiosity regarding the wider world. Hester Prynne, on the other hand, does not choose her mark; no matter what adjustments she makes to it, no matter how it is regarded by others in *The Scarlet Letter*, the mark is originally (and at various times throughout the novel) an imposition on her body. This difference between Hester and Queequeg is crucial to any understanding or comparison of their marked bodies. This is not to suggest, however, that Hester Prynne is completely without power; to do so denies the subversive critical potential of the grotesque body. While Hester is compelled to acknowledge the power of the Puritan magistrates to inflict the scarlet *A* on her bosom, for example, she denies their right or competency to remove it and therefore unmark her. "It lies not in the pleasure of the magistrates to take off this badge," she tells Roger Chillingworth when he informs her that the magistrates are discussing the removal of the letter. "Were I worthy to be quit of it, it would fall away of its own nature, or be transformed into something that should speak a different purport" (169).[2]

Hester's response to Chillingworth highlights the two aspects of the marked body that concern me throughout *Identifying Marks*: first, the response of the marked individual to the mark itself; and second, the reading and interpretation of the mark by others. As the following chapters reveal, these two aspects are distinct yet interconnected in the literary and cultural discourse of the marked body. Victoria Pitts, author of *In the Flesh: The Cultural Politics of Body Modification*, explains this quite succinctly: "When bodies are understood as social and political—as inscribed by and lived within power relations—anomalous body modifications do not appear as inherently unnatural or pathological, but they also don't illustrate that individuals can freely or limitlessly shape their own bodies and identities. Rather, body projects suggest how individuals and groups negotiate the relationships between identity, culture, and their own bodies" (35). While my theoretical approach is similar to that of Pitts, her focus on the "body projects" of late-twentieth-century individuals allows for an agency in regard to the body that few nineteenth-century Americans could have experienced, particularly those already "marked" by gender, race, class, disability, or any "othering" form of identity. Sailors of the period perhaps saw their accumulation of tattoos as a "project"—a collection of souvenirs from a series of voyages across the globe. Yet as Simon P. Newman's study of early American seafarers reveals, such tattoos are indelible indicators of factors such as a sailor's religion, class position, and familial relationships. A sailor's "choice" to mark his own body must be considered within a cultural context that throughout the nineteenth century made the tattoo an accepted, perhaps even expected, modification for men who made their living from the sea.

For the most part, the mark was something to be resisted in the nineteenth century, as it carried along with it a necessary renegotiation of the self and a vulnerability to observation and interpretation by others. Yet this lack of agency in the initial acquisition of the mark may not, in fact, negate the usefulness of the term "body project," particularly the way in which it forces us to think about the body as a work in progress, a text that is repeatedly inscribed and interpreted by the self and others throughout one's lifetime. In the sense that a "body project" is, in the words of Joan Jacobs Brumberg, "a way to visibly announce who you are to the world," the intersubjective mediation of the nineteenth-century forcibly marked body can be considered a project with immense cultural significance (97). It is, therefore, this type of marked body—and these questions of agency, power, and identity—that are the focus of *Identifying Marks*. While neither Queequeg nor Hester Prynne represents the exact type of figure examined throughout the rest of this study, Queequeg's indigenous, freely chosen tattoos are less intriguing to me than Hester's forcible mark, which represents the complex relationship between individual agency and cultural discipline, a relationship that is literally inscribed on and worked out through Hester's body. This is not to say that these marks are unrelated; in fact, as discussed in the first chapter, any understanding of the marked body in nineteenth-century America must begin with the tattooed bodies of indigenous men who were brought to the Western world and displayed to white audiences. Although much more scholarship is needed to illuminate the politics of such performances in both Great Britain and the United States, I am narrowing my own study of the forcibly marked body to those individuals for whom the mark is not welcome and is, in fact, a symbol of their cultural and political subordination and, perhaps, rebellion.

With its awareness of self and other, its layers of interpretation, and its employment of the grotesque, the body project of the forcibly marked individual implicitly engages theoretical issues of vision and the gaze. To further explore this claim and its implications, I will continue my analysis of the forcibly marked body of Hester Prynne. Although she insists that no one can remove the scarlet letter, the differences between it and the tattoo and the scar—marks that are quite literally "carved in flesh"—seem clear. Yet because of the cultural prominence of *The Scarlet Letter* and the immediacy with which Hester Prynne springs to mind in any consideration of the nineteenth-century marked body, it is important to push this analysis as far as possible, using the familiar figure of Hester to introduce my approach and theoretical concerns. I then leave Hester behind to consider the bodies of the tattooed captives, scarred maidens, and branded slaves that allow one to think beyond her.

As film critic and theorist Laura Mulvey has so memorably observed, "In a world ordered by sexual imbalance, pleasure in looking has been split into active/male and passive/female. . . . In their traditional exhibitionist role women are simultaneously looked at and displayed, with their appearance coded for strong visual and erotic impact so that they can be said to connote *to-be-looked-at-ness*" (47–48, emphasis in original). While Mulvey is discussing classical Hollywood cinema, her comments apply here insofar as the marked women examined become—despite the nineteenth-century idealization of the private woman and the domestic sphere—public women, or women who are marked as spectacles. This element of Hester's punishment is clear; as the narrator of the novel points out, "[t]here can be no outrage, methinks, against our common nature . . . more flagrant than to forbid the culprit to hide his face for shame," and the letter forces Hester to tolerate "eyes, all fastened upon her, and concentred at her bosom" (55, 57). While "the culprit" is not gendered female in the first quote, the focus of the public's eye—Hester's "bosom"—in the second is clearly more painful for a woman than for a man. At least part of the significance of the letter—as well as of its positioning—is that it sanctions the gaze of others, a gaze that would not be permitted had Hester not transgressed. The letter effectively renders her body a public spectacle, emphasized by the way she is forced to stand on the scaffold after emerging from the prison door. Hester's "*to-be-looked-at-ness*," however, is apparent throughout the novel even after she steps down from the scaffold:

> Clergymen paused in the street to address words of exhortation, that brought a crowd, with its mingled grin and frown, around the poor, single woman. If she entered a church, trusting to share the Sabbath smile of the Universal Father, it was often her mishap to find herself the text of the discourse. . . . [Children] pursued her at a distance with shrill cries, and the utterance of a word that had no distinct purport to their own minds, but was none the less terrible to her, as proceeding from lips that babbled it unconsciously. . . . Another peculiar torture was felt in the gaze of a new eye. When strangers looked curiously at the scarlet letter,—and none ever failed to do so,—they branded it afresh into Hester's soul. (85–86)

Hester's very presence seems to inspire observation and commentary—most often from clergymen but also from the youngest of the townspeople, who learn what it means to be a part of the community by participating in the censure of the fallen woman.

Clearly, not all of Hester's observers are male, nor are they all white. (The Native American men who visit Boston are said to gaze at Hester's "bosom" as

well.) Yet it is important to recognize that the power to gaze at Hester originates with the white male magistrates and is sanctioned by them. This "conquering gaze" is layered throughout *The Scarlet Letter*: the magistrates, Roger
Chillingworth, and the Reverend Dimmesdale employ it, as does the narrator
of the novel and, one might argue, Hawthorne himself. Hawthorne's narrator
acknowledges the intense emotions accompanying the assumption of this powerful gaze when he recounts the discovery of the scarlet letter in the Custom
House: "Certainly, there was some deep meaning in it, most worthy of interpretation, and which, as it were, streamed forth from the mystic symbol, subtly
communicating itself to my sensibilities, but evading the analysis of my mind"
(31). Even detached from Hester's body, the letter seems to demand a reading,
an "interpretation," based on the narrator's "sensibilities" rather than on his
analytic capabilities. Intrigued, the narrator places the letter on his own breast
but "involuntarily let[s] it fall to the floor" when he feels an unbearable heat
radiating from it. To master the letter and its effect on him, the narrator rejects
this sensory method of determining its meaning and creates an explanatory
narrative based on the "main facts of that story . . . authorized and authenti-
cated by the document of Mr. Surveyor Pue," which is said to accompany the
letter (32). This narrative effectively restores the fluid connection between the
magistrate's punishment, the letter, and Hester's physical body, thus distancing the storyteller from the way in which "the mystic symbol" affected his own
body. Throughout the rest of the novel, the narrator appears omniscient. Like
the magistrates, whose authority he both assumes and questions, the narrator
even offers to extend the power of this gaze to those who are intrigued by his
narrative or perhaps doubt its veracity: "The original papers, together with the
scarlet letter itself,—a most curious relic,—are still in my possession, and shall
be freely exhibited to whomsoever, induced by the great interest of the narrative,
may desire a sight of them" (32–33). Thus the "truth" of Hester's body lives on
long after she is dead, apparently fixed by the reconstructed narrative as well as
by the testimonial power of Pue's papers and the letter itself.

Yet the multiple layers of this text—Hawthorne, the narrator, Mr. Surveyor
Pue, the townspeople themselves (who convey the story to Pue), and finally
the deeply submerged voice of Hester herself—provide the narrative ambiguity necessary for the authority and ultimate significance of the letter to be
called into question. The meaning of the mark is always contested, always fluid;
while political and social context can, on occasion, briefly fix its meaning, the
"transcoding" of body and culture soon begins again. As many critics have
noted, the scarlet letter takes on multiple meanings throughout the novel. In
one case, the narrator explains, "Such helpfulness was found in [Hester],—so
much power to do, and power to sympathize,—that many people refused to in-

terpret the scarlet A by its original signification. They said that it meant Able; so strong was Hester Prynne, with a woman's strength" (161). The ways in which others read the letter often reveal more about the observers themselves than about Hester. For example, after Hester emerges from the prison with the "fantastically embroidered" letter on her bosom, one woman scoffs, "She hath good skill at her needle, . . . but did ever a woman before this brazen hussy, contrive such a way of showing it? Why, gossips, what is it but to laugh in the faces of our godly magistrates, and make a pride out of what they, worthy gentlemen, meant for a punishment?" Another woman more sympathetically argues that "[n]ot a stitch in that embroidered letter, but she has felt it in her heart" (54). Insofar as the Boston community's attitudes toward authority and morality come to expression in their reactions to Hester and the letter, they are as much a part of *The Scarlet Letter* as Hester herself.

In Hester's case, however, as well as that of other nineteenth-century marked figures, what is ultimately at stake is the power to make meaning of one's own body or even to return the gaze from an embodied position. To be marked is, again, to open oneself up to observation, to interpretation, to possession even; it is, above all, to have one's corporeality publicly and physically impressed as text. How, then, does this textualization of the body affect one's ability to read either one's own body or the bodies of others? Does the mark rob the marked individual of this power? Or might it enhance the powers of the gaze, giving to the individual a way of looking back and reclaiming agency through the mark rather than despite it? The power inherent in the control of the gaze—one's own and that of others—is detailed by Marc Blanchard, who says of the contemporary tattoo: "Tattoo is about revealing, being revealed and gazing upon the revealing. The tattooed subject focuses the public gaze on his or her own body or part of the body while also delighting himself or herself as both exhibitionist and voyeur of his or her own spectacle, in a ritual of intense specularity. One could say that to wear a tattoo is to see and be seen by controlling the gaze, as the delight in revealing the tattoo is made more exquisite by the dreadful memory of a painful inscription" (295). Thus, Blanchard might argue, to wear a tattoo is to anticipate and invite the reactions of others, to make one's body an interactive text of sorts.

Blanchard hints at the tattooed individual's ability "to see" as well as "to be seen" but does not elaborate on the way in which the marked individual might be given insight into the "marks" of others via the inscription of his or her own body. Hester's case is intriguing in this regard; although the letter gives her heightened powers of vision, neither she nor her community is comfortable with these powers and what they reveal. The narrator of *The Scarlet Letter* explains that Hester "felt or fancied . . . that the scarlet letter had endowed her with a new sense. She shuddered to believe, yet could not help believing, that it gave her a sympathetic knowledge of the hidden sin in others' hearts. . . . In all her miserable experience, there was nothing so awful and so loathsome as this sense" (86–87). Hester's new "sense," her ability to see inside the hearts and minds of others, recalls Mary Ann Doane's assertion that "[t]here is always a certain excessiveness, a difficulty associated with women who appropriate the gaze, who insist upon looking" (187). Hester herself is uncomfortable with such "excessiveness," with the way in which the scarlet letter gives her powers to see and judge that surpass those of the white male magistrates. Yet to "insist upon looking" is to attempt to control the way in which one is looked at, to deny that one is completely "to be looked at."

Given the context of nineteenth-century American "body projects," control over the marked body and the gaze might be too much to ask of Hester and her counterparts—other marked women as well as marked men of color. Yet the texts I examine in *Identifying Marks* reveal a surprisingly complex array of representations of and responses to the marked body—some that are a product of essentialist thinking about race and gender identities, and some that complicate, critique, or even rebel against conventional thought. All must be examined within their own cultural context in order to understand the myriad ways in which the marked body functions in nineteenth-century America. I hope my work contributes to the growing body of scholarship that complicates the (dis)embodied nature of American identity in the nineteenth century. At the very least, my choice of texts and my approach to them is a manifestation of my commitment to the expanding diversity of nineteenth-century American literary and cultural studies. For many scholars of American literature, the question of the marked body begins and ends with Hester and Queequeg. As demonstrated in this introduction, these characters are by no means uninteresting and do, in fact, provoke fascinating conversations about the body, individual agency, and American identity. Yet as I have discovered in discussions with my students, Melville's Tommo, Elizabeth Stoddard's Cassandra Morgeson, and Louisa May Alcott's Robert only enrich these conversations—flesh them out, one might say. I hope that this study will reveal the way in which a supposedly resolved question—What is the significance of the marked body in nineteenth-century America?—takes on new dimensions when approached from a critical standpoint that embraces the politics of recovery and critical theory.

The chapters in this study are arranged thematically rather than chronologically. Although chapter 1 addresses some of the earliest texts treated and chapter 5 the latest, Pauline Hopkins's *Contending Forces* (1900), this arrangement does not indicate a linear progression through the century in which attitudes toward the marked body become more tolerant, representations of the marked body become more or less prevalent, or the body itself loses its symbolic power. As my conclusion demonstrates, even in the late twentieth and early twenty-first centuries the marked body remains a powerful symbol demanding that readers ask similar questions about culture, identity, agency, and, ultimately, power. On a surface level, *Identifying Marks* is split into two sections: the first three chapters primarily address representations of the white woman's marked body, while the last two focus on the marked black body and the legacy of slavery. What becomes apparent, however, is that these discourses are not entirely distinct in nineteenth-century America; white women's textuality, or their ability to be marked, for example, demonstrated a blurring of the cultural boundaries between race and gender, as did the cultural feminization of black men. The marking of white women, African American women, and African American men both highlight and complicate the myth of the unmarked white man, although it is, of course, crucial to contextualize the body being marked and the mark itself. Ultimately the difference between a white woman with a scarred face and a black man with a branded hand is the difference between two systems of oppression functioning together to shape the cultural politics of nineteenth-century America. No matter what their focus, however, all these chapters share a concern with the relationship of the marked body to the twin issues of agency and vision. The chapters build on one another, developing the argument that the marked body is at the epicenter of political and cultural mediation in these texts and tracing the deployment of power along the sight lines manifest in the "conquering gaze."

Chapter 1 establishes many of the key ideas of the book as a whole: the association of the mark with both racial and gender identity; the marked body as spectacle; and finally, the array of responses available to the marked individual, including, most importantly, the returned gaze. Here I look at the discourses of race, gender, and tattooing in two narratives of captivity: Herman Melville's *Typee* (1846) and Royal B. Stratton's *Captivity of the Oatman Girls* (1857). As I explain, the marked body in America had traditionally been associated with people of color. The dime-museum and circus performances of tattooed white people in midcentury, however, destabilized strict definitions of race and created unprecedented anxiety about the boundaries of identity and the body. Melville and Stratton both feed and feed on these anxieties by introducing figures captured by native peoples and threatened with the mark of the tattoo. Their responses to this threat play out according to cultural dictates of gender and race, with Melville's masculine hero successfully resisting the mark and Stratton's female victim being inscribed by the Mohaves who hold her captive. Perhaps because of this vulnerability, Stratton, especially, attempts to contain the disruptive potential of the tattoo by maintaining that Olive Oatman's facial tattoos—and the experiences they seemed to represent—have no effect on her identity as a Christian white woman. Yet as Melville demonstrates in his novel, the marked body ultimately calls the boundaries of racial or gendered identity into question.

Chapter 2 builds on the discussion of Olive Oatman and the spectacle of her tattooed body by examining the fictional representation of women with marked faces. These fictions play an important part in the navigation of new discourses of romantic love that would become increasingly central to the middle classes in the United States in midcentury. Such discourses are both tested and critiqued by the presence of the mark; although the courtship of the marked woman often reveals the triumph of romantic love (proving, one might say, that love is blind), it nonetheless exposes an apparent lack of any real power for women in this new sentimentalized relationship between the sexes. My argument here is based on both sensational and sentimental texts: George Thompson's sensational *City Crimes; or Life in New York and Boston* (1849), Maria Susanna Cummins's sentimental novel *The Lamplighter* (1854), and a complex short story by Harriet Prescott Spofford, "The Strathsays" (1863). These texts highlight the importance of vision to both romantic love and the concept of sympathy that runs through *Identifying Marks*, beginning with responses to Oatman's captivity. How does the mark attract sympathy from the audience (either other characters or the reader of the text)? Perhaps more importantly, what are the range of responses available to the marked woman when she is rendered a spectacle? In the texts examined in this chapter, women's vision tends to be completely denied or severely limited, thus denying them control over interpretations of their own bodies.

The questions raised in chapter 2 lead directly to the consideration of female agency and the marked body in chapter 3. To preface the remarkable delineation of female agency in Elizabeth Stoddard's novel *The Morgesons* (1862), the chapter begins with an analysis of Nathaniel Hawthorne's short story "The Birthmark" (1843), perhaps his most famous representation of a marked woman after Hester Prynne. While Georgiana's birthmark is clearly not forcibly received in this story, it *is* forcibly removed insofar as Georgiana surrenders any sense of self or agency to her scientist husband, Aylmer, and allows him to conduct experiments on her that will erase the birthmark. The erasure of Georgiana's mark, which ultimately kills her, represents Aylmer's attempt to mark his wife as his own, completely subsumed by her husband and his desires, however destructive they might be. *The Morgesons*, on the other hand, features the strongest display of female agency and the female body in nineteenth-century American literature. Marked by scars on her cheeks, Cassandra Morgeson employs a reverse discourse in two crucial ways. First, she calls the scars her tattoos, thus claiming them as chosen marks of her own suffering and experience. Second, and just as importantly, Cassandra learns to return the gaze directed at her body, reading the bodies of others and diluting their power to define her.

Following this discussion of a woman's active involvement in making meaning of her own marked body, I turn to the more complicated paradigm of the African American marked body. Many of the same questions are at issue here, yet the linking of sympathy to vision becomes increasingly important in the final two chapters of the book. What part does the marked black body play in the political deployment of sympathy during the antebellum, Civil War, and postbellum periods? How does this representation differ from that of the wounded white male body, so essential to patriotic rhetoric throughout the Civil War? And does a textual dependence on the mark, the result and symbol of the brutality of the institution of slavery, limit the potential for agency for the African American subject?

Chapter 4 focuses specifically on representations of the black male body in abolitionist rhetoric in conjunction with competing definitions of black manhood throughout the century. The chapter begins with an analysis of abolitionist representations of the marked slave body, which were heavily influenced by sentimental ideologies. Such representations were politically useful but were also limited by the abolitionist resistance to black male self-assertion and agency, which most white audiences regarded as threatening. The scarred body of the black man is also the center of Louisa May Alcott's "My Contraband" (1863), in which the marks on Robert's body correspond to the different stages of his transition from slave to contraband to Union soldier. Reminiscent of the tattoos of Olive Oatman, Robert's marked body symbolizes the fluid boundaries of race and gender in a society that desperately desired to fix such boundaries. However, although Alcott's text was written during a period of great changes and opportunities for African American men, this story remains mired in the sentimental rhetoric of the scar that preceded it; Alcott attempts to redefine black manhood but cannot avoid reducing Robert to the scars that mark him. It is not until after the Civil War that writers such as Lydia Maria Child and Frances Ellen Watkins Harper are able to reposition that marked black male body, examining it within a domesticated political discourse of reunited families and reconstructed lives.

The final chapter examines the marked body—or, more specifically, the *absence* of the marked body as I have defined it—in representations of women of color throughout the nineteenth century. Although African American women were occasionally represented as scarred in abolitionist literature, I use texts by Child and Stowe to argue that these grotesque figures were not sentimentally redeemable or amenable to sympathetic identification in the same way as the women who suffered sexual exploitation and abuse. Thus the marked woman remained largely absent from abolitionist rhetoric, posing a particular problem for postemancipation African American writers such as Pauline Hopkins. Hopkins engages the issue of the marked black female body in *Contending Forces*, examining the paired but distinct experiences of physical and sexual abuse. Both, she claims, play an important role in the legacy of embodied black female subjectivity left to African American women at the turn of the twentieth century. Using the rhetoric of the stigmata, Hopkins reclaims the mark for black women as a symbol of healing and survival of which African Americans should be proud. In effect, Hopkins reverses what had been a violent textual imposition of the mark by removing the shame associated with the stigmata of slavery.

Although this study begins with a focus on a very specific kind of mark—the forcible tattoo—it concludes with a recognition of the fluidity between the tattoo and the scar, the (usually) chosen mark and the forcible one. To flesh out the discourse of the mark is to emphasize both the particularities of each body and each mark as well as the commonalities between them. It is to consider the specifics of race, gender, and identity as well as the larger desire to mark and unmark the body throughout the nineteenth century. Above all, it is to acknowledge that real bodies, the realities of corporeality in nineteenth-century America, lie behind these fictions, and to take responsibility for my own treatment of them.

CHAPTER ONE

Capturing Identity in Ink

Tattooing and the White Captive

Claiming to have 365 designs tattooed onto her body, Nora Hildebrandt was employed by Bunnell's Museum in New York City in 1882 as a "tattooed lady," one of the first in U.S. history. Her tattoos and the narrative behind them attracted curious audiences to her performance. Whether the tale was told to appease the inevitable critics of a woman who would allow her body to be thus marked and displayed or simply to increase interest in (and revenue from) her show, Hildebrandt claimed that her father, tattoo artist Martin Hildebrandt, had been forced to tattoo her while both were being held captive by "red skin devils."[1] Even more scandalous, however, was Hildebrandt's assertion that one of these "devils" was none other than the prominent tribal leader of the Hunkpapa Lakota Sioux, Sitting Bull. According to the memoir sold at Hildebrandt's performances, Sitting Bull had promised to spare the lives of father and daughter if Martin Hildebrandt would agree to tattoo his tribe. Yet, "[o]ne of Sitting Bull's warriors accused [Hildebrandt] of trying to poison them, and the chief told the prisoner if he would tattoo his daughter he would give him his liberty—that he must tattoo her from her toes to her head. . . . She was tied to a tree and the painful operation commenced. He was compelled to work six hours a day for one year before she was rescued, accomplishing three hundred and sixty five designs" (qtd. in Mifflin 18).

Sitting Bull's presence in Nora Hildebrandt's captivity narrative is ironic in that Sitting Bull was a captive himself at the time of Hildebrandt's stage debut. After having surrendered to U.S. troops on July 20, 1881, at Fort Buford, Dakota Territory, Sitting Bull was held as a prisoner of war for two years. He settled on the reservation at the Standing Rock Agency in present-day North Dakota after his release, becoming a successful farmer and stockman while also struggling to preserve the traditional values and customs of the Lakota. During 1884 and 1885, however, Sitting Bull left the reservation to participate in Buffalo Bill's Wild West Show.[2] This story of captivity and subsequent exhibition of the self strangely mirrors that of Nora Hildebrandt, with one very important difference: Hildebrandt's narrative was a complete fabrication. Yet Sitting Bull's experience also complicates Hildebrandt's narrative, removing it from the supposedly harmless realm of "entertainment" and revealing its complicity with the horrendous treatment of Native Americans by the U.S. government. For Hildebrandt's audience, her forcible tattooing may have functioned as justification for the succeeding treatment of Sitting Bull: codes of white womanhood throughout the history of the United States virtually guaranteed that a man of color would be punished for his involvement in this sort of violation. Yet from another point of view, Sitting Bull's captivity deromanticizes Hildebrandt's narrative, revealing Sitting Bull himself to be a victim of the U.S. government rather than a despotic chief who had the power or the inclination to force a white man to tattoo his own daughter.

Regardless of how observers read Sitting Bull's role in Hildebrandt's narrative or in the context of his own captivity, the captivity story provided by Hildebrandt was clearly constructed to maximize its effect on her audience. The inclusion of Sitting Bull and his tribe in her narrative scandalously positioned her performance in the exotic mode of freak show presentation, which originated with the display of indigenous peoples in Europe in the seventeenth century. Prince Giolo, brought to Europe in 1691 and thereafter known as "The Painted Prince," was the first recorded tattooed person to be exhibited in England. Captain James Cook returned to England with Omai, a tattooed South Sea Islander, in 1774. The public was drawn to these early exhibits, fascinated with what seemed to be a primitive process, practiced by savages in exotic locales. According to Robert Bogdan, performances in the exotic mode in Europe and the United States were arranged "to appeal to people's interest in the culturally strange, the primitive, the bestial" (105). This paradigm seemed to necessitate a simplification and distortion of indigenous cultures to reassure audiences of their own "self-worth and the civility of urban life" (Dennet 7). As Hildebrandt's narrative reveals, the stories presented in the memoirs of tattooed white people retained the racist assumptions and stereotypes of the original exotic mode. Yet the performer being promoted was a white person rather than a person of color. The people of color in these narratives functioned in two contradictory but simultaneous ways: they emphasized the whiteness of the performer at the same time they revealed the tentative boundaries of that white identity. The performer's white skin was capitalized on precisely because of its vulnerability to the mark, a mark associated in white cultures with people of color.[3]

Certainly Hildebrandt was not alone in claiming she had been kidnapped by a native tribe and forcibly tattooed; that assertion had already been used for decades in selling tickets to museum and sideshow entertainments. James

O'Connell, the first tattooed white man to exhibit himself in the United States, and Captain Costentenus, perhaps the most famous, both claimed to have been forcibly tattooed by beautiful young women in exotic but primitive locales. An 1877 advertisement for Costentenus's performance reveals the complex sexual and racial dynamics of these narratives (see figure 1). The ad shows Costentenus tied spread-eagle to stakes in the ground while an attractive, young indigenous woman uses a long tool to mark his upper thigh—the only site on his body not yet covered by tattoos. In the background, a group of indigenous men observe the process with interest. Hildebrandt's narrative plays with these conventions in titillating ways, positioning a woman as the victim and, in an incestuous twist, her father as the tattoo artist who works diligently over her body for 365 consecutive days. Importantly, however, Martin Hildebrandt's apparent unwillingness to tattoo his daughter transfers responsibility for the act from him to Sitting Bull, who, like the men in the Costentenus illustration, is clearly meant to be seen as the aggressor in this situation, despite (or perhaps because of) his voyeurism.

Although the tattoo had always inspired a strange mixture of fascination and anxiety, the appearance of tattooed sailors in the West and the subsequent stage debut of tattooed white men and women prompted a reconsideration of the tattoo's significance in Western cultures. Michel Foucault's work suggests that the bodies of Western men and women have always been marked in culturally prescribed ways.[4] The bodies of middle- and upper-class women in mid-nineteenth-century America, for example, were frequently marked by the corset, or "tight lacing," which dress reformers argued caused cosmetic misfortunes as well as more serious health problems such as "atrophied and 'annihilated' chest muscles, restricted blood circulation, convulsive coughing, consumption, heart palpitations, excessive nervousness, cold hands, deformed ribs, bruised livers, improperly developed nipples, lateral curvature of the spine, displaced organs, . . . and finally, displaced breasts" (Cogan 60). Class also played a role in the marking of the laboring body, both male and female, which often, depending on the workplace, exhibited a tan from exposure to the sun as well as signs of malnutrition. The permanence and exoticism of the tattoo, however, forced a distinct recognition of cultural marking, causing concern over the disruption of identity that might result from this particular mark.

Like Hildebrandt's narrative and performance, two nineteenth-century American texts, Herman Melville's *Typee: A Peep at Polynesian Life* (1846) and Royal B. Stratton's *Captivity of the Oatman Girls* (1857), demonstrate the struggle to simultaneously exploit and contain the disruptive potential of the tattoo. Both Melville and Stratton position the tattoo narrative within the more

Figure 1. Captain Costentenus. *Harper's Weekly*, May 26, 1877. Courtesy of the Library of Congress.

familiar captivity narrative, thus ensuring themselves a ready and sympathetic audience. As many critics have noted, the captivity narrative has endured for centuries in the work of American authors, beginning with Mary Rowlandson's 1682 account of her captivity among the Narragansett Indians. Frontier novels such as Charles Brockden Brown's *Edgar Huntly* (1799), James Fenimore Cooper's *Last of the Mohicans* (1826), and Catharine Maria Sedgwick's *Hope Leslie* (1827) include subplots featuring narratives of captivity. These novels also, interestingly, represent native peoples as tattooed—with "uncouth figures" in *Edgar Huntly* (164), blue tortoises in *The Last of the Mohicans* (226), and a snake in *Hope Leslie* (104). Melville and Stratton carry on the legacy of these frontier novels, as do tattooed performers like Hildebrandt who later promote their shows with tales of captivity. All these texts and performances recognize and respond to the fascination with which nineteenth-century audiences regarded tattoos and the tattooing process. However, writers and performers who incorporated tattoo narratives into their texts also had to address their audiences' anxieties about this "primitive" method of marking the body.

Although captivity narratives such as *Typee* and *Captivity of the Oatman Girls* purport to offer information about the cultures in which the captives live (and do so successfully, to some degree), the texts are shaped by their authors' constant awareness of audience. As John Evelev points out, rather than actually representing indigenous peoples and their cultures, these texts represent a "highly mediated portrait" of the captives' experiences, "not only a portrayal of their encounter with the 'primitive,' but also the encounter with their civilized audience and their demands" (36). The politics of tattooing in these narratives are similarly complex. Loosely based on actual captivity experiences, tattoo narratives in both *Typee* and *Captivity of the Oatman Girls* reveal the cultural anxieties of a white, American audience concerning race, gender, and identity. Although both texts seem to offer an anthropological study of the captor's culture—especially the practice of tattooing—the focus is on the white body and whiteness itself rather than on the native culture.[5] Melville and Stratton anticipate audience reactions to tattooing and use facial tattooing in particular to symbolize the horrifying possibility of the white body being permanently marked by an indigenous culture. In this sense, both texts—even *Typee*, which in many ways is a critique of colonialism—take part in a traditional discourse of conquest and colonization. Yet combined with a politics of vision, tattoos also raise questions about the construction of race and gender in nineteenth-century American identity politics. As in the case of Nora Hildebrandt, we might ask just what constitutes whiteness if the skin is indelibly marked with ink? To what extent does the tattoo compromise one's identity as "white"? Similarly, how might tattooing accord with or disrupt nineteenth-century notions of gender identity?

Saving the Face of White Masculinity

Scholars continue to debate the extent to which *Typee* is based on Melville's own experiences in the Marquesas; another related point of contention is the distance between Melville, the author, and his narrator, Tommo. I am inclined to agree with those who see the line between author and narrator here as an ambiguous one. It is important to note that Melville published *Typee* as the "unvarnished truth" of his adventure, and that many who read it soon after publication regarded it as such. The novel and its sequel, *Omoo* (1847), were extremely popular with both American and British audiences, and Melville was so closely associated with the narratives that he was often called "Typee" and "Omoo" by friends and admirers (Anderson 284). According to Melville's latest biographer, Herschel Parker, the writer even enjoyed some celebrity as a nineteenth-century sex symbol, because of his discussion of and alleged participation in the supposedly licentious sexual culture of the Typees. Yet Melville's creation of the character Tommo, whom the author uses to make some of his most pointed critiques of the colonization of the Pacific, is crucial to the argument here. Thus although I treat *Typee* as a novel, I always keep in mind the autobiographical basis of the text and the questions raised by such ambiguity.[6]

Despite its generic complexity, the plot of *Typee* is easily summarized. The novel's questionable hero—called, for various reasons, Tommo—is a sailor who decides to jump ship while anchored in the bay of Nuku Hiva. Repelled by the treatment of his despotic captain and seduced by the "strange visions . . . spirit[ed] up" by the Marquesas, Tommo and a companion named Toby make their arduous way across the island and into the Typee Valley (5). Although the Typees' reputation for brutality and cannibalism initially unnerve the duo, they settle quite happily into their life with the Typees, who treat them alternately as captives and as honored guests. These extremes are made even more apparent— and disconcerting—when Toby is allowed to leave the valley in search of medical assistance for Tommo, who suffers from a mysterious wound to his leg. Left alone, Tommo faces the twin perils of cannibalism and tattooing.[7]

To understand the threat that tattooing poses to Tommo and the power dynamics implicit in tattooing and the display of the tattoo, one must turn first to one of the most compelling images in Melville's *Typee*: that of the queen of Nuku Hiva's backside. This image, which neatly demonstrates the intimate relationship between race, gender, and tattooing in this novel, appears early in the text, prior to (but chronologically after) Tommo's captivity. Although only a few years have passed since his escape, much has changed: in this scene, Tommo is a sailor on an American man-of-war and the French are in control of the Marquesan Islands, eager to parade their colonial influence and control in front of the visiting Americans.

This influence, they hope, is to be embodied in the king and queen of Nuku Hiva, who are escorted on board the American man-of-war for a visit. The impression made by the royal couple, however, is questionable. The military uniform of the king, for example, is juxtaposed with his facial tattoos, which Tommo claims, "suggested some ludicrous ideas" (7–8). Yet, as Melville explains, "it was in the adornment of the fair person of [the king's] dark-complexioned spouse that the tailors of the fleet had evinced the gaiety of their national taste." Draped in scarlet cloth and yellow silk, a purple turban adorning her head, and tattooed legs peeking out from her skirts, the queen is clearly intended to be a spectacle, an object of both fascination and ridicule. She is above all to be observed and commented on by her white audience. Interestingly, though, the queen turns the tables of both race and gender by rejecting the distance between spectacle and observer and replacing it with reciprocity. Instead of simply allowing herself to be looked at, the visiting queen herself looks at an old sailor whose body, like hers, is covered in tattoos. In an effort to see more of his tattoos than are immediately visible, she even rolls up his trousers and pushes aside his shirt; Melville writes, "[S]he gazed with admiration at the bright blue and vermilion pricking, thus disclosed to view" (8). With this simple act, the queen disrupts the Frenchmen's carefully planned display, refusing to be a passive object herself and celebrating enthusiastically the tattooing culture she shares with the "old salt."

As might be expected, this act of agency does not please the French officers, yet they clearly have no idea how limited their control over the queen actually is. "The embarrassment of the polite Gauls at such an unlooked-for occurrence may be easily imagined," Tommo reports, "but picture their consternation when all at once the royal lady, eager to display the hieroglyphics on her own sweet form, bent forward for a moment, and turning sharply round, threw up the skirts of her mantle, and revealed a sight from which the aghast Frenchmen retreated precipitately, and tumbling into their boat, fled the scene of so shocking a catastrophe" (8). Significantly, the queen does not necessarily reject the position of spectacle or object; rather, she revels in what Marc Blanchard calls the "ritual of intense specularity" (295). By returning the gaze, looking back at the sailors and appraising their bodies in the same way they do hers, the queen wrests control of the spectacle away from the French. Culminating with the revelation of her tattooed backside, these acts reveal an agency from which the French must escape in terror.

The French, however, are not the only ones running from the native culture in the Marquesas. Although Tommo attempts to distinguish himself from the French here through mockery and laughter, he too has fled the tattooed bodies of the islanders and the (perceived) threat to his raced and gendered body that they and their culture pose. Despite his delight in the carnivalesque repudiation of the French imperial gaze, Tommo himself participates in this "conquering gaze" throughout *Typee* and, like the French officers, ultimately runs away because he can't bear to have his position of power compromised. The importance of vision in this text, as well as perhaps Melville's sense of Tommo's abuse of the gaze, is indicated in the word "peep" in the subtitle of the book. To "peep" is to employ a forbidden, salacious gaze that usually protects the viewer from observation. Promising that his narrative encompasses a "peep at Polynesian life," Melville exposes Tommo from the beginning of the text as a man who wishes to remain invisible, taking prurient pleasure in the visibility of others. (Interestingly, Melville also implicates his reader here insofar as the reader has chosen to "peep" along with Tommo. The reader allows Tommo to take the risks and remains safe on the other side of the page.) Ultimately, Tommo knows that to be tattooed is to risk objectification, representation, and feminization. If he were tattooed, he could at most hope for a reversal of the gaze enacted by the queen. As someone who "peeps," Tommo would presumably find such exposure unbearable.

Until tattooing becomes a threat to him, however, Tommo adjusts his own appearance to conform to and participate in Typee society. He dresses in native *tappa*, stops shaving, and even decorates himself with flowers for the celebration he calls "the Feast of Calabashes." He participates actively in such cultural events and even becomes intimately involved with a young Typee woman named Fayaway. Tommo's name, from the Marquesan verb meaning "to enter into, to adapt well to," appropriately indicates his initial willingness to acculturate to some degree to Marquesan society (qtd. in Samson 30). Yet these changes are by no means permanent, and Tommo is constantly aware of the importance of his physical appearance should he return to white society; in fact, he adopts *tappa* only because he desires to preserve the clothing he was wearing when he arrived in the Typee Valley.

Although Tommo is willing to make temporary concessions to native traditions, he refuses to allow these gestures to affect his conception of himself as a Westerner. Similarly, his adoption of native customs and clothing do not alter the anthropological tone of much of his narration and his subsequent confidence in his own authority to describe and interpret Typee culture for his audience. Lacking anything but the most rudimentary understanding of their language, Tommo nonetheless professes to comprehend Typee religious practices, food and clothing preparation, and courting rituals. He ultimately bases much of his interpretation of the hierarchy of Typee society on his "readings" of their tattooed bodies. For example, after describing the broad stripes of tattooing covering the eyes of one man, Tommo concludes, "The warrior, from the excellence of his physical proportions, might certainly have been regarded as one of Nature's noblemen, and the lines drawn upon his face may possibly have denoted his exalted rank" (78). Tommo attempts to maintain this anthropological distance despite his obvious vulnerability among the Typees, compounded by a wounded leg as well as by an inability to communicate successfully with anyone, either inside or outside the tribe.

Curiously, Tommo's representation of himself as unmarked observer is contradicted early in the novel when he first arrives in the Typee Valley. It is not, after all, as if Tommo's body had never been modified before his residence with the Typees. Like Melville's better-known narrator, Ishmael, Tommo has a mysterious past, but there is no doubt that as a sailor, he wears the clothing required to perform this role successfully: the duck trousers, the sturdy pumps, the heavy Havre frock. The physical alteration of his body is revealed as well when the Typees marvel over the contrast between the "swarthy hue" of his face and the fairness of the skin previously hidden under his clothing (74). Although these modifications are rare and curious to the Typees, they are the norm for Tommo (and for other men of his race, class, and profession) and do not, therefore, alter his sense of himself as unmarked. As long as Tommo can preserve his Western clothing and perform the role of acculturated captive, his "conquering gaze" remains intact and unquestioned. The permanent nature of tattooing, however, presents a threat that might actually necessitate a reconstruction of self and a subsequent loss of the gaze.[8] If Tommo were to accept tattooing, he would then become what anthropologist Alfred Gell calls a "reproducer" of Typee culture, accepting their traditions as his own and becoming a representative of their culture who may, in turn, pass these traditions on himself (7). (In fact, by bearing these traditions on his own body, he can hardly help passing them *on himself.*) Tommo's rejection of the opportunity to "enter into" the culture of his captors entirely and his desire to remain unmarked are unsatisfactory to the Typees, who clearly see Tommo's happiness in the Typee Valley as an indication of his willingness to continue as an active participant in their culture.

The significance of tattoos in the expression and transmission of Typee culture renders the tattoo artist a powerful figure; appropriately, the pressure to be tattooed originates in an encounter between Tommo and Karky, the artist. When Karky notices Tommo observing the tattooing process, he understandably believes (given his other adjustments to Typee society) that Tommo has come to be tattooed himself. Tommo attempts to convince him otherwise, but Karky—described as a "tormenter" and an "artist, with a heart as callous as that of an army surgeon"—refuses to accept his denial (217, 218). Tommo finally offers his arms to the tattoo artist, but realizes that Karky wants nothing less than to mark his face. Melville writes:

> The idea of engrafting his tattooing upon my white skin filled him with all a painter's enthusiasm: again and again he gazed into my countenance, and every fresh glimpse seemed to add to the vehemence of his ambition. Not knowing to what extremities he might proceed, and shuddering at the ruin he might inflict upon my figure-head, I now endeavored to draw off his attention from it. . . . At last, half wild with terror and indignation, I succeeded in breaking away . . . and fled . . . , pursued by the indomitable artist, who ran after me, implements in hand. (219)

Thus Tommo sees his white skin as an irresistible attraction to Karky, the artist who has presumably never had such an attractive canvas on which to work. Tommo is horrified, however, at the incongruous prospect of white skin, particularly the white face, being permanently marked by the tattoo. For Tommo, the tattooing process would be an "attack" and would "ruin" his face.[9] After the encounter with Karky, Tommo reflects, "This incident opened my eyes to a new danger; and I now felt convinced that in some luckless hour I should be disfigured in such a manner as never more to have the *face* to return to my countrymen, even should an opportunity offer" (219). Although clothing can be changed and facial hair removed or grown, facial tattooing is almost impossible to hide and would irrevocably alter Tommo's ability to blend in with his "countrymen" upon his departure from the Marquesas. As a white man returning home with tattoos, Tommo would be regarded as an acculturated captive with questionable loyalties to his own culture and to the white race. He would be unable to save (his) face or retain his reputation as an unmarked white man.

As Samuel Otter notes, "The face is the conspicuous surface of contact between the individual inside and the social outside, the only such surface, with the exception of the hands, regularly exposed in Western fashion" (40). Facial tattooing would therefore rob Tommo of the reciprocal recognition and respect afforded white men in Western society based, primarily, on the "social outside" of the face (however it might be marked by class). Even within Typee society, facial tattoos would necessarily prevent Tommo from assuming his position as distanced white observer of the nonwhite "other"; in the United States, they would render him the very other who is observed, as in the tradition of the dime museum and the freak show. The markings on his skin and the acceptance of Typee culture they indicate might even rob Tommo of his whiteness, rendering him a man "of color" albeit of no particular race.[10] The extent to which tattooing can affect appearance and identity regardless of race is frighteningly apparent in Tommo's observation of the oldest members of the Typee tribe, "four or five old wretches, on whose decrepit forms time and tattooing seemed to have obliterated every trace of humanity." "Owing to the continued operation of this latter process," he explains further, "which only terminates among the warriors of the island after all the figures sketched upon their limbs in youth have been blended together . . . the bodies of these men were of a uniform dull green color—the hue which the tattooing gradually assumes as the individual advances in age" (92). These elderly men function merely as the background to Tommo's tale, never emerging as individuals or playing any important part in Typee culture. In fact, their tattoos and their green skin seem to indicate the extent to which they have left humanity and its social interactions behind. As Otter accurately observes, "Tattooing has bequeathed to these men not simply a different skin, but the skin of a different species" (39). Similarly, Tommo risks losing his racial identity and therefore his humanity if he allows Karky to tattoo his face.

The threat that tattooing poses to Tommo's masculinity, however, is just as significant as that which it poses to his whiteness.[11] Despite his relationship with Fayaway and what he perceives as his popularity with most of the young Typee women, Tommo's position within the Typee tribe is, by his own admission, more feminine than masculine. When a stranger enters the valley, for example, Tommo is horrified to find himself ignored and reflects, "Had the belle of the season, in the pride of her beauty and power, been cut in a place of public resort by some supercilious exquisite, she could not have felt greater indignation than I did at this unexpected slight" (136). Tommo's comparison of his face to a "figure-head" in the confrontation with Karky also raises the possibility not only that Tommo is in a feminized position but also that tattooing would solidify that status. Throughout the nineteenth century, many American shipbuilders modeled female figureheads after Greek and Roman goddesses; around the middle of the century, it became common practice for a shipowner to commission a figurehead with the likeness of his wife or daughter, dressed in the fashions of the day, and to name the ship in her honor. Hence to be or to have a "figure-head" may imply that one is feminine and/or subordinate. More importantly, however, Tommo's description of young Marquesan women being tattooed echoes his own experience with Karky and highlights the sexualized and gendered implications of tattooing. Tommo insists, for example, that the hand that tattooed Fayaway is "audacious . . . in its desecrating work" (86–87). The pursuit of the maiden by the "audacious" tattoo artist is reminiscent of a seduction, an analogy furthered by the sexual imagery of tattooing in which the skin is pierced by a phallic object, resulting in the mixing of fluids. The technical schema of tattooing as an analogue for sexual intercourse has been noted by many theorists of the tattoo; Gell, for one, writes, "The sight of a tattoo evokes imagery of sexual subjection, piercing, and flux" (36).[12] Furthermore, Tommo's emphasis on "saving face" clearly recalls the risk of sexual activity to a woman's reputation (comparing tattooing to the irreversible transformation represented by a woman's loss of virginity) and further positions the tattoo recipient—regardless of gender—in a feminized role.

Contributing to this imagery in Melville's imagination would be the stereotypes of forcible tattooing as perpetuated in texts such as Horace Holden's *Narrative of the Shipwreck, Captivity & Sufferings of Horace Holden and Benj. H. Nute* (1836). Holden's narrative was in the library of the *Charles and Henry*, the ship on which Melville left Tahiti in early November 1842, three months after his escape from the Marquesas and four years before the publication of *Typee*. Presumably a model for Melville's depiction of tattooing in *Typee*, Holden's narrative recounts his own captivity on the Palau Islands in the early 1830s. Holden's captors, like Tommo's, insist on tattooing their captives, but unlike Tommo, Holden and his fellow captives are unable to resist: "We were compelled to submit to this distressing operation," Holden writes (102). The narrative and an illustration accompanying the text depict the captives bound to the ground, being tattooed with native implements on their breasts and arms (see figure 2). Although the scene is reminiscent of tales told by tattooed men like James O'Connell and the infamous Captain Costentenus, it is also distinctly different in that this captive is being tattooed by indigenous men rather than by women. Thus the heterosexual fantasy is replaced by a nightmare of subordination and feminization further emphasized by Holden's assertion that "[b]esides the operation of tattooing, they compelled us to pluck the hair from different parts of our body, and to pluck our beards about every ten days" (103).

Although not involving forcible tattooing, a scene witnessed by Tommo just prior to his encounter with Karky shares several characteristics with the scene in Holden's narrative. The man being tattooed is "extended flat upon his back on the ground and, despite the forced composure of his countenance, it was evident that he was suffering agony" (*Typee* 217). Like the islanders who tattoo Holden, Karky is described as "a tormentor." Tattooing, then, evokes images of submission, subordination, and suffering—a humiliating experience that would threaten a conception of masculinity and a gaze dependent on control and authoritative distance. The humiliation inherent in the tattooing process is at least partly what prompts Tommo to insist that, should he be tattooed, he would not "have the *face* to return to [his] countrymen." This loss of not only his racial identity but also his masculinity would confirm his vulnerability, making him into a feminized object to be observed and thereby dominated.

The enactment of Tommo's gaze on the female body further reveals just how real the threat of tattooing is for Tommo and why he will go to great lengths to escape the Typees and their efforts to mark him. Tommo usually describes Fayaway in terms of her great beauty and innocent sensuality. For example, her "figure" is said to be "the very perfection of female grace and beauty." "Her complexion," he goes on to say, "was a rich and mantling olive, and when watching the glow upon her cheeks I could almost swear that beneath the transparent medium there lurked the blushes of a faint vermilion" (85). The use of the word "vermilion" here is intended to highlight Fayaway's modesty, the natural blush that links her to Melville's white female readers, yet it also recalls Tommo's description of the old sailor's "bright blue and vermilion pricking" in the scene with which I began my discussion of *Typee*. The tattooed queen of Nuku Hiva and the old salt with whom she is enamored seem initially to have little in common with the demure Fayaway. Yet like these grotesque figures, Fayaway too is marked with tattoos, a fact Tommo curiously attempts to minimize. "The females are very little embellished in this way," he explains, "and Fayaway and all the other young girls of her age were even less so than those of their sex more advanced in years. . . . All the tattooing that the nymph in question exhibited upon her person may be easily described. Three minute dots, no bigger than pinheads, decorated either lip, and at a little distance were not at all discernible. Just upon the fall of the shoulder were drawn two parallel lines half an inch

Figure 2. "Description of the process of tattooing." From Horace Holden,
A Narrative of the Shipwreck, Captivity, & Sufferings of Horace Holden & Benj. H. Nute
(Boston: Russell, Shattuck, and Co., 1836). Manuscripts and Rare Books Department,
Swem Library, College of William and Mary.

apart, and perhaps three inches in length, the interval being filled with deli-
cately executed figures" (86). Later Tommo acknowledges that married women
also have their right hand and left foot tattooed.

Yet, as Charles Anderson points out in his book *Melville in the South Seas*,
Melville's information about the tattoos of Typee women is "slightly inconsis-
tent and somewhat inaccurate" (150). According to Anderson as well as Gell,
complete tattooing for all women included the lips, the lobes of the ears, the
curve of the shoulder, both hands, both feet, and the legs; apparently there
were no distinguishing marks to symbolize either marriage or rank. Indeed,
as Melville's description of men's tattoos are correct in all particulars, it seems
significant that the details of women's tattoos are *so* inaccurate in *Typee*. When
the native woman being described is "of a mature age and rather matronly appearance," as are the married women and the queen, Tommo doesn't hesitate to
fictionally inscribe their bodies with tattoos (*Typee* 190). His hesitancy about the
disfigurement of the female body only reveals itself when the woman in question
is young and beautiful. Fayaway's facial tattoos, he insists, are "minute," "no bigger than pinheads," and definitely not discernible at a distance, in contrast to the
rather shocking facial tattoos of the Typee warriors. The tattoo might initially
seem to be a natural extension of the native woman's love of decoration; Tommo

goes into great detail about the young women's use of flowers to adorn their hair, ankles, and wrists. Yet he resists conflating tattooing with any other form of bodily decoration or modification, insisting that no such embellishment is needed to make Fayaway or her companions more attractive.

Tommo's desire (or Melville's desire, depending on how closely identified Melville is with his main character) to keep the young Typee women unmarked—or as minimally marked as possible—is indeed dictated by "the romantic needs of the narrative," as Anderson claims, but is also evidence of Western assumptions about gender and tattooing (151). As Margo DeMello observes, "Tattooed women overstep the physical boundaries of their bodies by permanently modifying them, and they overstep the boundaries of femininity by embodying a formerly masculine sign, the tattoo" ("Carnivalesque Body" 77). In Melville's nineteenth-century America, tattooing was indeed a "masculine sign," one that usually marked men as sailors, sometimes marked them as lower class, but *always* marked them as male. Although Fayaway and the other Typee women are not overstepping any boundaries in their own culture, it is the boundaries of Western culture with which Tommo is concerned. Tommo may admit that Fayaway wears a minimal amount of clothing—what he calls "the primitive and summer garb of Eden"—yet he also wants his female readers to recognize something of themselves, perhaps even their better selves, in the young Typee maidens, who, like their Western counterparts, spend much of their time in household duties and "skipping about from house to house, gadding and gossiping with their acquaintances" (87, 85). Extensive tattooing would presumably get in the way of such recognition.

The identification of the tattoo with feminization in the case of the threat to Tommo's face and with masculinization in the case of the threat to young Typee women may initially seem to be a contradiction. Yet Tommo's resistance in both situations derives from the sexual imagery of tattooing and the way in which tattooing necessitates a violation of the flesh and, quite possibly, of the racial and gender identity of the subject. The tattoo may initially appear to fix identity, marking it forever in the flesh, but it can also be seen as a symbol of fluid identity boundaries resisting any definitive interpretation. The subversive potential of the tattoo to disrupt identity links it to twentieth-century theories of the grotesque, most widely disseminated by Mikhail Bakhtin, but also developed by feminist theorists such as Susan Stewart and Mary Russo. As opposed to the classical body, which is, in Russo's words, "transcendent and monumental, closed, static, self-contained, symmetrical and sleek," the grotesque body is "open, protruding, irregular, secreting, multiple, and changing" (8). The relationship between the tattoo and the grotesque is most obvious in the tattoo's confusion of the interior/exterior boundaries of the human body. Although the wounds caused by the tattooing process, unlike other apertures on the surface of the skin, do eventually heal and close over, the tattoo is a constant reminder of the vulnerability of identity and flesh. One need only think of the elderly Typee men and the way in which tattooing had "obliterated every trace of [their] humanity" to understand the grotesque nature of the tattooed body.

As Tommo's observations of the Typees demonstrate, tattooing opens the body up for interpretation. Robbed of his whiteness *and* his masculinity by tattooing, Tommo would have two choices: to become like the queen of Nuku Hiva, a grotesque figure who attempts to control the display and interpretation of her tattoos, or to become like Fayaway, sexually and textually available to the first man who comes along to claim her. Rather than follow either of these models, he retains his authoritative distance, limits the queen to the beginning (but the future) of his narrative, and minimizes the significance of Fayaway's tattoos. Both gestures are aggressive, a point recognized by Frances E. Mascia-Lees and Patricia Sharpe in their discussion of "the differential meaning of tattoo for men and women" (148). As they note, "[E]ither the marking or the removal of the mark can serve as a representation of the imposition of a restrictive, unitary femininity" (162). In textually marking the body of the queen and withholding the tattoos of Fayaway and her friends, Tommo imposes his own understanding of the mark on the bodies of native women. As with his uninformed translations of the Typee language and culture, Tommo's (mis)readings of the Typees' tattoos, particularly those of the women, have more to do with his desire to solidify his own identity than with his desire to educate his reader. Although Tommo continually positions Karky, the tattoo artist, as the aggressor in *Typee*, Tommo himself is ultimately the aggressor here, the artist whose words have the power to erase or to mark the bodies of the Typees according to his own agenda.

Melville's *Typee* was based loosely on his own residence among the Typees in 1842. The actual four weeks of his captivity were transformed into four months, and Melville added to his firsthand knowledge of the Marquesas with information borrowed extensively from texts such as Captain David Porter's *Journal of a Cruise Made to the Pacific Ocean* and C. S. Stewart's *Visit to the South Seas*, along with a number of other texts that he mentions briefly, if at all, in *Typee*.[13] Like the stories of the tattooed white men who were exhibiting their bodies in the early 1840s, aspects of Melville's account were occasionally—and justifiably—doubted, as he was said to have no hard evidence of his captivity. His word and the text itself were apparently not enough to verify the truth of his story. A letter written by Richard Tobias Greene, the "Toby" who had deserted with Melville and had also spent time in the Typee Valley, did more to satisfy doubtful readers and reviewers. Published in the Buffalo *Commercial Advertiser*, the letter confirmed Melville's version of events in *Typee* and vouched for the author's integrity. Taken together, these two texts represented the "truth" of Melville's narrative independent of any physical evidence. Yet another captivity narrative, published eleven years after *Typee*, produced no such demand for textual verification; the apparent truth of this narrative relied instead on the visual evidence of the tattooed body of its heroine, Olive Oatman. Examining these two texts in relation to each other highlights Western assumptions about race and tattooing as well as the simultaneous fascination with and repulsion from the grotesque figure of the tattooed woman. This process also raises disturbing questions about gender and agency in nineteenth-century America.

The Captivities of Olive Oatman

In August 1850 the Oatman family left Independence, Missouri, as part of a wagon train of Brewsterites, a Mormon splinter group traveling westward to the mouth of the Colorado River. Their destination, at the intersection of what is now the borders of Arizona, California, and Mexico, had been revealed to James C. Brewster by prophecy as the intended refuge of the Mormon people.[14] After several disagreements regarding the Brewsterites' route and final destination, however, Royce and Mary Ann Oatman and their eight children split from the rest of the group and continued along the Gila River to Fort Yuma alone. On February 18, 1851, while still 150 miles away from the fort, the Oatmans were attacked by Yavapai Indians.[15] Seven family members were killed. Severely injured, fourteen-year-old Lorenzo managed to reunite with several Brewsterite families who had remained in the town of Pimole after their split from the Oatmans. Olive, thirteen years old, and Mary Ann, seven, were taken captive by the Yavapais, with whom they lived for about a year until they were sold to the Mohaves. Mary Ann died of starvation after about two years, but Olive remained with the Mohaves until February 22, 1856—approximately five years after being taken captive—when she was apparently rescued and returned to Fort Yuma.

Oatman's captivity became the subject of *Life among the Indians: Being an Interesting Narrative of the Captivity of the Oatman Girls*, which first appeared in print in 1857. Written by Royal B. Stratton, a Methodist clergyman, the narrative went through three editions. Part of the subtitle of the first edition, *Captivity of the Oatman Girls*, became the title of both the second and the third edition although the story remained essentially the same in all three.[16] Ostensibly a composite of the voices of Olive Oatman, her brother Lorenzo, and Stratton, the narrative recounts Oatman's captivity among the Yavapai and the Mohave Indians as well as her brother's five-year search for evidence of her survival. It is not known how much Olive and Lorenzo actually contributed to Stratton's account; Kathryn Zabelle Derounian-Stodola, an expert on the Oatman captivity, suggests that "Stratton constructed—indeed, *created*—their story, which became a bestseller as soon as it appeared in 1857" ("Indian Captivity Narratives" 35). In the conclusion to the narrative, Stratton himself admits that the first-person point of view of much of the narrative is a construction intended to evoke sympathy for Oatman and her family (3rd ed. 283). Yet as early as May 1858, a little more than two years after her return to white society, Oatman herself lectured publicly to promote the narrative; she is known to have been performing seven years later, at the close of the Civil War. The popularity of these lectures contributed to the success of *Captivity of the Oatman Girls*, which had sold twenty-six thousand copies by 1860.

Although Oatman's captivity narrative is a fascinating example of the genre, her story would most likely not have had such immense appeal for nineteenth-century American audiences were it not for one distinctive detail—the fact that both Mary Ann and Olive Oatman received chin and arm tattoos while living with the Mohaves.[17] The tattooing process is described briefly in Stratton's narrative, but the tattoos themselves became central to the appeal of the lecture series used to promote *Captivity of the Oatman Girls* throughout the late 1850s and early 1860s. More than twenty years before the appearance of Nora Hildebrandt, the reputed first "tattooed lady," drawings of Oatman's tattooed face were reproduced and used in broadside advertisements for the lecture series under headings such as "Five Years Among Wild Savages" (see figure 3). Newspaper reporters writing about Oatman's appearances inevitably commented on the tattoos. "She will bear the marks of her captivity to her grave," a writer for the *Evansville Enquirer* reported, "her savage masters having tattooed her after the custom of their tribes" ("Five Years"). An article in the *Daily Alta California* called Oatman's tattoos "the 'chief's mark'" and explained, "This savage embellishment does not materially enhance the personal charms of the lady, but it is an indelible evidence of the scenes she has undergone" ("Six Years' Captivity" 5). Quotes such as these would frequently appear on the broadsides as well, reinforcing the impact of the illustrations.

Olive Oatman clearly embodies Tommo's fear of facial tattooing as well as his anxieties regarding gender and tattooing. Facial tattooing has rendered Oatman an object to be displayed and observed on her lecture tour. The indelible marks simultaneously feminize her, making her into a victim to be pitied, and defeminize her, as is revealed in the reporters' comments on her (lack of) "personal charms." Perhaps most importantly, because Oatman, unlike Tommo, is unable to escape the tattoo, it is the interpretation of *her* tattoos rather than those of

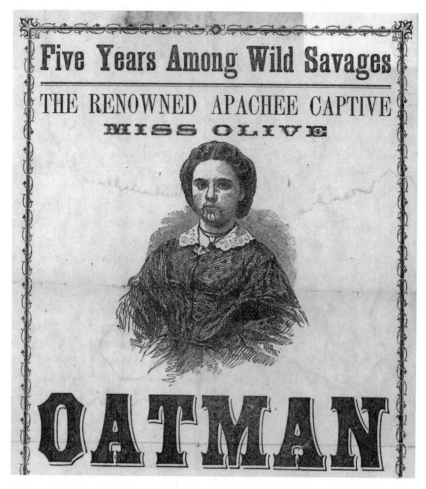

Figure 3. "Five Years Among Wild Savages." Undated broadside. Courtesy Everett D. Graff Collection, the Newberry Library, Chicago.

the native other that is given primacy in the narrative of her captivity. Stratton, author of the narrative and choreographer of the lecture series, presents the tattoos as evidence of the savagery of Native Americans and of Oatman's persistent desire to resist and ultimately to escape from her captors. In doing so, he makes a spectacle of the tattooed female body to reassure audiences of the unassailable nature of racial and gender identity, even within the extreme conditions of Indian captivity. Yet because of the nature of the tattoo as well as Stratton's desire to exploit Oatman's marked body to attract and titillate audiences, the tattoos in both the narrative and the supporting performances do not reflect or confirm the fixedness of identity; rather, as in Melville's *Typee*, these marks raise the possibility that identity boundaries are ultimately permeable and unreliable.

In *Captivity of the Oatman Girls*, there is little sense of ambiguity surrounding Oatman's experiences of captivity among both the Yavapais and the Mohaves. Unlike Tommo, Olive takes no pleasure in her captivity, does not develop any significant relationships with her captors, and does not, if she can help it, participate in cultural events or rituals. In fact, Stratton attempts to avoid any mention of issues that might complicate what he saw as the culturally intact white female returning to civilization from the savage culture in which she was held captive. The Native Americans in Stratton's text are described as "brutal savages and human-shaped demons," as well as "man-animals" (97, 98).[18] Both the Yavapais and the Mohaves are repeatedly represented as dirty, lazy, ignorant, and depraved. At no time during her captivity as depicted by Stratton does Oatman appear to be in danger of losing her white, Christian sense of propriety and adopting a more native way of life. Similarly, given the hostility toward Mormons in the mid-nineteenth century, the potential complication presented by Oatman's Mormonism is avoided by the complete erasure of the Oatman family's motivation for emigrating. Ironically, Stratton seems to use this erasure—and Olive's subsequent Christianity—as a defense against claims that she had assimilated into Mohave society during her captivity.

Oatman does seem to have abandoned her Mormon faith in favor of a more mainstream Christian sect after her return to white society. Rather than confirming Oatman's purity or piety, however, this apparent conversion suggests a flexibility of identity that might lend itself to transculturation. Derounian-Stodola has cast doubt on the narrative Stratton presents in *Captivity of the Oatman Girls*, insisting that Oatman was not only transculturated into Mohave society but may in fact have been married into the tribe and become a mother. Her claim rests on a number of documents, including the 1903 account of TokwaOa, a Mohave who remembered Olive Oatman and had, in fact, been one of the party accompanying her to Fort Yuma. TokwaOa's account stated that Olive and Mary Ann had been happy with the Mohaves and that the chief had ordered tribe members to tend to their needs (Kroeber 2). Interviews with Oatman also indicate that Stratton's representation of her treatment among the Mohaves was inaccurate. In an interview with Captain Martin Burke, the commandant of the fort, Oatman indicated that the Mohaves treated her and Mary Ann "very well." Burke adds parenthetically, "From her manner seemed perfectly pleased" (Kroeber and Kroeber 312). Another interview with Oatman appeared in the *Los Angeles Star* on April 19, 1856, almost two months after her return to white society. According to this interview, Olive insists that she and

Mary Ann were adopted into the family of the chief of the Mohaves and were treated well (Rice 102). Finally, evidence suggests that Oatman may have left a husband and children on her return to Fort Yuma. Susan Thompson Lewis Parrish, a friend of Oatman's whose family traveled with the Brewsterite wagon train, insisted in her memoir that "Olive became the wife of the chief's son and at the time of her rescue was the mother of two little boys" (Root 8). Parrish also claimed that after her "rescue," Oatman was a "frightened, tatooed [sic] creature who was more savage than civilized, and who sought at every opportunity to flee back to her Indian husband and children" (7).

The notion of transculturation—or at least the threat of a female captive forsaking her own culture for that of her captor's—was familiar to American readers of captivity narratives. Indeed, as Christopher Castiglia notes, the popularity of captivity narratives often depended on the textual presence of this threat (4). Although most captivity narratives conclude with the return of the captive to white society, several, most notably James Everett Seaver's *Narrative of the Life of Mrs. Mary Jemison* (1824), recount the experiences of captives who remain with their captors, marry into the tribe and eventually attain positions of authority within their adopted culture. Such narratives could be seen as a critique of white patriarchal culture, particularly since transculturation into native culture frequently afforded white women such as Jemison "physical, matrimonial, and economic space" unattainable in their own societies (Castiglia 36). "More often than not" though, Gary Ebersole notes, "representations of Indian captivity and of going native were used to reinforce existing cultural categories and conceptual systems of exclusion" rather than to question the status quo (193). In this sense, *Captivity of the Oatman Girls* and many other captivity narratives are indeed part of a tradition of "propagandist texts that rationalized white superiority" in nineteenth-century America (Derounian-Stodola, "Captive and Her Editor" 172).

In *Captivity of the Oatman Girls*, Oatman's physical body becomes essential to this nationalistic project in that Stratton attempts to use both clothing and tattoos to represent her supposed retention of Christian values and her eagerness to return to white society. According to the narrative, clothing (or the lack thereof) factors greatly into Oatman's response to the Yavapais: "Their mode of dress, (but little dress they had!) was needlessly and shockingly indecent, when the material of which their scanty clothing consists would, by an industrious habit and hand, have clothed them to the dictates of comfort and modesty" (135). The Indians who attacked the Oatman family are described as "scantily-clad, and what covering they had borrowed from the wild beasts, as if to furnish an appropriate badge of their savage nature and design" (114).[19]

Although the Mohaves do not wear fur, they are "[b]ark-clad, where clad at all, the scarcity of their covering indicating either a warm climate or a great destitution of the clothing material, *or something else*" (166–67, italics mine). Thus Oatman's Christian decency and feminine modesty are reflected in and perhaps even textually constructed by her judgment of the Indians and their apparently inexplicable lack of any desire to cover their bodies with clothing.

Oatman's clothing is not mentioned until close to the end of the narrative, when she resists entering Fort Yuma in her native dress. Prior to this moment, the details about her clothing and that of her sister are sparse: the girls' shoes and head coverings are taken from them on their journey to the Yavapai camp, and later they are given beads, which they wear "about [their] necks, squaw fashion" (122, 175). Yet the fact that Olive and Mary Ann wear native dress—consisting solely of a bark skirt—is confirmed by the illustrations that accompany all three editions of the text.[20] When Olive and Mary Ann arrive at the Yavapai camp, an illustration depicts them in the middle of a circle of dancing Indians, their arms around each other. Both wear short-sleeved dresses that reach almost to their ankles (see figure 4). The next illustration depicts Olive and Mary Ann sitting under a tree, presumably discussing the possibility of being sold to the Mohave. Both girls are wearing native bark skirts, which barely reach to their knees. Both are also bare-breasted. Behind the tree lurks an Indian man, whose presence indicates the sexual vulnerability of the girls as well as their complete lack of privacy (see figure 5). The girls are shown in the same way throughout the remaining illustrations. In fact, when depicted in the company of Indian women, as in the drawing illustrating Mary Ann's death, the girls are distinguishable only because they are shaded differently by the artist; otherwise, they appear to be Indian themselves (see figure 6).[21]

Such uncertainty about racial identity is evident in Stratton's text as well. For example, the heading of the first chapter of the narrative announces a scene called "Two Girls taken for 'Injins.'" The readers' expectations, however—and perhaps their voyeuristic desires—are thwarted in that the girls "taken" are not Olive and Mary Ann, and they are not literally taken captive. Rather they are mistaken—"taken"—for Indians by a fellow traveler who has gone to the river to draw water: "His busy brain must have been preoccupied with 'Injins,' for he soon came running, puffing, and yelling into camp. As he went headlong over the wagon-tongue, his tin pail as it rolled started a half-score of dogs to their feet, and setting them upon a yell, he lustily, and at the topmost pitch of voice, cried, 'Injins! Injins!' He soon recovered his wits, however, and the pleasant little lasses came into camp with a hearty laugh" (44). Soon after, another group of children are "suddenly transformed into huge Indians to the eyes of" a pair of white men

Figure 4. Mary Ann and Olive Oatman at the Yavapai camp. From R. B. Stratton, *Captivity of the Oatman Girls*, 3rd ed. (New York: Carlton and Porter, 1858).

Figure 5. Mary Ann and Olive Oatman in native dress. From R. B. Stratton, *Captivity of the Oatman Girls*, 3rd ed. (New York: Carlton and Porter, 1858).

hunting antelope (46). As in the first scene, the men make fools of themselves in their efforts to escape, but order is restored upon their sheepish realization of the mistake. This rash of children mistaken for Indians suggests not only the travelers' uneasiness about the Native American presence on the frontier but also a deep-seated fear of transculturation. If these children can be mysteriously transformed into Indians while under the watchful eye of their parents, what might happen to them if they are taken captive, separated from the family and the society that has shaped their racial identity? As in the illustrations, then, the body becomes an unreliable marker of race; the power of clothing to signify race becomes all the more important, particularly toward the end of *Captivity of the Oatman Girls*.

Olive's reluctance to appear before the white officers at Fort Yuma in her bark skirt is thus an important transitional moment in the narrative. The exchange of native clothing for civilized clothing symbolizes the captive's willingness to return to white society (and therefore to "escape" from the natives) and her retention of the norms of white civilization. The significance of this exchange to Stratton and to the way in which readers interpreted the narrative is confirmed by an examination of the illustrations depicting this scene in various editions of the text. The first edition includes an illustration of Oatman wearing a black dress while greeting the commander of Fort Yuma but does not provide any textual clue as to how she obtained the dress. In the second edition, however, Stratton explains that Oatman's appearance at the fort was delayed because of her lack of proper attire for the meeting: "Olive, with her characteristic modesty, was unwilling to appear in her bark attire and her poor shabby dress among the whites, eager as she was to catch again a glimpse of their countenances. . . . As soon as this was made known, a noble-hearted woman, the wife of one of the officers . . . , sent her a dress and clothing of the best she had" (271).[22] Curiously, this edition replaces the earlier illustration with one of Oatman wearing the native bark skirt; she can be distinguished from the Indians surrounding her only because she is being approached by the commander of the fort (see figure 7). With her eyes cast down, as if in shame, Olive extends her hand to the commander, thereby capturing the liminal moment in this transaction, the moment in which Olive is both white and Indian, "civilized" and "uncivilized." The third edition retains the textual explanation of the second but depicts Oatman in a dress again (see figure 8). In this case, though, the whiteness of the dress highlights the difference in appearance between her and the Mohave woman in native dress standing next to her. This illustration and the revised text accord better with Stratton's version of events in that Olive appears never to have lost her civilized values and sense of femininity. There is no evidence here of liminality or transculturation.

Figure 6. The death of Mary Ann Oatman. From R. B. Stratton, *Captivity of the Oatman Girls*, 3rd ed. (New York: Carlton and Porter, 1858).

Figure 7. Olive Oatman at Fort Yuma. From R. B. Stratton, *Captivity of the Oatman Girls*, 2nd ed. (San Francisco: Whitton, Towne, 1857).

Overall, despite her five years "among the Indians," Olive is represented in Stratton's narrative as a white woman who not only desires to return to white society but also retains her Christian faith and her ability to communicate in English. Her desire for a dress rather than a bark skirt neatly symbolizes Stratton's implicit assertion that you can take the woman out of civilization, but you can't take civilization out of the woman. This assertion is complicated, however, by the illustrations and, at times, the text itself, but most importantly by the presence of Oatman's tattoos, which she cannot remove and repudiate as easily as she can "her bark attire." As Gordon Sayre notes, tattooing "is the negative limit of clothing. It implies the vanity of ornament without the utility or modesty of clothing and is an enduring mark of primitivism. . . . [A]s the negation of both clothing and modesty, tattoos, even on a European's skin, were a mark of savagery" (165–66). Yet neither Stratton's text nor the accompanying illustrations actually address the threat posed by Oatman's tattoos; the illustrations, in fact, ignore the presence of the tattoos entirely, representing Olive and Mary Ann's chins and arms as unmarked.

Stratton acknowledges the tattoos themselves in his account of Olive Oatman's captivity but attempts to dictate the way in which they are interpreted by ostensibly presenting the tattooing process from the point of view of Olive herself:

> We had seen them [tattoo] some of their female children, and we had often conversed with each other about expressing the hope that we should be spared from receiving their marks upon us. I ventured to plead with them for a few moments that they would not put those ugly marks upon our faces. But it was in vain. To all our expostulations they only replied in substance that they knew why we objected to it; that we expected to return to the whites, and we would be ashamed of it then; but that it was their resolution we should never return, and that as we belonged to them we should wear their "Ki-e-chook." They said further, that if we should get away, and they should find us among other tribes, or if some other tribes should steal us, they would by this means know us. (182–83)

The narrative makes no mention of the arm tattoos that the girls almost certainly received at the same time; the focus here is on the more visible and therefore (to a white audience) more disturbing facial tattoos. According to the narrative, the girls resist these "ugly marks" to no avail, so strong is the Mohaves' wish to protect their property. Unlike Tommo, however, their resistance is verbal rather than physical: instead of running away, they "plead" with the Mohaves not to tattoo them. Although these limitations might be ascribed to the "reality" of the Oatman narrative, they are more likely connected to the Oatman girls' retention of "proper" female values and standards for behavior—even when

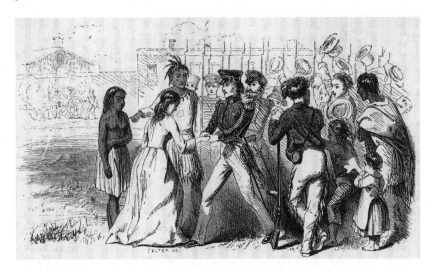

Figure 8. Olive Oatman at Fort Yuma. From R. B. Stratton, *Captivity of the Oatman Girls*, 3rd ed. (New York: Carlton and Porter, 1858).

these standards place them in danger.[23] The narrative insists that the tattoos are marks of captivity rather than marriage or adoption, of outsider rather than insider status. According to the narrative, "They told us this could never be taken from the face, and that they had given us a different mark from the one worn by their own females, as we saw, but the same with which they marked all their own captives, and that they could claim us in whatever tribe they might find us" (183).

This distinction is crucial to Stratton's presentation of the tattoos; rather than transforming Olive and Mary Ann into "reproducers" of Mohave culture (and perhaps more tantalizingly, reproducers of Mohave children), the tattoos are said merely to reinforce the girls' status as slaves. Yet such assertions are by no means evidence that the marks actually meant what Stratton said they meant. White audiences in the mid-nineteenth century knew little or nothing about Native American tattooing practices and would have taken what seemed to be Oatman's firsthand knowledge of Indian cultures and rituals as fact. Oatman's tattoos could just as easily have been a symbol of participation in or adoption into the Mohave tribe. Had Olive been adopted into the tribe, as she herself appears to have claimed immediately after her return to Fort Yuma, her tattooing would have been seen as a spiritual necessity. According to Mohave legend, a man or a woman without facial tattoos "would be refused entrance to the 'land of the dead' and had 'to go down a rat-hole' instead" (Taylor and Wallace 4–5). Moreover, Stratton's distinction between Oatman's facial tattoos and those of

Mohave women seems spurious given the fact that in Mohave culture designs for chin tattoos were chosen by the tattooer based on the shape and features of the face and, occasionally, on gender (4). Ultimately, however, it is impossible to know exactly what the tattoos meant to the Mohaves or to Oatman herself during her captivity.

It is certainly tempting to regard Oatman's tattoos as proof of one version of captivity or another, as Stratton and audiences of the narrative and lecture series seem to have done. Was Oatman an unwilling captive? Or was she married into the tribe? Did she leave children behind when she returned to Fort Yuma? Historians and literary critics seem driven to find answers to similar questions, and most are now convinced that Oatman's tattoos are evidence of at least some sort of acceptance into Mohave culture. By the mid-nineteenth century, precedence had undoubtedly been set for such an interpretation. Although many similar examples may have been lost to history, one surviving report tells of a female captive refusing to leave her Indian captors in the Mississippi Valley to return to her white family. She explained that "the Indians had disfigured her face, by tattooing it according to their fancy and ideas of beauty, and a young man of them had taken her for his wife, by whom she believed herself pregnant; that she had become reconciled to her mode of life, and was well treated by her husband; and that she should be more unhappy by returning to her father, under these circumstances, than by remaining where she was" (qtd. in Ebersole 229). The young woman's tattooed face is seemingly inseparable from her relationship with her Indian husband, her pregnancy, and her ultimate decision not to return to white society.

The search for the "truth" behind Oatman's captivity and tattoos is most interesting, however, because it reveals the urge to identify and fix identity boundaries and then to rally around traditional notions of race and gender when these boundaries are threatened. Although used to promote the narrative, Oatman's tattoos and the potential of her grotesque body threatened Stratton's representation of her captivity as well as the American understanding of captivity in the mid-nineteenth century at large. A brief look at another nineteenth-century representation of captivity can help illustrate the magnitude of this threat and the disruptive power of the grotesque. A prime example of American ideal sculpture, *The White Captive*, completed by Erastus Dow Palmer in 1859, depicted a nude young woman bound by her wrists to a tree (see figure 9). What makes *The White Captive* especially relevant here is the suggestion, made by Palmer's daughter, that the sculpture was inspired by the story of Olive Oatman, whose narrative had been published in 1857.[24] As an interpretation of Oatman's captivity narrative, the sculpture illustrates the extent to which the nineteenth-century American understanding of captivity relied on a classical representation

Figure 9. Erastus Dow Palmer, *The White Captive*, 1857–58. Marble, 65" × 20¼" × 17". Metropolitan Museum of Art, New York, Bequest of Hamilton Fish, 1894; No. 94.9.3. All rights reserved, The Metropolitan Museum of Art, New York.

of the white female body, a representation clearly contradicted by the grotesque body of Olive Oatman herself.

The White Captive was extremely well received by nineteenth-century viewers; during a public exhibition of the sculpture in New York, for example, attendance increased from one hundred to four hundred per day in the first month (Kasson, *Marble Queens* 74). In her book *Marble Queens and Captives: Women in Nineteenth-Century American Sculpture*, Joy S. Kasson notes that at least part of the thrill of viewing sculptures like *The White Captive* was "the dramatic tension evoked by the statue's nudity and the suggestion of physical and sexual violence" (78). Yet the audience was able to indulge in this titillating exercise of the imagination precisely because the young woman's identity was not ultimately at risk; in the viewing of the statue, there was an "assurance that the captive, no matter how hopeless her plight, would never change her essential nature or relinquish her spiritual power" (88). In one review subsequently reproduced as a viewing guide to the sculpture, the author insisted that the young captive's Christianity was essential to her survival and strength: "[T]he Christian heart was within her, and the Christian soul upheld her, and the Christian's God was by her side; and so she stood, and waited, and was brave" (qtd. in Kasson, *Marble Queens* 79). Despite the nudity of *The White Captive*, which excited some controversy, the majority of commentators regarded the young girl as spiritually and sexually innocent. Henry T. Tuckerman's review of *The White Captive* is indicative of the most widely accepted view of the subject's inherent morality; his emphasis, which recalls that of Stratton in *Captivity of the Oatman Girls*, is on the captive's retention of her Christianity and "virgin purity." Tuckerman also claims that the "keen distress" that "marks her expression" does not reveal the "inward comfort" and "elevated faith" that "combines with and sublimates the fear and pain" (Webster 29). Indeed, Tuckerman reads the captive's body in the same convoluted way he reads her expression, thus negating the impropriety of her nudity: " 'The White Captive' illustrates the power and inevitable victory of Christian civilization: not in the face alone, but in every contour of the figure, in the expression of the feet as well as the lips, the same physical subjugation, and moral self-control, and self-concentration are apparent" (qtd. in Kasson, *Marble Queens* 81).

Similar to the illustrations in Stratton's narrative, then, *The White Captive* relies on a belief that the classical body—closed and self-contained—can withstand any disruption or penetration, even if that body is nude and female. The classical body of the female captive confirms the superiority of white society (coded as "Christian") for sympathetic viewers. As Castiglia notes, "To the degree that the captive resists taking on the attributes of her captors, she represents the impermeable, defensible borders of the white, Anglo nation" (9). Indeed, the white marble out of which *The White Captive* is made seems indicative of the sculptor's desire to present the young girl's virtue—and that of the culture she represents—as "impermeable" and "defensible."

Although both the illustrations and the sculpture to some degree represent not just captivity but Olive Oatman's captivity, neither attempts to represent the tattoos on Oatman's chin and arms. Although the medium in which Palmer worked may have precluded representing tattoos or any other bodily marks, this omission seems much more intentional and is perhaps similar to the sculptural "convention by which the female genital region was portrayed unrealistically, as a smooth and unbroken triangle, without any indication of a vulva" (Kasson, *Marble Queens* 84). Like female genitalia, Oatman's tattoos would have disturbed what Palmer's biographer has called "the artist's sensitivity to the ideal" as well as nineteenth-century notions of femininity, passionlessness, and purity (Webster 47).[25] Although the nudity of the sculpture and the illustrations is, in fact, suggestive and mildly erotic, it is tamed, contained, even transcended by the rhetorical frame in which it is presented. As is demonstrated in a comparison of *The White Captive* and Oatman's promotional images, rather than unequivocally symbolizing the transcendence of the corporeal, Oatman's tattoos have the potential to represent the exact opposite—the corporeality of experience.

The disruptive potential of Oatman's tattoos and performances is perhaps most apparent in the visual images printed and distributed to promote Oatman's lecture tour. Both photographs show Oatman in rather traditional poses: in one, she is seated, her hands clasped in her lap, while in the other, she stands, one hand placed on the back of a chair (see figure 10). She wears an elaborate dress with a row of shiny buttons down the front and a white lace collar and cuffs. Yet the design on Oatman's dress—at her wrists, elbows, and ankles—replicates the lines on her chin, thereby drawing attention to the tattoos rather than away from them. The design also hints at the presence of Oatman's arm tattoos, hidden beneath her clothing. The standing portrait is particularly striking in that more of Oatman's dress is visible, and unlike in the seated portrait, Oatman stares boldly into the camera, seemingly challenging her audience to read and interpret the marks on her chin. This direct gaze, along with the revelation of Oatman's tattoos, is reminiscent of Melville's queen of Nuku Hiva in that both women seem to intentionally interact with those who view them. Yet the careful posing of Oatman's body, the elaborate dress, and the traditional use of the chair as prop indicate that Oatman's purpose in her lecture series is quite different from that of the rebellious queen.

According to the only surviving typescript of her lecture notes, Oatman's gaze mirrors the bold strategy she uses to draw her audience's attention to her

Figure 10. Portrait of Olive Oatman, ca. 1865. AHS#1927. Courtesy of the
Arizona Historical Society/Tucson.

tattoos. The lecture begins with a traditionally feminine statement of her reluctance to speak publicly:

> Neither the position of public speaking nor the facts that I am to relate are in
> harmony with my own feelings, for my nature intuitively shrinks from both.
>   But I yeald [*sic*] to what I conceive to be the opening of providence & the sterne
> [*sic*] voice of duty. (qtd. in Pettid 1)

Similar to the dress worn in the promotional images, this statement asserts Oatman's femininity, her adherence to white societal values. Perhaps in anticipation
of any criticism, she protests that her feminine "nature . . . shrinks" from pub-
licity and that only the "voice of duty" can convince her to place herself in the
public eye as she does in her performances. Yet later in the lecture, after having explained the circumstances of the massacre of her family, Oatman boldly
directs her audience to take notice of the lines on her chin:

> Their captives whether Indians or whites become slaves. They give them the tribes
> *slave marks* so that in case they desert to any other *tribe* they can be recognized at
> once.
>   You perceive I have the marks indelibly placed upon my *chin*. (qtd. in Pettid 19)

The strategy here is similar to that employed in the design of Oatman's dress and
the staging of her photograph. Oatman may be reluctant to speak, but she is an
authority on Indian culture and the experience of captivity. She may appear
and behave quite feminine, but she also directs her audience's attention to her
tattoos. Along with her labeling of herself as a "slave," this directive highlights
the performative nature of her lectures and the importance of her body as well
as her words to that performance. Oatman takes risks here, placing herself in
the position of an acculturated captive, a Native American woman, and perhaps even an African American slave, yet she is safe and respectable as long as
she can—as she does in Stratton's narrative—return to her "real" identity as
a white, Christian woman. Overall, both the images and the lecture itself attempt to balance the exploitation of the tattoos and the assertion of Oatman's
white womanhood in order to both attract audiences to the performances and
avoid the criticisms commonly leveled at women public speakers throughout
the century.

   In general, women who spoke publicly in nineteenth-century America were
seen as having crossed the boundaries of "natural" feminine behavior; as many
critics agree, this "cultural regime . . . dictated that it was a man's nature to in-
habit the public rhetorical sphere and woman's nature not to" (Johnson 3). Just
twenty years before the publication of *Captivity of the Oatman Girls*, Sarah and
Angelina Grimké were rebuked by a group of Congregationalist ministers for

their "unfeminine" abolitionist lectures. "We invite your attention to the dangers which at present seem to threaten the female character with widespread and permanent injury," the ministers wrote in a public letter. "The appropriate duties and influence of women are clearly stated in the New Testament. The power of woman is her dependence, flowing from that consciousness of that weakness which God has given her for her protection" (qtd. in Riley 117).

Women of color who dared to speak publicly were often attacked even more vehemently by critics. Frances Ellen Watkins Harper lectured many times over a fifty-year span during the latter half of the nineteenth century. In a letter written in 1870, just a few years after Oatman ceased her public appearances, Harper told a friend, "I don't know but that you would laugh if you were to hear some of the remarks which my lectures call forth: 'She is a man,' again 'She is not colored, she is painted' " (*Brighter Coming Day* 126–27). Thus Harper's gender, race, and virtue were questioned because of her lectures, presumably in an attempt to remove her authority to speak on issues such as the women's movement, abolition, and temperance. Similarly, Sarah Winnemucca, a Paiute, lectured hundreds of times in the late 1870s and early 1880s to "win hearts and minds and to bring the pressures of public opinion to bear on the national government" in support of her ailing tribe (Zanjani 197). Winnemucca's femininity was frequently called into question; the *Reno Crescent*, for example, called her "a common Indian strumpet" (qtd. in Zanjani 113). Another regional newspaper, the *Silver State*, accused Winnemucca of drinking heavily after a lecture. When Winnemucca challenged the editor to a duel in defense of her honor, he called her a "drunken savage" in his newspaper and implied that she should be sent to jail for threatening him (qtd. in Zanjani 209). As with Harper, Winnemucca's authority was undermined insofar as these articles' accusations of indecency and drunkenness diminished the Paiute woman's standing in the white community to whom she appealed in her lectures.

One of the most important differences between Oatman's performances and the lectures of the Grimké sisters, Harper, and Winnemucca, however, is that Oatman claimed not to have a political purpose for her public speaking. Although her lectures clearly supported a racist national policy toward the Native American tribes of the Southwest, Oatman herself identified her project as entirely personal, even telling her audiences, "I appear before you at this time, not as a public lecturer but as a Narrator of events. Events connected with my own personal experience and observation" (qtd. in Pettid 1). Her closing remarks merely ask "the young ladies of this Audience" to "appreciate the word *Home*" (qtd. in Pettid 25). The absence of an overt political agenda, along with Oatman's apparent conversion to Christianity, her association with Stratton and his church, and her seeming vulnerability after the massacre of her family, may have protected her from much of the criticism endured by other female public speakers of the period. As Nan Johnson notes, the most successful women rhetoricians of the nineteenth century—Elizabeth Cady Stanton, Mary Livermore, Frances E. Willard—similarly positioned their "public influence" as "an inspired extension of their feminine domain" (16). Whatever Oatman's personal feelings about lecturing, she seems not to have quit the lecture tour because of such pressure.

Yet like the lectures of the other women discussed here, both white women and women of color, Oatman's performances ultimately call racial and gendered identity into question. Her simultaneous flaunting of her tattoos *and* her femininity pushes her audience to consider the possibility that identity is indeed fluid and that she might be, in fact, transculturated or at the very least not exactly the same girl she had been when she was taken captive. In this sense, Oatman could be seen simultaneously as "one of us" and "one of them." She was a white person whose tattoos and words demonstrated the danger and savagery of the frontier and the necessity of taming it. Yet she was also an "other," a white woman who looked native, who had lived in a native culture, and was rumored to have been adopted or even married into a native tribe. As Castiglia notes, captive white women "deny the binary opposition of white and Indian societies; moving between cultures, at home in neither yet ultimately constituted from elements of both, the captives articulate 'hybrid' subjectivities that destabilize white culture's fiction of fixed and pure identity" (7). Oatman's tattoos provided audiences with visual evidence of such hybridity that may have caused them to doubt the official version of her captivity.

Despite all of Stratton's assertions to the contrary, the disruptive potential of the tattoos is evident even within the narrative itself; when Olive is reunited with her brother Lorenzo, for example, Stratton writes, "She was grown to womanhood; she was changed, but despite the written traces of her outdoor life and barbarous treatment left upon her appearance and person, he could read the assuring evidences of her family identity" (277). Olive's face reveals the mixed nature of her identity at this point in the narrative, as do the conflicting illustrations depicting her meeting with the commander of Fort Yuma. While the family resemblance reveals Olive to be an Oatman, the facial tattoo just as strongly reveals her to be a member of the Mohave community. Even Stratton cannot neatly disregard this liminal moment in the narrative.

Other representations of similar moments assert that Oatman's tattooed face made it difficult for observers to categorize her as a white woman; this confusion was testified to by Henry Grinnell, who assisted in Olive's rescue and was present at Fort Yuma when she was returned. An article in *Harper's New Monthly Magazine* reported that "[s]he was brought down to a place on the Colorado at an appointed time. Here Mr. Grinnell met her. She was sitting on the ground, with her face covered by her hands. So completely was she disguised by long exposure to the sun, by paint, tatooing [*sic*], and costume, that he could not believe she was a white woman" ("Tour through Arizona" 701). Oatman's skin, physically transformed by "sun, . . . paint, [and] tatooing," is no longer a reliable marker of identity; yet while Grinnell "could not believe she was a white woman," neither did he believe that she was Native American. Her grotesque body remains horrifyingly undefined, open for interpretation. Grinnell's uncertainty is also implied in Stratton's text; in his representation of this moment, Stratton writes, "With eager eyes [Grinnell] stood gazing for some time, when three Indians and two females, dressed in closely woven bark skirts, came down to the ferry on the opposite side of the river. At that he bounded toward them, crying at the top of his voice, 'They have come; *the captive girl is here!*' " (271). Although the other "female" accompanying Oatman's party is the daughter of the chief—clearly an Indian—Stratton simply calls both women "females" and the males "Indians." Thus he avoids the issue of the racial identity of the "females" and, other than the bark skirt, Oatman's physical appearance. It is not clear whether these two girls are "taken for 'Injins' " or these two "Injins" are taken for "females." What does seem clear is Stratton's inability to sufficiently contain the disruptive potential of Oatman's appearance throughout his narrative and the lengthy lecture series.

To Stratton, Oatman's tattoos represent both an embarrassment (how can we claim that she resisted transculturation if she has tattoos on her face?) and an exploitable commodity (now that she has these tattoos on her face, let's use them to obtain an audience for the narrative itself). To most of her audiences, Olive's tattoos represented the brutality of native peoples, who would "disfigure" the white, female body in an effort to enslave her or, worse yet, to force her to marry into the tribe. Yet, as Grinnell's observation of Oatman demonstrates, her tattoos may also have blurred the boundaries between Native Americans and whites for her audience. It was this combination of horror and fascination, repulsion and curiosity that likely persuaded audiences to purchase Stratton's narrative and attend the lecture series. This may, in fact, have been the kind of response that Stratton was counting on, both literally and figuratively.

Olive Oatman's sense of her own tattoos is unclear, as is the "truth" of her captivity. Susan Thompson Lewis Parrish, Oatman's childhood friend, claimed that Oatman's tattoos were successfully "erased . . . from her face," unlike the "wild life" that could not be erased "from her heart" (Root 8). Yet, as later photographs reveal, Oatman's tattoos were not, in fact, removed, although she would eventually wear a veil to hide them when in public. After her marriage to John B. Fairchild in 1865, she quit the lecture tour. Rumors suggest that Fairchild did what he could to erase his wife's previous identity, including buying up copies of Stratton's narrative and burning them (Derounian-Stodola, "Captive and Her Editor" 185). It seems safe to assume, however, that Fairchild's efforts to erase his wife's history were no more effective than efforts to erase her tattoos, if only because both are impossible procedures. There can be no erasure of the marked body—only additional markings. The assumption behind most interpretations of tattooing is that the tattoo is an attempt to freeze identity, and the forcible tattoo an attempt to impose one culture on the body of someone who does not "naturally" belong to that culture. Yet, as is the case in Herman Melville's *Typee*, the effort to remove the tattoo is no less an imposition of identity and culture— in Oatman's case, of a static feminine identity in a culture that, in theory at least, prefers its women to be as physically, emotionally, and mentally unmarked as a marble statue.

CHAPTER TWO

"Burning into the Bone"

Romantic Love and the Marked Woman

In George Thompson's sensational novel *City Crimes; or Life in New York and Boston* (1849), the sensual libertine Josephine Franklin is punished for denying her sexual favors to the villainous Dead Man, a criminal who murders, mutilates, and blackmails indiscriminately throughout the novel. Armed with the knowledge of Josephine's responsibility for her own father's murder, the Dead Man attempts to blackmail her into having sex with him. When she refuses—out of disgust at his hideous appearance rather than any qualms of virtue—he responds with an act of vengeance planned to rob her of any power within her world of seduction and extortion. He vindictively explains, "You are beautiful and you pride yourself upon that beauty—but I will deprive you of your loveliness. . . . Your cheeks shall become ghastly, your complexion livid, and your brilliant eyes shall become sightless orbs—for the curse of *blindness* shall be added to your other miseries. Obstinate girl, bid an eternal farewell to eyesight and beauty, for from this moment you are deprived of both, forever!" (298). The Dead Man throws a vial of sulfuric acid in Josephine's face; as a result, the narrator tells us, "her face was horribly burnt and disfigured, and her brilliant eyes were destroyed; she was stone blind!" (300). Josephine is robbed not only of her beauty but also of her ability to see, to elicit either pleasure or power through vision. In the demented environment of *City Crimes*, such punishment is oddly appropriate for the sin of refusing herself to the Dead Man.[1]

Predictably, however, Josephine's blinding and disfiguration do not prevent her from continuing to deceive and seduce hapless men; in fact, perhaps because she is aware of her physical limitations, Josephine is even more determined to achieve financial security at the expense of one of her male victims. Just two months after the mutilation of her face, Josephine and her mother conspire to marry Josephine to the wealthy Mr. Thurston. Although Josephine wears a thick veil reaching to her waist in public and insists that she is both disfigured and blind, Thurston romantically convinces himself (with Josephine's subtle assistance) that the young woman "is trying to play [him] a trick"—hiding her beauty from the world in order to find a man who truly loves her for who she is (305). Aware of her own vulnerability and Thurston's wealth and public stature, Josephine does not disabuse her suitor of his "disbelief in her deformity, and, while she persist[s] in her assurances that she [is] hideously ugly, she ma[kes] those assurances in a manner so light and playful, that Mr. T. would have taken his oath that she was beautiful" (306). Believing that marriage will force Thurston to financially support her and her mother, Josephine underhandedly convinces him to marry her and only reveals her visage to him in the "nuptial chamber" (308).

Curiously, however, although Thompson has dwelt elsewhere with some detail on Josephine's "ghastly cheek, her eyeless sockets, and [her] vivid lips," he ends the wedding night scene with the lifting of her veil (308). In the following chapter, we are simply told that "Josephine Franklin terminated her miserable existence by poison . . . on the day after her marriage with Mr. Thurston, who, when he beheld the hideous deformity of his bride, instead of the beauty which he expected, recoiled with horror—and after bitterly reproaching her, drove her from his presence, bidding her never to let him see her again, and refusing to make the smallest provision for her support" (309).[2] Notwithstanding Josephine's guilt—she is a murderess and a seductress who allows nothing to stand in the way of her insatiable greed and sexual appetite—Thompson's reluctance to describe the scene of Josephine's humiliation is telling. This rhetorical strategy appears strangely similar to Stratton's inability or refusal to describe Olive Oatman's tattoos or to allow their representation in the illustrations accompanying the text of *Captivity of the Oatman Girls*. Although these two texts—sensational novel and piously sentimental captivity narrative—are very different in nature, they share a simultaneous fascination with and repulsion from the marked female body.

In Thompson's case, of course, the marked body plays a much larger role in the narrative—and in some of his other sixty-plus novels. The violence done to Josephine, her deceptive behavior, and her husband-to-be's romanticization of their courtship all contribute to Thompson's mockery of sentimentality, marriage, and domestic life. Yet even as he intentionally horrifies his readers with Josephine's blinding and mutilation and assures them that this is, indeed, the apt wages of sin, he creates some measure of sympathy for her and uses this character to demonstrate women's economic dependence on men and the marriage market. According to Karen Halttunen, such moral complexity was not uncommon in nineteenth-century sensational fiction. In fact, sensational fiction and the violence featured so prominently in it was a response to larger cultural movements, particularly "the shift from the traditional patriarchal family, with its central concerns for economic productivity and hierarchical order, to the modern sentimental family, with its central concerns for emotional closeness and mutual affection." Sensational fiction both "affirmed the new domesticity in terrifying tales of people who violated its tenets" and "appealed to a backlash against the new ideal by providing readers with the pornographic pleasure of witnessing . . . violations" (*Murder Most Foul* 135).

In this light it is possible to read Josephine's fate as a cautionary tale for nineteenth-century readers, warning them neither to manipulate nor to romanticize a potential mate. Rather, according to the dictates of romantic love and companionate marriage, which are the necessary prerequisites to the sentimental family (or the "new domesticity," as Halttunen labels it), lovers should practice honest self-expression, thus revealing their private selves to each other.[3] According to Karen Lystra, "This most often involved an attempt by both parties to *unmask*, to abandon all outward forms of propriety, and to shed all normative social roles except the romantic self" (38, emphasis mine). Lystra's emphasis on the unmasking of lovers prior to marriage highlights Josephine's transgressive and deceitful use of the veil and the importance of the moment of revelation in *City Crimes*. Her "unmasking" *after* the wedding breaches the norms of romantic love; by waiting, she allows her lover to deceive himself as to her true physical appearance and character in order to convince him to marry her. She and her new husband are therefore punished for settling for marriage with someone they hardly know and do not love rather than insisting on a truly rewarding companionate partnership.

As Lystra points out, romantic love also had its drawbacks, including heightened experiences of pain as well as pleasure (46). Romantic love could cloud one's vision, allowing individual desires regarding courtship to overpower objective truths about the preparation for and maintenance of a marriage and family. Mr. Thurston's self-deception regarding Josephine is, for example, a clear indication of the influence of the *notion* of romantic love but not its reality. Allowing himself to believe that he alone knows the true Josephine, he marries her, despite what she has told him about her physical condition. In this sense, *he* is truly the blind one, while Josephine at least sees her way through to the culmination of her wedding day (if not to the end of the plan itself).

While Mr. Thurston's experience highlights the danger of the illusions of romantic love, Josephine's reveals how this new paradigm ignores the fact that women's sole opportunity for economic security often lay in courtship and marriage. Women in *City Crimes* may possess immense sexual power, but they are otherwise helpless and completely unable to support themselves economically. Their well-being depends on their power—sexual or moral—to attract and keep a man. Josephine's veil, then, appropriately recalls the veil worn by Oatman at the request of her husband; both women use this device to deny their past, as it is inscribed on their faces, to please—and in Josephine's case, to deceive—the man who is to provide them with security and status in a world that has allowed them to be marked in such a way. Oatman and Josephine attempt to hide their marked faces and avoid the public gaze by wearing the veil, yet the garment only serves to heighten what Laura Mulvey calls their "to-be-looked-at-ness," or their cultural status as visual object. Both figures embody what John Berger sees as the condition of woman in Western society in general: "She has to survey everything she is and everything she does because how she appears to others, and ultimately how she appears to men, is of crucial importance for what is normally thought of as the success of her life" (46). The necessity for such intense awareness of the visual self makes Josephine's blinding particularly ironic: at the very moment when she needs this ability to self-survey most desperately, she is violently denied the means of seeing herself, let alone anyone or anything else.

This chapter extends the argument of chapter 1, focusing specifically on the way in which women's marked faces both disrupt and confirm cultural conceptions of middle-class white womanhood and, more importantly, narratives of romantic love. Romantic love and the marriage plot figured prominently in much nineteenth-century American fiction—sensational, sentimental, or otherwise—and to a large extent, the particular mode shaped these narratives, dictating what was, in fact, imaginable or representable. Yet the marked woman presented challenges for all these forms, challenges ultimately calling into question the extent of women's power in nineteenth-century American culture. Using *City Crimes* as a starting point, I examine the use of the marked female body in various nineteenth-century American fictions to represent and complicate nineteenth-century courtship, especially as it shifts from a focus on property and social standing to the ideal of romantic love. Perhaps because of the emphasis on female beauty as a valuable commodity in the marriage market and the (supposedly) contradictory valuing of the "unmasked" self in romantic love, the marked woman makes frequent appearances in these narratives, often providing an extreme example of the triumph of love over economics. Yet these narratives are by no means monolithic and, as the texts discussed here reveal, the marked woman ultimately highlights the compromises inherent for women in notions of romantic love.

Sentimental Womanhood and the Invisible Mark

Maria Susanna Cummins's novel *The Lamplighter* (1854) is recognized by literary scholars as a quintessential sentimental text, one that allots women the domestic and, perhaps more importantly, spiritual power through which they achieve love, community, and even financial and material comfort.[4] The novel "is premised on an emotional and philosophical ethos that celebrates human connection, both personal and communal" and rewards women who establish and maintain such connections in an extended domestic sphere (Dobson, "Reclaiming" 266). The sentimental paradigm of womanhood and community that Cummins helped establish in *The Lamplighter* was reproduced and revised in women's novels throughout the century. Exceeded in sales in the 1850s only by Harriet Beecher Stowe's *Uncle Tom's Cabin* (1852), its influence on nineteenth-century American literature and culture is immense, and like other sentimental novels, it contributed to a reassessment of women's power and agency in America. When read with a focus on the female body and romantic love, however, the novel presents a much more compromised picture of female subjectivity, one that reveals quite blatantly the corporeal limits of sentimentalism. Although the blind Emily Graham is not the heroine of the novel, Cummins's representation of her disabled but impossibly unmarked body demonstrates the persistence of the classical ideal even (or especially) in a narrative form that was premised explicitly on "the problem of the body" (Samuels, "Identity" 169).

The Lamplighter traces the maturation of the orphaned Gertrude, who is saved from physical and spiritual destitution by the kindness and generosity of others. While the titular lamplighter, Trueman Flint, accommodates Gerty's physical and emotional needs as a child, her spiritual and social education is provided by Emily Graham, a blind woman who becomes her mentor. Their relationship begins when Gerty is merely a child but continues into adulthood, as she goes to live with the Grahams after the death of Flint and becomes a caretaker and companion to her beloved Emily. Although Emily must be physically led by others because of her disability, it is she who leads Gertrude, among others, on a much more important journey, that of the soul to God. Indeed, as Mary Klages points out, Emily's blindness fits her for such leadership as well as for salvation (89). Cummins writes: "God had chosen an earthly messenger to lead his child into everlasting peace; a messenger from whose closed eyes the world's paths were all shut out, but who had been so long treading the heavenly road, that it was now familiar ground. Who so fit to guide the little one as she, who with patience had learned the way? Who so well able to cast light upon the darkness of another soul as she, to whose own darkened life God had lent a torch divine?" (67). Such light and dark imagery pervades the novel, especially in regard to Emily. Her appearance in the novel is foreshadowed, for example, when the narrator takes pity on little Gerty's sufferings and asks, "Will [Christ] not send man or angel to light up the darkness within, to kindle a light that shall never go out, the light that shall shine through all eternity?" (4). Ultimately, we are told, "the blind girl imparted light to the child's dark soul" (67). Emily's disability thus enables her to accept others as God would, thereby inspiring them to "tread the heavenly road" along with her. While Josephine's blindness only highlights her grotesque corporeality and her complete lack of morality, Emily's allows her to transcend the body and become the epitome of morality and spirituality.[5] Throughout the novel, Emily is repeatedly labeled "too good for this world," "one of [the Lord's] holy angels" (19, 21).

Although Emily's blindness is central to her sense of self and to the novel, it is said to be invisible and inoffensive to those around her. Rather than staring sightlessly into the distance, Emily is always represented as having her eyes closed. At their first encounter, for example, Emily's closed eyes prompt Gerty to suspect that Emily is sleeping. Emily corrects her, explaining, "They are always shut, my child. . . . I am blind, Gerty; I can see nothing" (54). "Can't your eyes be opened, anyway?" Gerty asks, and Emily replies, "No, . . . never; but we won't talk about that anymore" (55). The narrator insists, "[I]t was hard to realize that Emily *was* blind."

> It was a fact never forced upon her friends' recollection by any repining or selfish indulgence on the part of the sufferer; and, as there was nothing painful in the appearance of her closed lids, shaded and fringed as they were by her long and heavy eyelashes, it was not unusual for those immediately about her to converse upon things which could only be evident to the sense of sight, and even direct her attention to one object and another, quite forgetting, for the moment, her sad deprivation; and Emily never sighed, never seemed hurt at the want of consideration, or showed any lack of interest in objects thus shut from her gaze; but, apparently quite satisfied with the descriptions she heard, or the pictures which she formed in her imagination, would talk pleasantly and playfully upon whatever was uppermost in the minds of her companions. (64)

Emily's sweet disposition and unwillingness to complain prevent her from being an imposition or a harsh reminder of the frailty of human embodiment. Her closed eyes remind observers of a gentle sleep rather than a restrictive handicap; staring, sightless eyes would apparently be too offensive and too much a reminder of the limitations placed on Emily's existence by her disability.

Klages regards this erasure of Emily's blindness as a leveling technique allowing her to be read as the quintessential sentimental woman precisely because her disability makes her more sympathetic to others. She writes, "Emily's being is . . . defined not as the product of her blind eyes but as the product of her abundance of feeling. In showing how easily Emily's blindness is forgotten by herself and others, Cummins declares Emily's equality with the sighted on the basis of her capacity for True Womanly self-sacrifice and empathy" (93). Klages argues that Emily is regarded not simply as an object of sympathy but as an empathic adult in her own right who is able to use her power to improve the lives of others because she allows—indeed, promotes—the erasure of her self (and her disability). Eva Cherniavsky essentially agrees that Emily is a powerful sentimental figure, especially in her relationship with Gertrude, but questions Emily's possession of agency precisely *because of* her lack of vision. "Emily's blindness effects a de-formation, or dissolution, of her corporeal and subjective boundaries," Cherniavsky explains, "and thereby locates her beyond (or prior to) the visual dialectic of intersubjectivity. Unable to return the gaze, to see the other seeing her, Emily becomes the locus of her interlocutor's self-completion" but is not, importantly, complete herself (84). In other words, Cherniavsky argues that Emily is incapable of empathy not only because she is incapable of sight but also because she embraces the way in which her disability disconnects her from worldly experience. This distance allows her to function as a Tiresias-like seer whose self and voice are constantly in the service of others. For the purposes of my argument, it is also crucial to recognize that although Emily never actually sees the other or—just as importantly—herself, others *do* see Emily and can observe her unchecked because of her disability. This is perhaps why it is so important for Emily's blindness to be relatively invisible to observers. Ultimately, although (or perhaps because) her blindness may make her an ideal sentimental figure—dependent yet powerful, experienced yet innocent, closed (in terms of her eyes) yet open to interpretation—it also makes her corporeality essential to any consideration of Cummins's representation of disability and the marked female body. How and why does Emily's body contain such seeming contradictions?

The story behind Emily's blindness is not revealed until late in the novel, after she has already been established as an "angel" figure. She tells Gertrude that she has not always been so angelic, so submissive, or so dutiful. In fact, she had once been "a child of the world, eager for worldly pleasures, and ignorant of any other" (321). At age sixteen, Emily was in love with her stepbrother, Phillip Amory, against the wishes of her father. Although Mr. Graham made every effort to keep the two apart, Phillip contrived to meet Emily in her father's library, where she sat recovering from a fever. While bathing her temples with cologne, Phillip was confronted by Mr. Graham, who accused the young man not only of courting Emily for her money but also of committing forgery in Mr. Graham's counting house. Distraught at the violence of the encounter, Emily fainted. In a frenzied attempt to revive her, Phillip reached for what he thought was the bottle of cologne and spilled the contents of the bottle on Emily's face and eyes. Emily's reaction revealed, however, that the bottle contained acid; as Emily writhed in pain, Mr. Graham banished Phillip from his home. Years later, Emily tells Gertrude that after several months, the doctor thought there was some hope of restoring Emily's eyesight, but when Emily heard a false rumor that Phillip had died, she literally "wept all . . . hopes away" (321).

The importance of this story within the larger narrative of *The Lamplighter* is accentuated by the fact that it is told twice in the novel—once when Emily relates it to Gertrude in conversation and again in a letter from Phillip to Gertrude. (In a twist of fate typical of the sentimental novel, Phillip is revealed to be Gertrude's long-lost father.) The accounts are for the most part the same, making the repetition of the tale seem gratuitous. Yet in many ways this tale forms the crux of *The Lamplighter*, bringing the primary characters together as a family and, more importantly, highlighting the relationship between the representation of the female body and romantic love.

The theme of romantic love dominates much of the novel, most prominently in Gertrude's relationship with her childhood friend William Sullivan. After Willie goes to India to make his fortune, Gertrude nurses his grandfather and then his mother as they die, then patiently waits for her childhood friend to return and marry her. Similar to many mid-nineteenth-century heroines—Jane Eyre, most famously—and according to the model of "Real Womanhood" outlined by Frances B. Cogan, Gertrude seeks a companionate marriage based on friendship, love, and perhaps most importantly, a shared past. When Willie returns from India to find Gertrude, he asks if she is free to accept his love, and she tellingly answers, "Free from all bonds, dear Willie, but those which you yourself clasped around me, and which have encircled me from my childhood" (409). Because Gertrude is relatively independent—she has educated herself to be a teacher and insists at various times on living alone rather than depending on the hospitality of wealthier friends—she is allowed and determined to make her own decisions regarding her future. She does not need to ask anyone's permission to love Willie or to accept his proposal. In this sense, their relationship is part of the weakening of patriarchal control over the family identified by Lystra as one of the repercussions of romantic love and companionate marriage (158).

While Emily's relationship with Phillip Amory is also an example of romantic love, her father's resistance to the match and the twice-told tale of Emily's blinding indicate the opposition of the patriarchal culture to such independently formed families. Phillip suspects that Mr. Graham's resistance to the relationship results from "an old enmity between himself and [Phillip's] father," but the origin of Mr. Graham's disapproval is less important than the fact that he goes to such lengths to separate the young lovers while making no effort to explain his reasons to them (371). Although his behavior in this regard is typical of this obstinate but protective father, it also reflects a belief in a mode of courtship that by the mid-nineteenth century was quickly becoming outdated and an awareness of the threat that the relationship between Emily and Phillip poses to his ownership of his daughter and to his own authority.[6] According to Lystra, "At least a portion of patriarchal authority rested upon customs, traditions, and roles that discouraged intense emotional attachments and suppressed individuality. Relating to each other as romantic selves, men and women foreshortened their emotional distance through empathy and personal identification. Therefore, by bridging the gender gap and encouraging men's empathy in women's lives, romantic love weakened certain aspects of patriarchal family relations" (229). Romantic love thus diminished the role of parents in courtship and marriage, enabling young couples to make their own decisions—if they chose to do so—independent of considerations of social status or wealth. This is not to say that romantic love erased the economic and political power differential between nineteenth-century men and women; rather "women gained more status, standing, and power through the medium of affection and self-expression in their relationships with men" (231).

The blinding of Emily Graham, then, takes place at a crucial moment in her relationships with her father and with Phillip. That she is alone with Phillip—in a clandestine encounter, no less—highlights the potential for sexual experimentation in a relationship based on premarital emotional intimacy. Emily's presence with Phillip in the library clearly indicates her growing independence from her father as well as her willingness to engage in a companionate, romantic relationship with Phillip despite her father's disapproval. Yet more than any other factor (including Phillip's disappearance), it is Emily's blindness that clearly puts a stop to this relationship. Lystra points out that both "empathy and personal identification" are necessary to the development of a romantic relationship, as is the related "feeling of being immersed in and assimilating a portion of someone else's interior life" (229, 42). As Cherniavsky demonstrates, Emily's capacity for empathy is diminished if not erased by her blindness in that she is unable to see the other, develop a distinct sense of self, and therefore experience an intersubjective relationship with another human being. Her disability, therefore, prevents Emily from experiencing several of the key components of romantic love.

Framed within this context, the question of who is responsible for Emily's blindness takes on added significance. As Emily readily admits, Phillip was the "unhappy cause" of the accident that blinds her (320). Yet she does not hold him responsible, as she reveals when the two are reunited as adults and Phillip asks her if she can ever forgive him for "[t]he deed that locked [her] in prison darkness." Emily exclaims, "Phillip! . . . [C]ould you for one moment believe that I attributed that to you?—that I blamed you, for an instant, even in my secret thought?" She goes on to insist, "Never, even in my wild frenzy, did I so abuse and wrong you. If my unfilial heart sinfully railed gainst the cruel injustice of my father, it was never guilty of such treachery towards you" (396). Phillip's innocence and Emily's more complex interpretation of her father's role in the incident are apparent even earlier in the novel when Emily describes her last visual memory to Gertrude: "A few dim pictures, however, the last my poor eyes ever beheld, are still engraved upon my memory, and visible to my imagination. My father stood with his back to the light, and from the first moment of his entering the room I never saw his face again; but the countenance of the other, the object of his accusation, illumined as it was by the last rays of the golden sunset, stands ever in the foreground of my recollection" (319). Given the novel's emphasis on light and its connection to spirituality and righteousness, Emily's perception of Phillip's innocence and the sanctity of their love for each other is clear. Yet Emily's reliance on this last "dim picture" to interpret the accident that blinds her and the relative guilt of the parties involved also indicates the paralysis of her self-development at the moment she loses her sight, indicating yet again the importance of vision to subjectivity.

The reunion of Emily and Phillip signifies, to some extent, the victory of romantic love over patriarchal control; using the rhetoric of romantic love, Phillip asks Emily to marry him, insisting, "We loved each other in childhood, our hearts became one in youth, and have continued so until now. Why should we be longer parted?" Emily answers, "No word of mine shall part hearts so truly one, and your home shall be mine" (420). The nature of their relationship, however, is distinctly spiritual rather than romantic. Although they do marry at the end of the novel, they conveniently marry late enough in life that children are apparently not an issue. Emily's disabled body does not—to the presumed relief of nineteenth-century readers—have to be transformed into a sexual body, and her disability will not affect any offspring.[7] The central purpose of their marriage, Cummins implies, is the religious conversion of Phillip; while Emily "will leave behind one to follow in her footsteps" after her death, to "fulfill her charities, and do good on earth," her successor is her husband rather than their own biological child (421). Mr. Graham never truly reforms or recognizes his own culpability in the tragedy that blinded Emily and separated the lovers. When initially reunited with Phillip, he admits that he was mistaken in accusing him of forgery but never apologizes for his obstruction of the young lovers' relationship. Nevertheless, Emily, schooled by her disability to trust in God and patriarchy, cannot quite bring herself to blame her father for the accident or for separating her from Phillip; although her father's dictum is "cruel," it is a sin for her "unfilial heart" to act or even feel anything that might be against his will.

If Phillip is not to blame and it is a sin to question her father's authority, no matter how unjust, then who is to blame for Emily's blindness? Unable to hold either her father or Phillip responsible, Emily attributes her disability to God's will, to the necessity of experiencing earthly trials in order to reject the physical world and find salvation in God. "Speak not of my blindness as a misfortune," Emily tells Phillip. "I have long ceased to think it such. It is only through the darkness of the night that we discern the lights of heaven, and only when shut out from earth that we enter the gates of Paradise" (397). This gesture, however, is not so different from the gesture she makes toward her father. Both God and Mr. Graham are largely invisible patriarchal figures who claim to know what is best for Emily, often arranging and rearranging her life without her knowledge or approval. Rather than experience the pain of rebellion and possible rejection, Emily embraces both the law of her father and the law of her Father; her blindness simultaneously negates the possibility of rebellion and makes her more malleable to manipulation by those dual patriarchs. Emily's last recourse is to accept blame for the accident herself. Several critics comment on the ways in which the scene in the library recalls the ghastly blinding of Oedipus and suggest that Emily's choice to have an incestuous relationship with her "brother" caused her accident.[8] Emily's responsibility for her own condition is similarly reinforced throughout her recollection of the incident. Not only is her blindness a heavenly reprimand for being "a child of the world," but Emily apparently also finalizes the effects of the accident by weeping over Phillip's presumed death.

Separated from her lover and forced to remain in her father's home, Emily remains forever childlike; it is almost as if she is prevented from changing precisely because she cannot see herself and therefore cannot visually witness or effect change. In fact, Emily's body seems impervious to *any* type of change or inscription, including simply the effects of the passage of time. After referring to her as an "invalid girl," the narrator explains that "in spite of ill health, she still retained much of the freshness and all the loveliness of her girlhood" (394). Emily is often referred to as a work of art, a perpetually perfect, classical statue that does not and cannot change. In one scene, for example, the moon is said to "cast her full beams upon Emily's white dress, and [give] to the beautiful hand and arm, which escaping from the draperied sleeve, rested on the side of her rustic arm-chair, the semblance of polished marble" (127). Even after years have passed, Emily is said to look "more like a statue than a living figure" (395). Such references recall Olive Oatman's invisible influence on Palmer's *The White Captive* and raise a similarly muted issue in Cummins's *The Lamplighter*: the strange absence of scars resulting from the accident in which Emily Graham was blinded.

Although Emily has had acid poured directly onto her face, the accident has apparently not resulted in any sort of scarring or disfigurement. Rather, as mentioned earlier, the perfection of Emily's face is continually noted and celebrated. This is in distinct contrast to the sensationalistic Josephine Franklin of

City Crimes. As the result of a similar accident, Thompson explains, Josephine's "once radiant countenance was of a ghastly yellow hue, save where deep purple streaks gave it the appearance of a putrefying corpse. Her once splendid eyes, that had so oft flashed with indignant scorn, glowed with the pride of her imperial beauty, or sparkled with the fires of amorous passion, had been literally burned out of her head! That once lofty and peerless brow was disfigured by hideous scars, and a wig supplied the place of her once clustering and luxuriant hair!" (307). Although Emily's "sins" are by no means as extreme as those of Josephine, the similarities in the accidents that blind them should logically produce similar results, even if the description of the aftermath differs predictably from text to text.

Although Cummins focuses primarily on Emily's blindness as a result of the accident, she also briefly implies that Emily's eyeballs have been literally consumed by the acid thrown in her face. When another young woman asks Gertrude if Emily has always been blind, Gertrude tells her that until Emily was sixteen, she "had beautiful eyes and could see as well as" anyone else. The young woman asks, "What happened to her? how did she lose them?" (229). Later, when Emily tells Gertrude the story of the accident, her narrative is disrupted by the difficulty of explaining precisely what *did* happen to her "beautiful eyes":

> "Listen, Gertrude. He—the poor, ruined boy—sprung to help me; and, maddened by injustice, he knew not what he did. Heaven is my witness, I never blamed him; and if, in my agony, I uttered words that seemed like a reproach, it was because I was too frantic, and knew not what I said!"
>
> "What!" exclaimed Gertrude; "he did not—"
>
> "No, no! he did not—he *did not* put out my eyes!" exclaimed Emily; "it was an accident. He reached forward for the cologne which he had just had in his hand. There were several bottles, and, in his haste, he seized one containing a powerful acid which Mrs. Ellis had found occasion to use in my sick room. It had a heavy glass stopper,—and he—his hand was unsteady, and he spilt it all—"
>
> "On your eyes?" shrieked Gertrude.
>
> Emily bowed her head. (320)

Although Emily insists that Phillip "*did not* put out [her] eyes," she goes on to explain that "it was an accident." The implication is that although her eyes were "put out," Phillip did not physically do it; the acid that he spills into her face is the cause.

Yet the suggestion of disfigurement remains merely that: a suggestion without any corresponding physical reality. In fact, Emily's classically beautiful face and body are essential to the success of the sentimental narrative in that they exemplify a key sentimental convention: the direct relationship between character and the face. Cummins alludes to this convention when describing the physical appearance of Gertrude as an adult. After posing the question, "Is Gertrude a beauty?" the narrator answers,

> By no means. Hers is a face and form about which there would be a thousand differ-
> ent opinions, and out of the whole number few would pronounce her beautiful. But
> there are faces whose ever-varying expression one loves to watch,—tell-tale faces,
> that speak the truth and proclaim the sentiment within; faces that now light up with
> intelligence, now beam with mirth, now sadden at the tale of sorrow, now burn with
> a holy indignation for that which the soul abhors, and now, again, are sanctified by
> the divine presence, when the heart turns away from the world and itself, and looks
> upward in the spirit of devotion. Such a face was Gertrude's. (129)

Gertrude's face is essential to her unconventional beauty, which is a result more of moral goodness and spiritual purity than of the color of her eyes or the tex-ture of her hair. According to Cummins, the sentimental heroine is identifiable by her "tell-tale face" in which all her emotions and her character are clearly revealed.[9] Karen Sanchez-Eppler notes a similar dynamic in the sentimental fic-tion of Harriet Beecher Stowe: "Sentimental narrative functions through stereo-types, so that upon first encountering a character there is no difficulty in as-certaining his or her moral worth. In sentimental writing, the self is externally displayed, and the body provides a reliable sign of who one is" (27).[10] In the example that Sanchez-Eppler provides from Stowe's *Dred: A Tale of the Great Dismal Swamp* (1856), the sentimental heroine insists that a stranger's face is "very repulsive" and therefore decides that she hates and will not trust him (qtd. in Sanchez-Eppler 28). Sanchez-Eppler explains that "she weighs the evidence of his character in the reaction of her body to his body. . . . The succeeding chap-ters prove the accuracy of Nina's reaction to Mr. Jekyl, and so endorse her and the sentimental novel's mechanisms of assessment" (28).

Within such a paradigm, a blind woman can hardly become the ideal senti-mental heroine because her lack of vision prevents her from truly seeing and reading the faces of those around her. Moreover, facial disfigurement would make the self difficult to read and would perhaps even suggest that a disfigured person could not be trusted to convey a "true" self. The mutilation of Josephine Franklin, for example, seems apt in that her moral character is, one might say, unattractive and even deformed. Her blindness similarly indicates her inability and lack of desire to read the hearts and characters of others because of her own self-involvement. However, the ability of *The Lamplighter*'s heroine, Gertrude Flint, to read others is not in question in the passage describing her physical appearance. As Cummins explains, "one loves to watch" such faces; although

Gertrude is a more active sentimental heroine than Emily, she is similarly positioned as the object of attention, a text to be read by others. The only active
looking done by this heroine is directed "upward in the spirit of devotion." Both
Emily and Gertrude are denied an active gaze in the sentimental paradigm; their
selfhood is shaped not through vision but solely through the twin ideals of religion and romantic love.

The haunting reference to Emily's disfigured or missing eyeballs threatens
The Lamplighter's neat resolution of the plot, however, in that they represent
the grotesque underbelly of the sentimental family, which is a supposed avenue
to power for women only if they are willing to be exchanged from one level
of the patriarchy to the next, their bodies on the line every time. Although romantic love seems to be the answer to the challenges facing both Emily and
Gertrude in this novel because it allegedly accords more power to women in
relationships, it is important to recognize that romantic love causes Emily's
disability and (hidden) disfigurement no matter which human agent accepts
(or rejects) responsibility. As in Olive Oatman's lecture series, the suggestion
of disfigurement reveals the threat posed by a grotesque body to a society that
privileges the classical. This threat is kept at bay by barely hinting at such disfigurement and by erasing any other signs of the accident from Emily's face even
though the absence of the mark, in Oatman's case as well, is as important as its
presence. Indeed, the boundaries between the two states—the classical and the
grotesque—are more flexible than they initially appear.[11] As Peter Stallybrass
and Allon White note, "The classical body splits precisely along the rigid edge
which is its defence against heterogeneity: its closure and purity are quite illu-
sory and it will perpetually rediscover in itself, often with a sense of shock or
inner revulsion, the grotesque, the protean and the motley, the 'neither/nor,' the
double negation of high and low which was the very precondition for its social
identity" (113).

Similarly, the differences between sensational fiction and sentimental fiction
begin to erode when considered in light of the marked woman and the narrative of romantic love. Despite critics' claims that sensational fiction "constituted a cultural formation that was in fundamental opposition to the domestic
sentimental fiction of the same decades," neither sensational nor sentimental
frameworks seem capable of accommodating the marked woman (Looby 654).
Emily and Josephine represent two sides of the nineteenth-century fictional
coin. Both are blinded and somehow disfigured for their (potential) transgressions. Josephine hides her disfigurement behind a veil, while Emily hides hers
behind perfectly formed eyelids and thick eyelashes. Both narratives ultimately
seem to uphold the dictates of romantic love as opposed to marriage motivated
by financial or social considerations. Yet the disabled and mutilated bodies of

women left in the wake of these texts should cause more than a little discomfort and doubt. Teasing out the hidden contradictions in these representations of women's marked bodies reveals the old patriarchy lurking behind the new sentimental family in mid-nineteenth-century American culture.

The Marriage Mark(et)

Published almost ten years after Cummins's *The Lamplighter*, Harriet Prescott Spofford's short story "The Strathsays" reflects similar concerns about narrative form, romantic love, and the marked woman. Unlike Cummins, Spofford is a very difficult figure to position generically, stylistically, or modally; throughout her sixty-year writing career, her stories, novels, and poems were (and still are) indiscriminately classed as romantic, sentimental, sensational, and realistic.[12] She took on a variety of subjects and themes in her fiction: detective stories, frontier adventures, depictions of small New England communities, and tales of life in the nation's capital, to name just a few. This experimental attitude toward fiction writing extended to Spofford's treatment of the figure of the marked woman.

Although "The Strathsays" was published in the *Atlantic Monthly*, one of the most popular and prestigious literary magazines in nineteenth-century America, Spofford distances her critique of American fiction and culture by depicting a Scottish family living in New Brunswick. (The main character attends school for a time in Scotland.) To increase the romance of her narrative, Spofford does not specify the time in which the story takes place; internal clues indicate that the story is set sometime around the end of the eighteenth or the beginning of the nineteenth century.[13] Spofford counters these distancing techniques by employing first-person narration, which, as Susan K. Harris points out, eliminates the omniscient narrator, whose role is usually "to guide and control readers' interpretations of the heroine's adventures" (*19th-Century American Women's Novels* 152). First-person narration limits the viewpoint of the text to the main character and thus contributes to what might be considered a more realistic text.

For the purposes of my argument, it is important to recognize the ways in which an omniscient narrator guides readers' interpretations of female characters' bodies. In *The Lamplighter*, for example, readers are told to regard Emily's ageless, unmarked face as a reflection of her role as a "votary of Heaven" (128). Similarly, in *City Crimes*, after describing the mutilation of Josephine's face, Thompson's omniscient narrator exclaims, "Oh, it was a pitiful sight to see that talented and accomplished young lady thus stricken with the curses of deformity and blindness, through her own wickedness—to see that temple which

God had made so beautiful and fair to look upon, thus shattered and defiled by the ravages of sin!" (307). First-person narration in "The Strathsays" allows the marked woman to be heard rather than simply seen, objectified, and represented, as she is in both of the other texts discussed in this chapter and in Stratton's *Captivity of the Oatman Girls*. Perhaps because the main character in this story is merely scarred and not blinded, her vision is allowed to shape the narrative as well as, to a certain extent, her own destiny. As in *The Lamplighter*, however, the marked woman functions in this text to indicate the limitations of women's power, even within the new companionate marriage and sentimental family.

"The Strathsays" is narrated by Alice Strathsay, the youngest child in a fatherless family of four daughters. Her mother, Mrs. Strathsay, is a powerful Scottish matriarch who has been displaced from her European home by marriage and remains in New Brunswick with her children after the death of her husband, a shipping merchant. Aware that the survival of her daughters depends on her matchmaking skills, Mrs. Strathsay lives "for nought but the making of great matches for her girls" (100). Her skills as a matchmaker are supplemented by her financial acumen and her emotional inaccessibility, both of which are said to have given her the strength to survive her husband's early death: "A high, keen spirit was his wife; she did not bend or break. . . . None ever saw tear in those proud eyes of hers, when they brought in her husband dead, or when they carried him out; but every day at noon she went up into her own room, and whether she slept or whether she waked the two hours in that darkened place, there was not so much as a fly that sang in the pane to tell" (99). Along with Alice's insistence that her mother has "half a mind to hate" all her daughters "because they were none of them a son," Mrs. Strathsay's ruthless matchmaking establishes her early in the story as a distinctly *un*sentimental maternal figure who considers emotions a hindrance and will presumably scorn the claims of romantic love (99). Yet it seems that she has not always felt this way; Alice senses her mother's passionate love for her deceased husband in their own relationship, as Alice is said to resemble most the father she never knew. She is fully aware of her mother's preference as well as the reason for it: "[F]or the color in my cheek was deeper tinct than Scotch, it was the wild bit of Southern blood that had run in her love's veins; when she looked at me, I gave her back hot phases of her passionate youth again" (99–100). Alice recognizes, however, that this association will not prevent her mother from arranging a marriage for her, as she has for her eldest daughter, Margray.

While Alice is fortunately intended for Angus Ingestre, with whom she is in love, Margray has been married to a wealthy but elderly man, Johnny Graeme, who dies just before she gives birth to his son. When Angus, who is a sailor, visits Alice at school in Edinburgh and informs her of Graeme's death, Alice feels no grief and doubts that her sister does either; "[H]e bought Margray, you know he did, Angus!" she exclaims (102). She insists that neither she nor her sister Mary will allow themselves to be sold "for siller and gowd" (103). Alice is aware that she and her sisters are being bred for the marriage market, where each physical and personal attribute is assessed and assigned an economic value. By telling Angus that she and Mary will not participate in the marriage market, she attempts to confirm the fact that her relationship with Angus is somehow different from that of Margray and Johnny Graeme, although it too has been orchestrated by her mother. Her relationship, she contends, is one based on romantic love, simultaneously of her own choosing but—however seemingly contradictory—also somehow "meant to be." Like Emily and Phillip, and Gertrude and Willie, Alice and Angus have grown up together, and their relationship has an incestuous tinge to it. When Alice insists, for example, that Graeme is "no brother of mine," she goes on to say, "Brother indeed! there's none such,—unless it's you, Angus!" Angus, however, attempts to clarify the relationship, reminding her, "I'm not your brother, Ailie darling, and never wish to be,—but" (102). His clarification is interrupted by Alice, indicating perhaps that the distinction is easier and more clearly made for Angus than for her.

Alice's wish not to be commodified is violently granted when her face is horribly burned in an accident that occurs during Angus's visit. In catching her cape on fire while carelessly tossing a match out the window, Angus is the inadvertent cause of the fire that disfigures Alice's face. After the fire is extinguished, Alice loses consciousness and is immediately put to bed to recuperate. Like Phillip Amory in the aftermath of Emily Graham's accident, Angus must leave Scotland before Alice is well enough to see him. Her face is never described in detail, possibly because Alice's point of view shapes the story; we know the extent of the damage only by Alice's general lament for what she has lost. Regardless, it is apparent that her burns are severe, as is her depression when she wakes and realizes the extent of her disfigurement:

> I went near no moors, I looked no more out of my window, I only sat by my bedside and kept my face hid in the valences; and the little gray governess would sit beside me and cheer me, and tell me it was not so bad when all was said, and beauty was but little worth, and years would efface much, that my hair was still as dark and soft, my eyes as shining, my—But all to what use? Where had flown the old Strathsay red from my cheek, where that smooth polish of brow, where—I, who had aye been the flower of the race, the pride of the name, could not now bide to brook my own glance in the glass. (104)

Although Alice's hair and eyes are still lovely, her complexion, that sentimental indicator of true womanhood and morality, is mutilated; her cheek and brow are distinctly *not* red and *not* smooth but are otherwise apparently impossible to describe or even to look at in the mirror. In this sense, Alice's scarred face is similar to Emily's mutilated eyeballs; the important difference is that Alice cannot close her eyes and hide either her disfigurement or others' response to it from herself. As she can clearly see, the visibility of her mark disturbs rather than confirms the classical conception of the beautiful, angelic, middle-class white woman. The "gray governess" is able to look at Alice's face and insist that the situation is not as horrible as it appears—not because Alice's face isn't disfigured, but because "beauty was but little worth." Yet to Alice, who has been raised to be a wife, and to her mother, who depends on Alice's appearance to render her marketable, beauty has significant economic worth. Most importantly, however, more than beauty has been lost with the disfigurement of Alice's face: her physical resemblance to her father and her claim to her mother's special attention and affections are "effaced" when her face is burned. "[Y]ears would efface much," the governess tells her, but Alice knows that there will be no returning from the loss of the "Strathsay red."

Alice's disfigurement, then, symbolizes what Rosemarie Garland Thomson identifies as "the ultimate threat to nineteenth-century female selfhood: a body that prevents her from attachment to a man, women's conduit to power and status" (*Extraordinary Bodies* 97). Alice's body, which disrupts her tie to her father and is assumed to repulse potential suitors, is now without function in the culture in which she lives—a culture in which women are valued primarily for their physical appearance and concomitant marriageability. The sensationalistic response of Josephine Franklin to such disfigurement is deceit; although Alice is no Emily Graham, she is still morally above any such action. The governess would seem to provide another alternative for Alice—the world of fulfilling work and self-support—but Alice is apparently unable to accept this as an option.

As long as Alice is away from her mother and the realities of the marriage market, she is able to recover somewhat from the accident both physically and emotionally. Although she initially fears the reactions of the other girls at her school, their kindness encourages her to feel "normal" again and even to discover personal resources of which she was unaware. "And so seeing I had lost my fair skin," Alice explains, "I put myself to gain other things in its place, and worked hard at my stents, my music, my books. I grew accustomed to things, and would forget there had been a change, and, being young, failed to miss being bonny; and if I did not miss it, who should?" (105). In the company of other young women, for whom appearance (in this case) does not dictate social status, Alice is comfortable with herself and is able to accept, or at least forget about, her disfigurement. This world of women and girls allows Alice to imagine that what matters is her own comfort or discomfort with her appearance. What Alice forgets, of course, is that as a woman, she must always be aware of how she appears visually to others, especially men. Alice attempts momentarily to develop what Berger calls a "sense of being in herself," but as he goes on to explain, for Alice as for all women, this sense is ultimately "supplanted by a sense of being appreciated as herself by another" (46).

Alice's illusion of "being in herself" is shattered when she returns home and reenters her mother's world; in this exchange of economics and sexuality, her beauty *is* missed and she is regarded as different, both from the person she used to be and from the people around her. Alice is reminded most harshly of her appearance and its implications when she meets her mother for the first time in several years. While she is rushing to Mrs. Strathsay's open arms, Alice's veil is blown away from her face:

> I ran forward, and paused, for my veil had blown away over my face, to throw it back and away,—and, with the breath, her shining blue eyes opened and filled with fire, her proud lips twisted themselves in pain, she struck her two hands together, crying out, "My God! how horrible!" and fainted.
>
> Mrs. Strathsay was my mother. I might have fallen too,—I might have died, it seems to me, with the sudden snap my heart gave,—but all in a word I felt Mary Strathsay's soft curls brushing about my face, and she drew it upon her white bosom, and covered the poor thing with her kisses. (105–6)

Although Mary's loving acceptance of Alice works to counter the worst effects of her mother's rejection, it is important that Alice's face has become a "poor thing," worthy only of sympathy and somehow disconnected from the rest of her being. Needless to say, Alice no longer "fail[s] to miss being bonny." Although Mrs. Strathsay is her mother, as Alice reminds us, she does not respond to her daughter's injuries as a nineteenth-century sentimental mother would be expected to respond; she does not nurture or comfort her or assure her that all of God's creatures are beautiful in his eyes. When Alice and her mother are finally reconciled, Alice explains, "I felt her eyes upon me as if she searched for some spot fit for her fine lips, and presently . . . the kiss had fallen upon my hair" (106). Unlike Mary, Alice's mother is unable to kiss her daughter on her damaged face, and her kiss therefore does not indicate complete acceptance.

Mrs. Strathsay clearly regards Alice as damaged goods, removed from the marriage market because of an assumed lack of demand, and treats her as such. For example, when Alice insists that she will wear bright colors so that she "may please the eye one way or another," her mother responds, "No use, child" (107).

Alice is directed to wear white and gray and black at all times to avoid drawing attention to her physical appearance and is told that she "should slip into life as [she] could" (106). Although Alice will not financially support herself, she is expected to fade into the background visually, as does the "gray governess" who attempts to comfort Alice after the accident. When Alice muses about being married, her mother exclaims, "You! . . . And who is it would take such a fright?" (108). Ultimately, Mrs. Strathsay's scorn and disgust teach Alice "to have a strange shrinking from all careless eyes" (113).

As in the case of Emily Graham, Alice herself is regarded as somehow responsible for her own disfigurement and for others' responses to it. Her mother's response is, of course, the most extreme and therefore the most difficult for Alice despite her sisters' efforts to explain it. When Margray insists that it is the loss of Angus Ingestre's wealth that has so angered their mother, Mary disagrees with her: "You know, girl, that our mother loved our father's face in her, and counted the days ere seeing it once more; and having lost it, she is like one bewildered" (109). Regardless of the reason for her mother's response, as Margray reminds Alice, their mother had "counted much on your likely looks" and was surprised because Alice had "never told us the accident took them." Alice tells her sister, "I thought you'd know, Margray," but the blame for Mrs. Strathsay's response is effectively shifted to Alice herself, who is accused of not warning her mother about her physical appearance (106).

Similarly, Angus's direct responsibility for the accident, like Phillip's in Emily's case in *The Lamplighter*, is never acknowledged. In fact, Angus too is said to be ignorant of the extent of Alice's injuries even though he was a witness to the accident. Although Alice insists that he had to have known about the permanent damage to her face, her sister Margray claims that Angus's first encounter with Alice after the accident was a shock to him: "He said he'd been ever fancying you fresh and fair as the day he left you,—and his heart cracked when you turned upon him" (113). Alice was not, in fact, "fresh and fair" the day Angus left her, but both Mrs. Strathsay and Angus are simply unable or unwilling to accept the reality of Alice's scarred face until they are directly confronted with it.

With this reallocation of responsibility for her disfigurement and the reactions of others, Alice is marked as (socially) disabled—not because of the scars themselves but because of the way in which other people regard her after she is scarred. Susan Wendell, author of *The Rejected Body: Feminist Philosophical Reflections on Disability*, considers facial scarring an "important example" of "disabilit[ies] of appearance only, . . . constructed totally by stigma and cultural meanings." She writes, "The power of culture alone to construct a disability is revealed when we consider bodily differences—deviations from a society's conception of a 'normal' or acceptable body—that, although they cause little or no functional or physical difficulty for the person who has them, constitute major social disabilities" (44). It is, in fact, the gaze of those who watch Alice that defines her as disabled, not the facial scars themselves. Because she is disabled in this way, she, like Emily, is expected to relegate herself to her parental home, accepting the impossibility of marriage and a home of her own. Essentially, she is expected to remain a child.

Alice's oldest sister, Margray, who has been married off to the highest bidder, sees Alice's disfigurement as a chance for her to escape an arranged marriage. "If my mother cannot marry you as she'd choose, you'll come to less grief, I doubt," she tells Alice (106). Yet although Alice had disagreed with her mother's motives and her businesslike approach to matchmaking, she had no quarrel with the marriage Mrs. Strathsay had intended to arrange for her. When Angus returns from his voyage and visits the Strathsays, Alice is initially so conditioned by her mother to think herself worthless that she assumes he will fall in love with her sister Effie "or some other fair-faced lass" (113). When Margray insists that Angus will marry Alice out of a sense of responsibility, Alice refuses to participate in such an arrangement, even though it would permit her to escape her mother's home and her constant disapproval and disgust. Alice eventually discovers that Angus had never stopped loving her, and his acceptance of her disfigurement is compared to the reactions of Mary and Mrs. Strathsay: " 'Oh, Angus' I cried,—'can you love me with no place on my face to kiss?' But he found a place" (117). Alice does, after all, marry the man for whom her mother intended her. Yet Mrs. Strathsay's hand in the marriage becomes less important when Alice is disfigured and therefore written off as an investment worthy of any man's time, money, or—especially—love.

The accident effectively removes Alice from the marriage market yet creates a space in which she can be certain that she is loved as an individual rather than as an economic product. The match between Alice and Angus is a triumph of romantic love for this very reason. "Can I help loving you?" Angus asks Alice after their momentous kiss. "Oh, Ailie, I do! I do!—when all my years you have been my dream, my hope, my delight, when my life is yours, when you are my very self!" (117). In closing the story, Alice, as narrator, assures her reader that she and Angus live on happily, "revivifying our childhood with the strength of our richer years, heart so locked in heart that we have no need of words" (118). The rhetoric of romantic love is clear here; as Lystra explains, "Romantically attached individuals repeatedly evoked the inner sense of sharing the identity of another. Nineteenth-century romantic partners believed that they had assimilated part of each other's subjectivity" (42). Unlike Cummins, however, Spofford does not invoke Christianity to excuse the fervor of the lovers, nor does she deny the "disabled" woman the capacity to reproduce. Indeed, the story concludes with the birth of Alice and Angus's first child, a son who is named after Alice's father.[14] The birth of Alice's child indicates an acceptance of her body and her role as wife and mother. The adult Alice refuses to be relegated to a prolonged childhood because of her disability: "The joys of childhood are good, I trow," she reflects, "but who would exchange for them the proud, glad pulse of full womanhood?—not I" (99).

Alice's sister, Mary, attempts an even more radical rebellion against her mother and the marriage market, and this plot line is appropriately far more reminiscent of sensational fiction. After returning home from school, Alice learns that Mary has fallen in love with Helmar, "the descendent of a bold Spanish buccaneer who came northwardly with his godless spoil, when all his raids upon West-Indian seas were done" (111). Although Helmar is prosperous, Mrs. Strathsay is disgusted with the source of his wealth and refuses to condone the courtship. Mary agrees to renounce Helmar, but only if her mother will not pressure her to marry the captain for whom she is intended. When Helmar finds out about the arrangement, he vows "he'd darken [Mrs. Strathsay's] day, for she had taken the light out of his life" (112). Although Mary, like her mother, shows no outward sign of her loss, she inscribes her unspoken grief on her body. Margray tells Alice, "D' you mind that ring of rubies she wears, like drops of blood all round the hoop? 'T was his. She shifted it to the left hand, I saw. It was broken once,—and what do you think she did? She put a blow-pipe at the candle-flame, and, holding it up in tiny pincers, soldered the two ends together without taking it off her finger,—and it burning into the bone! Strathsay grit. It's on her white wedding-finger. The scar's there too" (113). Mary's scarred ring finger symbolizes her love for Helmar as well as her rebellion against the commodification of women and their bodies in the marriage market. In this sense, Mary's scar is similar to those of Alice, which Alice recognizes when she muses that "there were more scars than [she] carried, in the house" (113).

The scars of the Strathsay sisters mark the pain imposed on the entire family by the dictates of the marriage market as well as the particular moments in which each sister found it possible to escape the destiny her mother had shaped for her. While Margray succumbs to her mother's power and Mary and Alice are able to resist it in ways that enable them to remain within the family, however, the youngest daughter, Effie, rebels entirely, with the assistance of the vengeful Helmar. Ignorant of Mary's relationship with him, Effie falls in love with Helmar and agrees to run away with him. Helmar appears at the Strathsay home with Effie's corpse and explains that she had slipped and fallen into the river while boarding the boat in which they were to elope. "I never loved the girl," Helmar tells her mother. "Yet to-night she would have fled with me. It was my revenge, Mrs. Strathsay!" (117).

Although Alice's scarred face and Mary's scarred finger function in similar ways in "The Strathsays," it is significant that Alice is unintentionally wounded while Mary's wound is self-inflicted. Mary is an active agent in her own destiny; neither her rebellion nor her scarring is accidental. As might be expected, the story does not end happily for Mary as it does for Alice. Unlike Alice, Mary is represented as having transcended the body at the conclusion of "The Strathsays." She "lives now in the dream of hereafter" where she and Helmar will be reunited, "shrived by sorrow and pain, and by prayer." Hearing Mary sing, Alice remarks that "her soul seems to soar with her voice, and both would be lost in heaven but for the tender human sympathies that draw her back to our side again" (118). Although Mary seems distinctly unlike Emily Graham throughout most of the story, her suffering ultimately causes a similar spiritualization of this marked woman who lives only to die, perhaps a manifestation of the extent of her transgression: as the death of Effie reveals, Mary's relationship with the piratical Helmar is fraught with danger and sexual potential. Alice and Angus's relationship is very different in this regard. Unlike Emily and Phillip of *The Lamplighter*, Alice and Angus are supervised by the "little gray governess" during the scene in which Alice's face is burned; as Alice's naming of Angus as her brother indicates, their relationship (at least before marriage) is not dangerous or sexualized in any way (until, of course, the burning of Alice's face). Unlike Emily, Alice is clearly not burned to punish her for any potential sexual transgression.

Why, then, is Alice's face burned and scarred if not to warn young women against sexual experimentation?[15] Despite Alice's happiness at the end of "The Strathsays," Angus's role in the accident that disfigures her highlights not only the importance of romantic love but, more specifically, the disturbing way in which romantic love both *causes* and *resolves* the crisis in this narrative, as it does in *The Lamplighter*. Had the accident never happened, Alice and Angus would most likely have soon married and had children, as they eventually do. Alice's accident has two revealing consequences: first, Angus's importance to Alice and her romantic sense of self increase exponentially; and second, the power of the Strathsay matriarchy is distinctly diminished, replaced by a patriarchal—if sentimental—family headed by Angus.

Despite the ways in which, as Lystra points out, romantic love encouraged men and women to identify with each other and bridge the gender gap, Angus's love rather than his relationship with Alice becomes, in a sense, the focus of the story, something highlighted in the scene in which Alice and Angus are reunited. After having avoided Angus during his visits to the Strathsay home, convinced that he is there to see Effie, Alice encounters him in the hallway. Angus holds her hands and refuses to allow her to escape him again.

"I've a puzzle . . . to show thee,—a charade of two syllables,—a tiny thing, and yet it holds my world! See, the first."

He had led me to the mirror and stationed me alone. I liked not to look, but I did. "Why, Angus," I said, "it's I."

"Well done! and go to the head. It's you indeed. But what else, Ailie darling? Nay, I'll tell you, then. The first syllable,—just to suit my fancy—shall be bride, shall it not?"

"Bride," I murmured.

"And there behold the last syllable!" taking a step aside to the window, and throwing wide the blind.

I looked down the dark, but there was nought except the servant in the light of the hanging lamp, holding the curbs of the two horses that leaped and reared with nervous limbs and fiery eyes behind him.

"Is it horses?—steeds?—oh, bridles!"

"But thou'rt a very dunce! The last syllable is groom!"

"Now you shall see the embodiment of the whole word"; and with the step he was before the glass again. "Look!" he said, "look from under my arm—you are just as high as my heart!"

"Why, that's you, Angus,"—and a gleam was dawning on me.

"Of course, it is, little stupid! No less. And it's bridegroom too, and never bridegroom without this bride!" (117)

As this passage begins, the focus seems to be on Alice; Angus leads her to the mirror and encourages her to look into it and then identifies her as the embodiment of the word "bride." Despite her mother's lack of faith, Alice is asked to visually connect her disfigured face with the roles of bride and wife—ultimately to recognize the continuity between her self prior to the accident and her current self. Scarred or not, she is still the woman Angus loves and wants to marry. Before he can do that, Alice must learn to look at and accept herself as she is, no matter how much she "like[s] not to look."

Yet it is important that "bride" only functions here as the beginning of the word "bridegroom," the more difficult part of the puzzle to determine. Unlike Alice, Angus is not wholly identified through his role in the relationship between him and Alice; the charade cannot be solved simply by Angus standing in front of Alice and declaring himself "bridegroom" as he declares her "bride." Alice is part of this charade; he cannot be bridegroom without her, which is presumably why the puzzle is enacted before the mirror. Yet the ultimate focus is Angus himself, come to rescue Alice from the situation in which he has placed her by causing the accident that burned her face.[16] Also disturbing is Angus's patronizing attitude toward Alice in this scene; he calls her a "dunce" and "little stupid," revealing the drastic power differential in this relationship. Angus's control over Alice and the potential for violence inherent in their relationship is perhaps highlighted by the fact that this scene is followed quickly by Helmar bursting into the Strathsay home with Effie's body in his arms.

Angus's pivotal role in the resolution of the story is reiterated in Alice's description of the family dynamics after Effie's death and her own marriage. Earlier in the story, Alice insists that "marriage after marriage would not lighten the rod of iron that Mrs. Strathsay held over her girls' lives," yet these two events apparently "lighten the rod" and reallocate the economic and emotional power in the Strathsay family (114). Mrs. Strathsay lives with Alice and Angus in the Strathsay family home, where she lavishes Alice's son with attention, "bringing him up in the way he should go." Alice says, "I verily believe that she fancies him to be my father's child." Thus despite the loss of "the old Strathsay red" from Alice's cheek, the Strathsay family resemblance survives in the child that Alice bears. Mrs. Strathsay favors this child just as she did Alice. Yet Alice refuses to allow Mrs. Strathsay to manipulate her son in the way she and her sisters were manipulated: "She's aye softer than she was, she does not lay her moulding finger on him too heavily;—if she did, I doubt but we should have to win away to our own home" (118). As a married woman with access to her husband's financial resources, Alice is able to control her own life and that of her family; her mother's interference would result in her banishment from her grandson's presence. Alice's empowerment, however, depends on renewing the patriarchal family and chastening the powerful matriarch. Angus is the head of the family now even if they still live in the Strathsay home, and his mantle will presumably be passed on to his son.

At the end of her story, Alice insists, "[W]e have grown to be a glad and peaceful family at length; 't is only on rare seasons that the old wound rankles" (118). The "old wound," the scars of the Strathsay family, are reminders of the past, of the way in which economic concerns and the marriage market had torn this family apart. The extensive violence done to women's bodies in this text as well as in *City Crimes* and *The Lamplighter* reveals their vulnerability in courtship—both despite and because of the presence of romantic love—as well as in the larger society in which they live. The myth of the unmarked woman, Spofford's story suggests, ignores the realities of women's lives, which are carried out in the midst of economic and emotional struggles for power. Women's bodies bear the record of these battles and prompt a sobering reconsideration of female power and agency in all three texts. Such discordance is particularly disturbing in "The Strathsays" with its blend of fictional modes ultimately allowing for corporeality for one sister, transcendence for the other, and compromise for both.

CHAPTER THREE

"Tattooed Still"

The Inscription of Female Agency

The erasure of disfiguration from the female body, enacted rhetorically in Herman Melville's *Typee* and in the memoirs of Susan Thompson Lewis Parrish, became a reality in the late nineteenth century with advancements in medicine and, especially, aesthetic surgery.[1] Women no longer needed to rely exclusively on the veil, as did Olive Oatman and the fictional Josephine Franklin, to divert the public gaze from their marked faces. Essential to the presentation of these innovative surgical methods to the public, however, was an assumed relationship between bodily modification, class, and gender. Appealing to readers' reverence for "high art," religion, and domesticity, for example, an 1898 advertisement for the John H. Woodbury Dermatological Institute jubilantly informed readers of *Leslie's Weekly* that they could "go . . . and get a new face" (see figure 11). The human body is represented here as the "hurried canvas" of Nature, which demands to be "retouch[ed] . . . with the genius of the Raphaels of the scalpel." In capital letters at the top of the page, the advertisers insist emphatically that "THE NEW SURGERY FOLLOWS THE LINES OF HIGH ART," thereby reassuring readers that aesthetic surgery is an artistic process to be distinguished from other, presumably less-sophisticated forms of bodily modification such as the tattoo, as well as other medical procedures.

Because such arguments for aesthetic surgery appealed directly to the middle-class goal of potentially limitless social advancement, they had to be carefully phrased. As Sander Gilman points out, "the very wellspring of aesthetic surgery" is "the discourse of passing." "The boundary between reconstructive and aesthetic surgery was distinguished on the basis of the introduction of procedures that were seen as enabling individuals to 'pass.' 'Aesthetic' procedures were and are those that enable individuals to pass into a category that they perceive as different from themselves" (24–25). Although Gilman's discussion of passing clearly borrows from the racial discourse of the nineteenth century, it can just as easily refer to the subversion of class barriers. Thus the Woodbury Institute can be seen as simultaneously playing on clients' desires to subvert the social hierarchy and sanctioning such transgressions by using the rhetoric of high art. This tactic allowed middle-class readers to believe that if they found such an appeal convincing, they were already, somehow *inherently*, destined to be more than middle class anyway.

Anticipating protests against "the change of a single lineament with which birth had endowed us, for the sole sake of gaining comeliness," the Woodbury Institute claims that every human being is charged with "the higher duty of looking like a god in whose image we were created." Indeed, this duty is even translated into religious terms: "It may be held as a high and solemn precept of the religion which uplifts and spiritualizes that every man and woman should look as well as science, art, and artificer shall permit." The advertisement goes on to claim that aesthetic surgery is a domestic as well as a religious duty:

> "Change your face, if it be ugly," should be written in every home. Much of sorrow and misery this gospel would wipe away. A husband whose features are awry should have no shame or hesitation in bringing them as nearly as possible into conformity with the outlines of the Apollo Belvedere. A wife whose comeliness is marred by some congenital malformation of countenance owes it to herself, her children unborn, and above all to her future happiness, that the image which looks out at her from her mirror should grow as nearly as possible into the likeness of Venus Aphrodite.

Unattractiveness and deformity are represented as domestic problems that bring "sorrow and misery" to the home, which would be happy if only both husband and wife were physically attractive.

The impact of the husband's attractiveness, however, is not specified; he is merely told that he should have no "shame or hesitation" in seeking to improve his appearance through surgery. The wife's duty is more clearly articulated; she is reminded that her "marred . . . countenance" affects her own self-image as well as her unborn children. Although the advertisement is not entirely clear on this point, it seems to indicate that surgical alteration of the woman's "congenital malformation" will lessen the risk of her children inheriting the same condition. It implies that the "future happiness" of her marriage and her family depend on her decision to transform her unattractive appearance through surgery.

The illustrations accompanying the text demonstrate a similar focus on female consumers. Out of nine illustrations included in the one-page advertisement, seven show before-and-after drawings of female patients who represent various aesthetic processes such as "reducing a projecting chin," "trimming off a pendant lower lip," and "building out a snub nose." Such before-and-after images confirm the institute's ability to allow a client to pass invisibly into a

"TRUTH IS BEAUTY, BEAUTY TRUTH."

THE NEW SURGERY FOLLOWS THE LINES OF HIGH ART.

A RT follows utility. After the practical, the ideal. Marvelous have been the strides of surgery in the past decade, and its development advances by leaps and bounds. Its higher problems, however, have been principally solved on the lines of the repair-shop rather than of the skilled designer's studio. Its remedial leaders have been the sturdy geniuses of the anvil rather than the moulders of clay to the wielders of the pencil and the brush.

In other words, we have patched up the broken bones of an age of accidents before we turned to the aesthetic duty of holding up the mirror to Nature and retouching her hurried canvases with the genius of the Raphaels of the scalpel.

The first note of the new dispensation was received with incredulity. It seemed almost like sacrilege to remould the countenance, and like the apotheosis of vanity to permit the change of a single lineament with which birth had endowed us, for the sole sake of gaining comeliness.

REDUCING A PROJECTING CHIN.

The higher duty of looking like a god in whose image we were created was overlooked. The brutalizing sweep of centuries, turning thousands into grotesque caricatures of the glorious pair of Creation's Eden dawn, was lost sight of.

It may be held as a high and solemn precept of the religion which uplifts and spiritualizes that every man and woman should look as well as science, art, and artificer shall permit.

To-day the genius of surgical advancement proclaims a high note. Born and developed in the silence which follows the stately, sonorous march, it grows into a symphony of unparalleled sweetness. "All may be beautiful" is its theme.

Fortunately the problems of plastic surgery as applied to beautifying the features are comparatively simple; all easy surgically, and executed with little or no pain. Thousands have asked, Is it possible that a nose should be changed, an eyebrow straightened, ears set back, wrinkles removed? Nothing less difficult. Not half as dangerous or difficult operations as set-

SHORTENING A LONG NOSE.

ting a broken arm or amputating a lacerated toe.

For three years or more countless operations of the most gratifying character have been performed by the skilled surgeons of the John H. Woodbury Institute and its branches throughout the United States. It must be remembered that most or nearly all of these operations have been performed under the most favorable circumstances. Consequently their success has been proportionately gratifying.

A patient who wishes a Roman nose changed to Grecian outlines goes to the surgeon's chair in perfect health. The tissues, ligaments, muscles, and bones operated upon are in their normal condition. Consequently recovery is rapid and perfect.

Hospital practice has to deal with cataclysms of the human frame, no more to be compared with featural surgery than the blow of the pugilist to the caress of the powder-puff. Lacerated tissues, shattered bones, diseased organs, and physical shock are the lions to the path of curative surgery. None of these difficulties confront the surgeons on Woodbury's staff. The operations are painless and certain. The moral effect is worth an epic.

TRIMMING OFF A PENDENT LOWER LIP.

"Change your face, if it be ugly." should be written in every home. Much of sorrow and misery this gospel would wipe away. A husband whose features are awry should have no shame or hesitation in bringing them as nearly as possible into conformity with the outlines of the Apollo Belvedere. A wife whose comeliness is marred by some congenital malformation of countenance owes it to herself, her children unborn, and above all to her future happiness, that the image which looks out at her from her mirror should grow as nearly as possible into the likeness of Venus Aphrodite.

In another century and another land Woodbury would have worn the decora-

BUILDING OUT A SNUB NOSE.

tions of royalty and have been saluted the peer of princes and kings. The present age is materialistic. When its history shall have been written and emblazed with the idealizing influences of a broader age, he will be classed with the poets and painters whose merits are eternally lauded, but whose genius was for a time unsung.

A description of all the operations performed at the John H. Woodbury Dermatological Institute will be unnecessary to convince every one that no beauty need be merely "skin deep." Those operations most commonly performed will serve. A few illustrate the methods pursued throughout Woodbury's entire practice. To begin

with, the nose and mouth and ears have more to do with beautifying or marring the countenance than anything else excepting the eye. No one need put up with uncouth features who will appeal to the improved surgery of to-day. It corrects the seeming errors of nature and makes plain faces pretty with a success that is marvelous.

This building-out and cutting-down of noses is really a study in architecture or art. Bridges are made from plaster moulds, and the work is done by a goldsmith. The insertion of an artificial septum between the nostrils is a very nice piece of work. Transforming Roman noses into the Grecian type, and re-shaping noses of the pug order, are among the simplest operations to perform. It only requires a study of what sort of nose the face demands, a determination of how much should be cut off here

REMOVING THE ROMAN HUMP.

and there, and a few minutes with the knife.

The chief skill in this sort of an operation consists in removing the tissues from the bone and cartilage before the paring process is begun, in such shape that they can be replaced so as to give a smooth, natural appearance when the incision is healed.

In removing the "hump" of a Roman nose, the flesh of the nose is cut on either side of the hump, a hook is inserted in the flesh, and it is held away from the bone by an assistant. Cocaine prevents pain. While the skin is raised, a steel burr, which is a small drill run by an electric motor, is pressed against the hump of the bone and it is quickly ground away. All that then re-

BUILDING OUT A SNUB NOSE.

mains to do is to take the hook out of the skin of the nose, trim the edges where they have been cut, sew them together, bandage up the nose, and wait for it to heal. When it does, the removal of the bandage reveals a nose that hasn't the slightest suggestion of the noble old Roman hump to it.

In remodeling a pug nose, the surgeon removes a portion of the cartilage between the end of the nose and the point of juncture with the upper lip, and the edge of the cut are then sewed together with thin thread. Cocaine is sprayed on the nose to make the operation painless. When the cartilage has been removed and the edges of the wound drawn together, the operation draws the point of the nose downward to a graceful angle. This angle can be regulated at will by carefully judging the amount of cartilaginous tissue to be cut away.

Ears that project from the head in an unsightly way, or which have hanging lobes that mar the owner's personal looks, are readily restored to a normal appearance. The uncouth projection of the ear from the head is corrected by cutting the flesh of the ear at the point where it joins the head, and then making an elliptical dissection and removing a section of the cartilage near the head. The several edges of the ear near the

the wound are drawn together and sewed. The surplus of cartilage that made the ear project from the head having been removed, the ear when it heals is no longer unsightly and rests close to the head. A V-shaped dissection of the outer edge of the ear and the removal of a small section of the carti-

RE-SHAPING A BULBOUS NOSE.

lage will summarily remedy the defect of the misshapen lobe.

One of the most popularly astonishing operations is the one for the permanent removal of wrinkles on the forehead. This is accomplished by making a horizontal incision through the skin of the forehead at its junction with the scalp; a second incision, in the form of an ellipse, completes this part of the operation, after which the tissue bounded by the incision is dissected out and the edges brought together, thus overcoming the relaxation that resulted in the formation of the wrinkles. This is done without leaving any trace of the operation.

In removing wrinkles from the neck, the surgeon will cut so that any mark will be

EXTENDING A SHORT LIP.

screened as far as possible by the jawbone. Having described the patterns, he cuts through the real skin, lifting out enough to provide for the smoothing out of the undesirable fold when the edges of the skin are drawn together. In general the pieces removed are of an irregular oval, pointed at the ends. The outlines of these ovals, or "gores," vary according to the condition of the face and the amount of tension necessary to draw out the wrinkles.

The operation for the removal of a double chin is simple. The parts are first thoroughly anaesthetized by cocaine. Then a strip of tissue, varying in size according to the extent of the disfigurement, and including the fatty deposit under the chin, is removed, the edges of the incision are then carefully closed and held in place by sutures of absorbent ligatures, and complete union takes place in a few days without leaving any noticeable scar.

The removal of minor skin blemishes is of course a simple matter in the hands of Woodbury's skilled operators. Pimples, moles, warts, freckles, birthmarks, and the like disappear as if by magic, leaving no more trace than if they had never been.

In short, the great variety of feasible facial operations, and with the skin-grafting method, now practiced with such success, it is possible to completely change the expression of the human face. Literally, all that a man or a woman who doesn't like the face he or she possesses need do to secure contentment is to go to the surgeons of the John H. Woodbury Dermatological Institute, 127 West 42d Street, New York, and get a new face.

Figure 11. Advertisement, the John H. Woodbury Dermatological Institute. *Leslie's Weekly*, May 26, 1898.

higher class; unmarred by the unattractive chin, lip, or nose that might indicate ethnicity or simply difference, the client is more conventionally attractive and therefore less visible as an interloper. Only one male patient is represented in the advertisement, while the final portrait (actually the first on the page) is presumably John H. Woodward himself, the exalted surgeon-artist who is also aesthetically perfect enough to be represented by a single face. Thus while both men and women are invited to visit the John H. Woodbury Dermatological Institute, women are clearly the primary intended audience of the advertisement.[2] With their eyes constantly on their mirror image—a situation virtually depicted in the advertisement's illustrations themselves—women recognize all too clearly the cultural significance of physical appearance and internalize the gaze that observes and judges them. Female beauty is thought not only to reflect but actually to create personal, familial, and social happiness and success—not just in one generation but in generations to come. There is no excuse for ugliness in a society fortunate and civilized enough to foster the likes of John H. Woodbury.

This emphasis on female beauty is not new to the late nineteenth century, nor is the potential for bodily modification, even though surgical techniques were far more advanced during this period than even decades before.[3] Prior to this period, as Oatman's experiences and the fictions of Cummins and Spofford illustrate, the disfiguration of the female body was regarded as unalterable; the only conceivable question was whether that disfigurement could be overlooked or transcended by romantic or spiritual love. As Gilman explains, "It is not that the reconstructed body was 'invented' at the end of the nineteenth century, but rather that questions about the ability of the individual to be transformed, which had been articulated as social or political . . . , came to be defined as biological and medical" (19). Given the rise of eugenics, some Americans also became concerned with the genetic inheritance of disfiguration or disability; although this is not, of course, a concern with the tattoo, what the tattoo is thought to represent (e.g., questionable morals, intelligence, or class status) could have been considered inheritable. As I demonstrate in the first chapter of this study, competing cultural narratives of racial and gendered identity hindered the redefinition and subsequent transcendence of Oatman's body. As if aware of the anxiety of inheritance articulated forty years later in the advertisement for the Woodbury Institute, Oatman and her husband, John B. Fairchild, did not have any children of their own, although they did adopt a child in 1873 (Derounian-Stodola, "Captive and Her Editor" 20). Although Angus and Alice Ingestre *are* able to have children, that possibility is denied Phillip and Emily Amory. Thus, despite medical advances, the captivity narrative, sentimental fiction, and the late nineteenth-century discourse of aesthetic surgery reflect a similarly intense anxiety over the implications of the marked female body for the health, survival, and social mobility of the American middle classes.

More than fifty years prior to the advertisement for the Woodbury Institute, such anxieties were clearly demonstrated and played out in scientific terms in one of Nathaniel Hawthorne's best-known short stories, "The Birthmark" (1843). Many parallels exist between this story and the rhetoric used to advertise aesthetic surgery in the 1890s, the most important being the primacy of the scientist-husband's agency and the concomitant diminished importance of the woman as subject or agent in her own right. Such a paradigm gives the male gaze the power to control the interpretation and significance of the female body within scientific discourse, the marital relationship, and American society in general. Elizabeth Stoddard's novel *The Morgesons*, published in 1862, is the first text to effectively change this paradigm without relying on sentimental conventions such as the discourse of romantic love. By bringing together the seemingly disparate discourses of the tattoo and the scar, Stoddard reveals that there was more than one script for the marked woman in nineteenth-century America. The mark did not simply have to be ignored, tolerated, or overcome; instead, it is possible for women to embrace the mark and to use it as the impetus for an oppositional gaze that allows them to renegotiate the terms of female agency.[4]

Object of Horror and Disgust

No discussion of marked women and female agency would be complete without an analysis of "The Birthmark" by Nathaniel Hawthorne. The story—and Hawthorne's work in general—is particularly relevant to Stoddard's novel *The Morgesons* because Stoddard, like many of her contemporaries, especially admired Hawthorne. Many critics agree that "Hawthorne's influence on Stoddard's life cannot be understated" (Amstutz 76). Stoddard herself insisted that there were "[t]hree names [she] owe[d] much to: Hawthorne, [James Russell] Lowell, and [Edmund Clarence] Stedman" (qtd. in Matlack 556). She and Hawthorne were actually distant cousins according to Stoddard's biographer, and although Hawthorne was never aware of their kinship, he recognized many of his own progenitors in Stoddard's portrayal of the Somers family in *The Morgesons*.[5] After reading the novel, he wrote a letter to Richard Henry Stoddard, Elizabeth's husband: "I read *The Morgesons* at the time of publication, and thought it a remarkable and powerful book, though not without a painful element mixed up in it. It interested me very much, because I thought I could recognize a sort of misty representation of my native town, and likewise the half-revealed features of peoples whom I have known—some of my own relatives, in fact" (qtd. in Matlack 266). Hawthorne may have even recognized some of Hester Prynne's rebellious spirit in Stoddard's heroine, Cassandra Morgeson. Perhaps because of these connections, the copy of *The Morgesons* that Elizabeth and Richard sent to Hawthorne was still in his library at the time of his death (Matlack 266). Hawthorne's encouraging response to her first novel was crucially important to Stoddard. In 1885, anticipating a lukewarm reception of the reissue of *The Morgesons*, she told a friend, "I have one immortal feather in my cap. Nathaniel Hawthorne recognized me" (qtd. in Matlack 549).

As Margaret B. Moore explains, "[I]n theme the two writers were attracted by similar subjects. Of course, they both saw 'New Englandly' and coastal New Englandly at that. Each treated the sea and the houses by them, the confining constraints for women, the remnants of Puritanism, the mystery of the human heart, sudden death, the place of caste, the truth in portraits, and alienation of human beings, one from another" (124). To this list, I would add a shared interest in the female body, sexuality, and agency. These themes are clearly prominent in *The Scarlet Letter*, which I discussed in the introduction, as well as in much of Hawthorne's other work. Although *The Morgesons* was compared to *The Scarlet Letter* in one review (published in the *World* on July 4, 1862) and was most likely influenced by this novel, I am more interested here in "The Birthmark" and the link it provides between the John H. Woodbury Dermatological Institute's goal of giving women "new face[s]" and Stoddard's representation of a woman who learns to accept her face—and the experiences that it marks—as it is.[6] As the first two chapters of this study have demonstrated, facial marks were the most threatening to nineteenth-century women and those who observed them precisely because so much of the female body was generally covered by clothing at the time. To aggressively mark or unmark a woman's face was also to affect her ability to navigate the marriage market and, as this chapter will reveal, to attempt to rob her of her own agency, particularly her agency to define and present the body and the self publicly and privately. In this sense, "The Birthmark" is a paradigmatic text.

In late 1836 or early 1837, Hawthorne recorded an observation in his notebook: "Those who are very difficult in choosing wives seem as if they would take none of Nature's ready-made works, but want a woman manufactured particularly to their order" (qtd. in Harding 362). A few years later, in 1839, this observation began to develop into an idea for a story, but his opinion of the "difficult" wife-seekers seems to have improved in the interval. "A person to be the death of his beloved in trying to raise her to more than mortal perfection," he wrote, "yet this should be a comfort to him for having aimed so highly and holily" (363). Indeed, Hawthorne's second notation eerily foreshadows the claim on the part of the Woodbury Institute that "[i]t may be held as a high and solemn precept . . . that every man and woman should look as well as science, art, and artificer shall permit." The goal of "mortal perfection" and the use of science to achieve this goal are seen as morally commendable—even holy—in both texts.

The story that developed out of these and other notations is "The Birthmark," which features Aylmer, "a man of science," who marries a beautiful young woman named Georgiana. After their marriage, Aylmer inquires about a small birthmark on his wife's cheek.

> In the usual state of her complexion—a healthy though delicate bloom—the mark wore a tint of deeper crimson, which imperfectly defined its shape amid the surrounding rosiness. When she blushed it gradually became more indistinct, and fully vanished amid the triumphant rush of blood that bathed the whole cheek with its brilliant glow. But if any shifting motion caused her to turn pale there was the mark again, a crimson stain upon the snow, in what Aylmer sometimes deemed an almost fearful distinctness. Its shape bore not a little similarity to the human hand, though of the smallest pygmy size. (176)

Although Georgiana claims that she has often been complimented on this birthmark, Aylmer insists that the mark "shocks [him], as being the visible mark of earthly imperfection" (176). Dismayed by her husband's reaction to the birthmark, she agrees to allow him to remove it from her cheek. Aylmer accordingly constructs a lavish boudoir for Georgiana adjacent to his laboratories and sets out to concoct a potion that will successfully erase the mark. Upon swallowing the draught, Georgiana falls asleep, only to wake in time to tell Aylmer that she is dying. In his quest for the ideal woman, then, Aylmer makes a sacrifice of his wife.

Critical reactions to "The Birthmark" differ widely in their assessment of the righteousness or "holiness" of Aylmer's mission. Arlin Turner, for example, commends "the loftiness of Aylmer's purpose" and claims that in the story "an obsession with a noble purpose produces tragic results" (163–64). On the opposite end of the critical spectrum, Judith Fetterley has famously labeled the text a "success story . . . the demonstration of how to murder your wife and get away with it" (22). She explains,

> It is, of course, possible to read "The Birthmark" as a story of misguided idealism, a tale of the unhappy consequences of man's nevertheless worthy passion for perfecting and transcending nature; and this is the reading usually given to it. This reading, however, ignores the significance of the form idealism takes in the story. It is not irrelevant that "The Birthmark" is about a man's desire to perfect his wife, nor is it accidental that the consequence of this idealism is the wife's death. (22)

As is the case with much feminist criticism of Hawthorne's work since the late 1970s, my own "resistant reading" of "The Birthmark" builds on Fetterley's perception of Aylmer's misogynistic insistence on his wife's physical perfection at any cost. Aylmer's successful experiment highlights his own desire to control—and therefore inscribe—Georgiana's body, an impulse deriving not only from prescribed notions of nineteenth-century female character but also from a simultaneous fear and jealousy of female power.[7]

It is crucial that Aylmer's concern with the birthmark does not emerge until after the two have married—until, that is, Georgiana becomes Aylmer's property, dissolved into the very being of her husband as feme covert. Indeed, it seems inevitable that once the marriage takes place, Aylmer will find some fault with Georgiana, some reason to subject her to scientific experiment. The narrator explains that Aylmer "had devoted himself . . . too unreservedly to scientific studies ever to be weaned from them by any second passion. His love for his young wife might prove the stronger of the two; but it could only be by intertwining itself with his love of science and uniting the strength of the latter to his own" (175). Rather than Georgiana tempering or altering his "love of science," however, she becomes both muse for and object of his experiments.

Although it is likely that virtually anything would have served as justification for experimentation, the significance of the "crimson hand" on Georgiana's cheek cannot be ignored. Aylmer claims to see the mark as "the symbol of his wife's liability to sin, sorrow, decay, and death," everything that obstructs his vision of her as spiritually and physically perfect (177). Aylmer's ownership of Georgiana and his desire to see her as undefiled are disturbed by the mark on her cheek; not only is it "a crimson stain upon the snow" or a symbolic taint of her purity, it also takes the shape of a hand, suggesting that others have touched Aylmer's possession before him, perhaps even in a sexual manner. Many critics note the connection between Georgiana's birthmark and her sexuality; one, for example, says that the birthmark's "meaning of mortality conceals associated connotations including sexuality, the female body, reproduction, the sexual wound, or masturbation" (Lloyd-Smith 99). Fetterley similarly notes that the mark "is redolent with references to the particular nature of female sexuality; we hardly need Aylmer's insistence on seclusion, with its reminiscences of the treatment of women when they are 'unclean,' to point us in this direction" (25).

According to Christian doctrine, woman's sexuality caused the Fall, and Georgiana's mark thus recalls Eve's supposed weakness—a particularly feminine frailty that threatens the untainted, domestic Eden that Aylmer envisions as their marriage. The narrator of the story simultaneously and somewhat paradoxically confirms the comparison of Georgiana to Eve *and* defends the heroine from any mark on her character: "Some fastidious persons—but they were exclusively of her own sex—affirmed that the bloody hand, as they chose to call it, quite destroyed the effect of Georgiana's beauty and rendered her countenance even hideous. But it would be as reasonable to say that one of those small blue stains which sometimes occur in the purest statuary marble would convert the Eve of Powers to a monster" (176–77). The "Eve of Powers" referred to here is sculptor Hiram Powers's *Eve Tempted*, molded between 1838 and 1842, which depicts Eve contemplating the fatal apple. The narrator's parallel between Georgiana and Powers's sculpture can be read in two opposing ways. In one sense, he, like Aylmer, believes that the birthmark renders Georgiana dangerous, the possessor of an uncontrollable sexual curiosity that can destroy their idealized marriage. After all, even though the sculptor captures Eve in the moment before eating the apple, viewers understand that the outcome of the scenario is inevitable: Eve will disobey God and Adam, and the Fall will ensue. In another sense, however, the narrator, like the author of *The Lamplighter*, compares his female character to a perfect piece of sculpture. In this case, however, the woman is already marked, and the mark is dismissed as unimportant, no more corrupting than "those small blue stains which sometimes occur in the purest statuary marble." Hence the marked woman can presumably also be pure. Aylmer clearly does not see his way through to this latter interpretation. Although he insists that Georgiana is "fit for heaven without tasting death," he still views her physical body as a symbol of her (potential) spiritual condition. Ultimately, "Georgiana is an exemplum of woman as beautiful object, reduced to and redefined by her body," and the mark on her body signifies—at least to Aylmer—"her mor(t)al imperfections" (Fetterley 24).

As Lynn Shakinovsky points out, Aylmer's understanding of the birthmark as "symbol" ends with his own very personal reading of it: "Aylmer cannot see his own response as an interpretation; it is precisely the mark's capacity to signify, its availability for symbolization, that Aylmer is incapable of apprehending" (271). Although Aylmer cannot comprehend the multiplicity inherent in the birthmark, however, he seems to have some sense of this potential. His derision of the mark, seclusion of Georgiana, and eventual "treatment" (resulting in her death) effectively prevent others from reading and interpreting it. His response functions to mark Georgiana as his own, to reinforce the symbolism of their marriage. As I pointed out in my discussion of *Typee* and *Captivity of the Oatman Girls*, the attempt to physically or rhetorically erase the mark from the female body is as much a mark as is the tattoo or the scar itself. The birthmark, which indicates a life lived before Aylmer, perhaps even a body touched with hands prior to Aylmer's marital possession of it, causes Aylmer's desire to erase Georgiana's body, to begin anew with a spousal tabula rasa.[8] Georgiana would be, then, a symbol of her husband's success as a scientist and as a man whose wife bears only the imprint of his own hand.[9]

The power dynamics of this desire to inscribe Georgiana's body (and therefore, paradoxically, erase it) by removing the birthmark are highlighted by Aylmer's actual marking of his wife with his hands. In this scene, Georgiana wanders into Aylmer's laboratory despite his explicit instructions to remain in her boudoir. In one of the few instances in which Georgiana watches Aylmer without his knowledge or approval, she discovers that the "sanguine and joyous mien that he had assumed for [her] encouragement" is actually a mask covering the anxiety he truly feels about the experiment (187). Her observation of him is quickly disturbed, however, when he notices her presence:

> Aylmer raised his eyes hastily, and at first reddened, then grew paler than ever, on beholding Georgiana. He rushed towards her and seized her arm with a grip that left the print of his fingers upon it.
> "Why do you come hither? Have you no trust in your husband?" cried he, impetuously. "Would you throw the blight of that fatal birthmark over my labours? It is not well done. Go, prying woman, go!" (187–88)

Visual, physical, and rhetorical power are all at issue in this scene. First, Georgiana's observation of her husband is not permitted within the laboratory or within the larger context of their marriage. While Georgiana is removed to her boudoir to allow Aylmer's "intense thought and constant watchfulness" over her, she is expected to limit her movement and her gaze to the space allotted her both physically and mentally (180). He is allowed to watch her "intense[ly]" and "constant[ly]," but her own powers of vision are not permitted. When she does finally employ an observant gaze, she discovers evidence of his duplicity and insecurity on his face. Second, the violence of Aylmer's removal of the "crimson hand" is foreshadowed in the fingerprints left on Georgiana's skin after he grips her arm in anger. Incensed by her unauthorized looking at him, Aylmer restores his power over his wife first by regaining the authority of the gaze and then by marking her with his own hands. Finally, in a revealing statement Aylmer calls Georgiana a "prying woman," associating her again with Eve, whose curiosity brings about the Fall. Georgiana's curiosity, he suggests, could have similarly disastrous consequences.

The significance of these references to Eve is even more striking when placed into context with Aylmer's concern with yet another representative of female power: Mother Nature. Aylmer's scientific pursuits prior to his experimentation on Georgiana have been no less ambitious. In his laboratory, the narrator explains, Aylmer had "attempted to fathom the very process by which Nature assimilates all her precious influences from earth and air, and from the spiritual world, to create and foster man, her masterpiece. The latter pursuit, however, Aylmer had long laid aside in unwilling recognition of the truth . . . that our great creative Mother, while she amuses us with apparently working in the broadest sunshine, is yet severely careful to keep her own secrets, and, in spite of her pretended openness, shows us nothing but results. She permits us, indeed, to mar, but seldom to mend, and, like a jealous patentee, on no account to make" (180). Thus Aylmer, having long ago "recogn[ized] the truth," enters into his experiment on his wife with the knowledge that such acts are resented and even actively prevented by Mother Nature. This "great creative Mother" is an intriguing blend of the stereotypical qualities of both woman (secretive, jealous, and manipulative) and inventor (innovative, hard working, and decisively more successful than Aylmer). In fact, Aylmer's lack of success, which even Georgiana recognizes after reading the journal in which he records the details of his scientific experiments, and his subsequent frustration with Mother Nature seem to contribute to his desire to remove Georgiana's birthmark. As Fetterley notes, "Out of Aylmer's jealousy at feeling less than Nature and thus less than woman—for if Nature is a woman, woman is also Nature and has, by virtue of her biology, a power he does not—comes his obsessional program for perfecting Georgiana. Believing he is less, he has to convince himself he is more" (28).

To convince himself of his own superiority, however, Aylmer also has to convince Georgiana not only that she is less but also that she is completely defined by Aylmer and his gaze. Any agency that Georgiana possesses in the beginning of the story, when she reprimands Aylmer for "tak[ing] [her] from [her] mother's side" if he is "shock[ed]" by her birthmark, disappears under Aylmer's "constant watchfulness" and commentary on the mark (176, 180). The story is filled with references to Aylmer's eyes resting on the birthmark. According to the narrator, Georgiana soon learns to "shudder at his gaze" and begs Aylmer to attempt to remove the mark (178). "Danger is nothing to me," she insists, "for life, while this hateful mark makes me the object of your horror and disgust,—life is a burden which I would fling down with joy" (179). Eventually, "[n]ot even Aylmer hated [the birthmark] as much as she" (188). Thus Georgiana is trained to see herself and her birthmark through Aylmer's eyes. She acknowledges—indeed, embraces—his gaze and her subsequent position as object. Although she admits that the "little hand . . . was laid upon [her] before [she] came into the world" and suggests that "it may be the stain goes as deep as life itself," she finds Aylmer's revulsion more unbearable than the thought of disfiguration or death (179).

After reading Aylmer's notebooks, Georgiana understands his limitations as a scientist as well as the dangerous boundlessness of his imagination and ambition. Yet rather than seeing this as justification for removing herself from the experiment (or the marriage, which seem to be one and the same), she is motivated even more strongly to go through with the process, no matter the risk to her own life:

> Her heart exulted, while it trembled, at his honourable love,—so pure and lofty that it would accept nothing less than perfection, nor miserably make itself contented with an earthlier nature than he had dreamed of. She felt how much more precious was such a sentiment than that meaner kind which would have borne with the imperfection for her sake, and have been guilty of treason to holy love by degrading its perfect idea to the level of the actual; and with her whole spirit she prayed that, for a single moment, she might satisfy his highest and deepest conception. Longer than one moment she well knew it could not be; for his spirit was ever on the march, ever ascending, and each instant required something that was beyond the scope of the instant before. (189)

This passage seems to imply that Georgiana may, in fact, understand at this point that she *is* the birthmark and that the two cannot be separated; this conflation of the two is suggested by Aminidab, Aylmer's assistant, who insists, "[I]f she were my wife, I'd never part with that birthmark" (181). The experiment will ultimately kill Georgiana because she cannot live without the mark, no matter how much she would like to. She is willing to accept such a risk only because she is even less willing to live without Aylmer and his acceptance of her. A second possibility is that Georgiana realizes not her own mortality but the fleeting nature of Aylmer's satisfaction, especially where his wife is concerned. She may comprehend finally that Aylmer's approval of her cannot last long. Once the birthmark is gone, Aylmer will find something else "wrong" with his wife, something else that he can attempt to "fix." Either way, the tragedy of the story is not Aylmer's failure (or success, if we read the story in the way Fetterley does) or even the subsequent death of Georgiana. Rather, it is Georgiana's loss of agency—her ability to read and control her own body—and her complete acceptance of Aylmer's delusions as truth.

By giving in to Aylmer's interpretation of her birthmark, Georgiana concedes, as do many of the female characters examined in this study, that the unmarked body is the ideal for women and that white men have the right to the "conquering gaze" that interprets, subdues, and ultimately erases those female bodies that happen to be marked. Georgiana herself accepts the truth of this gaze and adopts its view of her as her own; her last act, in fact, is to look at herself in the mirror and smile "when she recognize[s] how barely perceptible was now that crimson hand which had once blazed forth with such disastrous brilliancy as to scare away all their happiness" (191). Aylmer has, in fact, created the perfect woman—not because she is unmarked, but because she sees herself only through her husband's eyes, denying her own perception of herself and their marriage.

Ineffaceably Marked

Elizabeth Stoddard's focus on the female body in *The Morgesons* comes as no surprise when understood in the context of what she considered her own "want of refinement." In a letter to James Russell Lowell, Stoddard told him, "I must own that I am coarse by nature. At times I have an overwhelming perception of the back side of truth. I see the rough laths behind the fine mortar—the body within its purple and fine linen—the mood of the man and the woman in the dark [or] the light of his or her mind when alone" (qtd. in Matlack 185). Indeed, much of Stoddard's work demonstrates an awareness of the "back side" as well as the front, the taboo as well as the conventional, the unconscious as well as the conscious. Above all, she created female characters who accept their corporeal desires as well as their intellectual and emotional ones. Stoddard asked, "Why will writers, especially female ones, make their heroines so indifferent to good eating, so careless about taking cold, and so impervious to all the creature comforts? The absence of these treats compose their women, with an eternal preachment about self-denial, moral self-denial. Is goodness, then, incompatible with any enjoyment of the senses?" (qtd. in Matlack 161).

In many ways, this question and its inherent consideration of the female body drive Stoddard's first novel, *The Morgesons*. Although the novel has only recently been recovered, an extraordinary amount of critical attention has been paid to its representation of the female body. Recent critics of the novel, for example, inevitably take note of the scars that mark Cassandra Morgeson's cheek; these scars, most critics claim, symbolize Cassandra's burgeoning sexuality as evidenced in her passionate yet unconsummated relationship with her married cousin, Charles. The carriage accident in which Charles dies puts an abrupt end to the adulterous relationship but also results in the scars that figure so prominently in the remainder of the novel. At the very least, critics see the scars as "an emblem of the encounter" with Charles (Matlack 290). Sybil Weir believes that Cassandra's scars "signify her victory over a society which proclaimed women sexual imbeciles and which would automatically condemn Cassandra for loving adulterously" ("*Morgesons*" 433). She points out that Cassandra's scars, "the visible evidence of her sexual past," are, later in the novel, part of what attracts her fiancé to her (435). Susan K. Harris adds that Cassandra's "scars ultimately aid rather than hinder her in finding a husband and signify her discovery of her own capabilities" (*19th-Century American Women's Novels* 163).

These comments alone make it clear that the story of the marked woman in *The Morgesons* is very different from any we have encountered so far in this study. Despite these affirmative interpretations of Cassandra's scars, however, the marked female body is not always read as a consistently positive symbol in Stoddard's novel. Tattooed on the arm with the initials of her lover, Cassandra's friend, Helen, has been interpreted as a woman eager to be possessed by a man. For example, Sandra A. Zagarell notes that "Helen exhibits the yearning to be defined through a man which had marked Cassandra's own ambivalent reaction to Charles, for Helen has tattooed her fiance's initials onto her wrist" (50). Many other critics ignore the issue of Helen's tattoo, apparently regarding it as irrelevant to the rest of the novel. However, critics who dismiss the theme of tattooing overlook an essential element of *The Morgesons*: Cassandra's assertion that her scars are a form of tattoo. This insistence is especially powerful because the novel, like Spofford's short story "The Strathsays," is narrated in the first person, thus giving Cassandra some measure of control over how her body is viewed and interpreted by the reader. Taking Cassandra's assertion as my point of departure, then, I propose that the marked female body has been underemphasized and misread in *The Morgesons*. With an understanding of the history of tattooing and the radical textual potential of tattoos, Stoddard's depiction of the marked female body emerges as a complex representation of one woman's "battles" with her society's expectations for female behavior (*Morgesons* 173). Although forced to negotiate, even to compromise, her freedom, she remains an agent rather than a victim or an object, defining herself and her body as much as is possible in the society in which she lives.

The Morgesons traces the growth and development of Cassandra Morgeson, daughter of a merchant, whose family consists of her father and mother, her sister, Veronica, and, eventually, her younger brother, Arthur. Although the Morgesons are "a stirring, cheerful family," they are also "independent of each other," and Cassandra and Veronica are self-governing, even as children (24). The relationship between the sisters is distant, however, as Cassandra is vigorously healthy and insatiably curious about the world, whereas Veronica is an ethereal invalid, with no desire to venture outside the domestic sphere. Cassandra admits, "The difference in our physical constitutions would have separated us, if there had been no other cause" (58). The volatile Cassandra is drawn to the ever-changing sea, while her sister arranges her room and her life so as always to look inland: "She could not bear to catch a glimpse of the sea, nor to hear it" (26). As a young woman, Cassandra meets Charles Morgeson, a distant cousin, and agrees to live with him and his wife, Alice, in order to attend finishing school. While living with her cousin, Cassandra meets her "first intimate friend," Helen Perkins, and a young Harvard student, Ben Somers, yet she also finds herself in a passionate relationship with Charles. "An intangible, silent, magnetic feeling existed between us," Cassandra admits, "changing and developing according to its own mysterious law, remaining intact in spite of the contests between us of resistance and defiance" (74). The tension between the two increases until Charles is killed and Cassandra wounded in the carriage accident. After her recovery, Ben Somers convinces Cassandra to travel with him to his home to meet his family and to facilitate his courtship of her sister, Veronica, with whom he has fallen in love. There Cassandra meets Ben's brother, Desmond, a sensual, indolent young man who is also a victim of the family curse of alcoholism. Over the objections of Desmond's mother, Cassandra and Desmond fall in love, causing Desmond to leave the country in an effort to overcome his addiction to alcohol. Upon her arrival home, Cassandra finds her mother dead and also soon discovers that her father has lost his fortune. These factors and Veronica's persistent helplessness force Cassandra to consider domestic and economic matters for the first time in her life. Two weddings—that of Ben and Veronica and, surprisingly, that of her father and Alice, Charles's widow—leave Cassandra alone in the house in which she was raised. After two years, Desmond returns, a healed man, and they marry as well. Despite this reunion, the novel ends rather bleakly, with Ben's death from alcoholism and the birth of a mentally disabled child to Veronica.

Woven throughout the plot of *The Morgesons* is the symbol of the marked female body, beginning early in the novel with the revelation of Helen's tattoo. In a moment of confidence, Helen "rolled up her sleeve to show [Cassandra and Ben] a bracelet, printed in ink on her arm, with the initials 'L. N.' Those of her cousin, she said; he was a sailor, and some time, she supposed, they would marry" (97). Helen's cousin's familiarity with and practice of tattooing would have surprised no one living on the New England coast in the eighteenth and nineteenth centuries. As Simon P. Newman points out in "Reading the Bodies of Early American Seafarers," "Tattoos marked the men who made a career out of the sea. Although their stature and illiteracy tell us of their lowly origins and their scars, injuries, and marks of disease record the dangers of their occupation, the words and images engraved on their skin disclose the most about their beliefs and values" (61).[10] Helen's wearing of a tattoo, however, crosses nineteenth-century gender boundaries, as does her willingness to reveal her mark to her friends. Shocked at the impropriety, Cassandra immediately asks her, "How could you consent to have your arm so defaced?" When Helen reacts with pride and indignation, however, Cassandra is quick to appreciate the potential of the tattoo:

> [Helen's] eyes flashed as she replied that she had not looked upon the mark in that light before.

"We may all be tattooed," said Mr. Somers.

"I am," I thought. (97)

Cassandra's initial reaction to Helen's tattoo reflects the predominant attitude toward women who *chose* to mark their bodies in nineteenth-century America; a woman who made such a choice was regarded as having "defaced" her body, thereby also making a permanent gesture toward removing herself from the proper female sphere. No matter what form such a mark took (Helen's tattoo, for example, can be regarded as the equivalent of an engagement ring), the "beliefs and values" represented by a woman's chosen tattoo were regarded as inherently transgressive. As critics' reactions to Helen's tattoo reveal, twentieth-century readers have—albeit for different reasons—also been resistant to the notion that a woman would mark her body as a symbol of her relationship with a man. The "deface[ment]" in this scenario not only confirms a woman's commitment to a presumably oppressive relationship but also deters any other man from presenting himself as a potential lover. Ultimately, neither the nineteenth- nor the twentieth-century interpretation of Helen's tattoo allows for a positive comprehensive reading of the marked female body in *The Morgesons*.

Frances E. Mascia-Lees and Patricia Sharpe note that "it is, of course, significant that in Western culture men choose to have their bodies marked more frequently than women" (152–53). To acknowledge tattooing as a typically masculine tradition in the West is not to admit that women with tattoos are disfigured or "defaced," as Cassandra initially believes. Nor does this require that men's and women's tattoos be examined through the same interpretive lens, or that tattooing should always be regarded solely as something that a woman does for or in response to a man. As Victoria Pitts notes, women's bodily modification frequently focuses "attention on the ways in which female bodies are invisibly marked by power, including by violence" (73). Therefore, although Helen's tattoo can be read as a commitment to the relationship with her cousin, it should also be contrasted to the violence with which the bodies of other women in nineteenth-century American literature—including Emily Graham, Alice Strathsay, and Georgiana—are physically marked. The act can also be read against the marking of other women's bodies in *The Morgesons*—Ruth and Sally Aiken, for example, seamstresses who sew for Cassandra's grandfather. "What a disagreeable interest I felt in them!" Cassandra reflects, looking back at her childhood. "What had they in common with me? What could they enjoy? How unpleasant their dingy, crumbled, needle-pricked fingers were! . . . I rushed into the garden and trampled the chamomile bed. I had heard that it grew faster for being subjected to that process, and thought of the two women I had just seen while I crushed the spongy plants. Had *they* been trampled upon?"

(31). Women like Ruth and Sally are irretrievably marked, or "trampled upon," by the stifling religious and moral climate of the society in which they live. Lower-class women in particular are even marked physically by their labor, their "needle-pricked fingers" a sure sign of their public marketing of their domestic skills. It seems doubtful that these women, like the chamomile, "gr[o]w faster" as a result of being "trampled."

It is possible, then, that a woman's choice of a tattoo could be a sign of rebellion, critique and/or disavowal of the status quo, and adoption of a personal moral code to replace that of society. The tattoo as a mark of difference is evidenced in Cassandra's reaction to a letter from Helen, who has returned home to nurse her father. Cassandra reflects that Helen's town "was dull but respectable and refined and no one knew that she was tattooed on the arm" (116). Thus Helen's tattoo is the opposite of all that is stifling about polite society and can be read as a secret rebellion against respectability and refinement.

Although Cassandra is not yet marked by her scars when she first sees Helen's tattoos, she agrees with Ben's assertion that they "may all be tattooed." Therefore, soon after her negative response to Helen's marked body, Cassandra begins to identify with the notion of being different—emotionally and morally, if not yet physically—from those around her. Her identification with the "other" whose manipulation of the body signals a transgression of Western religion and culture had been evident even in her childhood, as revealed early in the novel in a discussion of Cassandra's reading:

> [S]itting near the window at twilight, intent upon a picture in a book of travels, of a Hindoo swinging from a high pole with hooks in his flesh, and trying to imagine how much it hurt him, my attention was arrested by a mention of my name in a conversation held between mother and Mr. Park, one of the neighbors. . . .
>
> "Are the Hindoos in earnest, mother?" And I thrust the picture before her. She warned me off.
>
> "Do you think, Mr. Park, that Cassandra can understand the law of transgression?"
>
> An acute perception that it was in my power to escape a moral penalty, by willful ignorance, was revealed to me, that I could continue the privilege of sinning with impunity. (20–21)

As this passage reveals, even as a child Cassandra had been aware that transgression involved physical—not just emotional or spiritual—pain. She almost seems to yearn for such pain, "trying to imagine" what the "Hindoo" experiences as the hooks pull at his flesh. This desire to feel his pain, to experience it as her own, does not originate from a sentimental urge to identify or to act on his behalf. Rather, she is attracted to the ritualization of pain, the way in which it marks what is obviously a rite of passage for the man represented.

Both Helen and Cassandra recognize that the marked female body represents a threat to the society in which they live, a society that requires women to be spiritual rather than corporeal, innocent rather than experienced. This is, after all, the society that induces Aylmer to attempt to perfect his near-perfect wife in "The Birthmark." At one point in her life, Cassandra says, she "concealed nothing; the desires and emotions which are usually kept as a private fund I displayed and exhausted" (58). Yet as Cassandra recognizes her desires as a mature woman and the way in which they contradict strict societal codes of female behavior, she makes an effort to conceal them even from those close to her. The scars, obtained in the midst of the awakening of her sexual desires, however, reveal this part of her that society teaches must remain unspoken. Like Hawthorne's Reverend Dimmesdale in *The Scarlet Letter*, Cassandra's body seems to reveal the very story she is expected to repress and hide from view. Unlike Dimmesdale's unspecified bodily markings that seem to testify to his adulterous relationship with Hester Prynne, however, Cassandra's scars are not imposed on her by a guilty conscience or even societal pressure. After she receives the scars, she names them as tattoos to Ben; "Tattooed still," she tells him, as he looks at the scars on her face (156). Although wounds are known to heal and disappear, she denies that this will happen to her "tattoos": "[T]hey were not deep," Stoddard writes, "but they would never go away" (140). Whereas the scar is an inflicted mark, the tattoo is usually a chosen one. At the very least, as the case of Olive Oatman reveals, the tattoo confuses questions of agency. By identifying her scars as tattoos, Cassandra effectively chooses to be marked, thus reinscribing her body with new meaning. She does not accept them as punishment for her sexual desires; unlike many nineteenth-century writers, Stoddard does not allow her heroine to be punished for the "crimson stain" (or scarlet letter) of her awakening sexuality. In fact, the traditional equation is turned on its head when Charles, rather than Cassandra, dies in the carriage accident.

The cultural tensions surrounding the marked female body in the mid-nineteenth century make Cassandra's decision to embrace and redefine her scars a remarkable one. Stoddard would clearly have been aware of Hawthorne's story "The Birthmark," and although it is impossible to say which of the sentimental texts she would have read, she would have been familiar with the literary mode (which she critiques throughout *The Morgesons*). In addition, she began writing *The Morgesons* four years after Oatman's return to white society and would likely have known about the captivity and rescue of Oatman through her connection with the *Daily Alta California*, a newspaper for which she wrote semimonthly columns between 1854 and 1858.[11] The *Daily Alta* reported on Oatman's ordeal four times during the first four months of 1856.[12] Although none of Stoddard's columns appeared on any of these days, her articles—published under the heading "Our Lady Correspondent"—clearly indicate that she read the *Daily Alta* as well as contributed to it, and she may have come across details of Oatman's captivity in this way.[13] Moreover, Oatman's captivity and "redemption" were reported on May 4, 1858, in the *New York Times*, where Stoddard, a New York City resident, may have read the following description:

> The girl OLIVE is near twenty years of age. She is a modest, intelligent young woman, but has evidently suffered greatly from the hardships she has been compelled to undergo during a captivity of *six years*. Her chin bears the "chief's mark," a species of tattooing, set in fine parallel lines, running downward from the lower lip. This savage embellishment does not materially enhance the personal charms of the lady, but it is an indelible evidence of the scenes she has undergone. ("Six Years' Captivity" 5)

Direct influence is difficult if not impossible to prove, yet Oatman provides an important parallel to Stoddard's representation of Cassandra, as do the fictional representations of Emily, Alice, Mary, and Georgiana. Unlike Oatman, Cassandra embraces her mark as well as the notion of the tattoo, thereby encouraging observers to acknowledge her complicity in the mark in a manner that would have horrified Oatman and her audiences. Although Cassandra's mark is imposed on her, as is Alice Strathsay's, she is more like Mary Strathsay in that she accepts the mark as a symbol of an illicit relationship and the awakening of her own sexuality. Cassandra Morgeson is most remarkable, however, in that, unlike Georgiana, she survives and in fact revels in the mark and its exhibition, thereby repositioning the female body and its significance in nineteenth-century American literature.

Regardless of whether the mark is chosen or forced, tattooing always incorporates a certain measure of control over the observer, directing the gaze to the tattooed parts of the body. Certainly the revelation of a forcible tattoo would produce a more complicated response in the bearer, with perhaps less delight and more shame or pain. As *The Morgesons'* depiction of marked women reveals, however, the chosen mark on the female body is indeed a source of fascination, both to the bearer of the mark and to the observer. This control of the gaze is wielded accordingly by both Helen and Cassandra. As indicated by Helen's decision to hide her tattoo while she is home nursing her father, she carefully chooses when, where, and to whom she wishes to reveal her tattoo; she does so at one point while trying on a dress made for her by Veronica: "The trying on of this dress was the means of [Veronica] discovering the letters on Helen's arm, which never ceased to be a source of interest. She asked to see them every day afterward, and touched them with her fingers, as if they had some occult power" (150). Because of the location of Cassandra's scars, she has less control than Helen over the revelation of the mark, but she does not choose to wear a veil to hide the marks as do so many other marked women. By translating her scars into tattoos, she regains some control over their interpretation and the effect such interpretations have on her. She is at the very least aware of the desire to read her scars and of the power dynamic inherent in such a reading.

In the scene in which Cassandra, speaking to Ben, refers to her scars as tattoos, for example, Cassandra realizes that both her sister and Ben are observing her. "As they watched me, I saw myself as they did. A tall girl in gray, whose deep, controlled voice vibrated in their ears, like the far-off sounds we hear at night from woods or the sea, whose face was ineffaceably marked, whose air impressed with a sense of mystery. I think both would have annihilated my personality if possible, for the sake of comprehending me, for both loved me in their way" (156). Despite the conspicuousness and permanence of the marks on her face, Cassandra remains a "mystery" to those who know and try to understand her. She avoids becoming engulfed by their gaze, however, by looking back—not only by seeing herself as they do but also by seeing them more clearly than they can see themselves. In this sense, she learns to employ what feminist theorist bell hooks calls an "oppositional gaze." Hooks explains, "Subordinates in relation to power learn experientially that there is a critical gaze, one that 'looks' to document, one that is oppositional. . . . [T]he power of the dominated to assert agency by claiming and cultivating 'awareness' politicizes 'looking' relations—one learns to look a certain way in order to resist" (95).

Indeed, Cassandra's resistance to the gaze of those around her is an issue of survival, as is indicated by her realization that their understanding of her comes at the risk of her own annihilation, her own loss of self. She voices this realization to Ben during an argument about her relationship with Desmond:

> I looked at him; he began to walk about, taking up a book, which he leaned his head over, and whose covers he bent back till they cracked.
> "You would read me that way," I said. (226)

Again Cassandra recognizes the attempt to "read" her as a violent threat to her own personality. Yet she also seems to understand that the practice of reading is fraught with emotion. Ben and Veronica *do* love Cassandra—"in their way"—and this love, with all its complications, directly causes and shapes their reading of her body.

The relationship between Ben and Veronica endangers Cassandra's sense of individuality and independence, as the couple rely on Cassandra to ease the way for their courtship with Ben's family, to provide them with a home, and ultimately to subsume her personality to their needs. Cassandra's love for Desmond threatens to break the triangle on which Ben and Veronica thrive.

Ben tells Cassandra, "If you marry Desmond Somers . . . you will contradict three lives,—yours, mine, and Veronica's. What beast was it that suggested this horrible discord?" (200). Constantly confused and frustrated by Cassandra, Ben finds Veronica much easier to "read." Veronica's constant, debilitating illnesses make her unable to care for herself and severely limit her interaction with the outside world. As her father notes, home is Veronica's sphere, and unusual as she is, her behavior and her desires do not transgress societal expectations of middle-class white women (60).[14] Cassandra, on the other hand, resists the stifling roles society has prescribed for her. Ben tells Cassandra:

> [T]o my amazement, I saw that, unlike most women, you understood your instincts; that you dared to define them, and were impious enough to follow them. You debased my ideal, you confused me, also, for I could never affirm that you were wrong; forcing me to consult abstractions, they gave a verdict in your favor, which almost unsexed you in my estimation. I must own that the man who is willing to marry you has more courage than I have. Is it strange that when I found your counterpart, Veronica, that I yielded? Her delicate, pure, ignorant soul suggests to me eternal repose. (226)

Cassandra ultimately refuses to renounce her own desires to facilitate those of Ben and Veronica, forcing the couple to face the marriage and the future they have made for themselves. "I will have no voice between you," she tells Ben (160). She similarly rejects the feminine ideal and the subsequent transcendence of the female body that Ben so values in Veronica; Cassandra would rather be considered "unsexed" than fit into the parameters of Ben's definition of the feminine.

Ben's brother, Desmond, whom Cassandra will eventually marry, also attempts to understand the significance of the scars but, importantly, does not see Cassandra as "unsexed" because of her unfeminine appearance or behavior. While visiting the Somers family's home in Belem, Cassandra spends an evening with them and several guests. She is surprised when Desmond suddenly appears next to her:

> I heard a low voice at my ear, and felt a slight touch from the tip of a finger on my cheek.
> "How came those scars?"
> I brushed my cheek with my handkerchief, and answered, "I got them in battle."
> He left his chair, and walked slowly through the room into the dark front parlor.
> (173)

Later Cassandra receives a letter from Desmond telling her, "I am yours, as I have been, since the night I asked you 'How came those scars?' Did you guess that I read your story?" (227). Although Desmond's claim to have read Cassandra's story may appear to be an intrusive gesture, yet another "loving" attempt to annihilate or appropriate her personality, it is important to note that he is only able to read her story because she offers it to him. Unlike the others who observe her, Desmond accepts Cassandra's scars as the mark of an experienced woman, one who has been tested and refined by her trials. She frames these experiences in terms of "battle" presumably because there is no equivalent metaphor for women because they are expected to be inexperienced and therefore unmarked. Desmond's mother, who resists the match, attempts to deny Cassandra's experience, telling her that she is a "toy," liable to be broken by Desmond. Yet Cassandra refuses this categorization, explaining, "I am already scarred, you see. I have been 'nurtured in convulsions' " (194).

Desmond denies himself a relationship with Cassandra until he has confronted his own demons and conquered his addiction to alcohol. Unlike Ben, who depends on Veronica and Cassandra for his redemption, Desmond overcomes the family curse on his own, only returning to Cassandra when he is a healthy man. Reminiscent of Cassandra's scars, Desmond's struggles are also marked on his body, causing Cassandra to exclaim, "How old you have grown, Desmond!" when they meet again. Desmond tells her, "You see what battles *I* must have had since I saw you," thus comparing his own experiences to the battles Cassandra had claimed as the source of her scars (250). Cassandra and Desmond ultimately come together as two experienced, mature individuals, without illusions or misgivings.

The significance of the marked body in *The Morgesons* and its place in Cassandra's relationships with both Desmond and Veronica is indicated in a dream Veronica has the night before she marries Ben. When Cassandra comes to wake her sister for the wedding, Veronica recounts the dream she has had about Desmond:

> "It was a strange place where we met; curious, dusty old trees grew about it. He was cutting the back of one with a dagger, and the pieces he carved out fell to the ground, as if they were elastic. He made me pick them up, though I wished to listen to a man who was lying under one of the trees, wrapped in a cloak, keeping time with *his* dagger, and singing a wild air.
>
> 'What do you see?' said the first.
>
> 'A letter on every piece,' I answered, and spelt Cassandra. 'Are you Ben transformed?' I asked, for he had his features, his air, though he was a swarthy, spare man, with black, curly hair, dashed with gray; but he pricked my arm with his dagger, and said 'Go on.' I picked up the rest, and spelt 'Somers.'
>
> 'Cassandra Somers! now tell her,' he whispered, turning me gently from him, with a hand precisely like Ben's." (239)

After she awakes, Veronica unbuttons her sleeve to reveal "a red mark on her arm above her elbow" (239). Like Helen's tattoo, it is possible to read Veronica's dream as symbolic of Desmond's possession of Cassandra. Yet Stoddard's representation of the marked female body up to this point makes such a reading of the dream difficult, if not impossible. The dream seems instead to reinforce the significance of the marked body in the courtship of Cassandra and Desmond as well as the fluid boundaries between tattooing and scarring in this novel. The inscription of "Cassandra Somers" in the tree bark and the subsequent pricking of Veronica's arm recall the inscription of the initials of Helen's lover on her own arm. Similarly, the marking of the bark with Cassandra's future name recalls the scars on her face, which are evidence of her passionate relationships with both Charles and Desmond.

More important, perhaps, is Veronica's reaction to the dream and the way it highlights crucial differences between the two sisters and their relationships to the corporeal. Cassandra notes that as a result of the dream, Veronica "divined [her] feelings for the first time in her life": " 'I have indeed been in a long sleep, as far as you are concerned; this means something. My blindness is removed by a dream. Do you despise me?' " (240). Despite Veronica's fascination with the marked body, she has been unable to consciously mark herself as an act of agency. Throughout the novel, Veronica attempts to control her body through self-starvation, refusing to digest anything other than milk, buttered toast, and crackers. Although such denial certainly marks her physically, emphasizing her "large eyes" and "colorless, fixedly pale expression," these marks seem the incidental result of her peculiar appetite rather than the goal itself (130). Ultimately, as Susanna Ryan notes, Veronica's self-starvation "effectively transform[s] the conventional limitations placed on the Victorian woman into a means of protection from the outside world, a world of sexuality and exposure" (137). Such "protection" is the life that Veronica has selfishly chosen for herself, unaware of or unconcerned with the way in which her decisions affect those around her. Only by having her own body marked in the dream—with a mark reminiscent of those worn by Cassandra and Helen—is Veronica forced to recognize that Cassandra has a life and desires of her own apart from Veronica's relationship with Ben and her (self-inflicted) poor health.[15]

Cassandra's scars, then, are crucial to her sense of self and her redefinition of womanhood as the result of experience rather than blissful ignorance or self-destructive illness. Rather than hiding her scars, Cassandra attempts to harness and direct the power of the marked female body by drawing attention to them as in her conversation with Mrs. Somers. Although such a gesture recalls Olive Oatman's directing her audience to observe her tattoos during the lecture series, Cassandra does so to validate her struggles and claim the agency she has won. It is important to note, however, that Cassandra does not always retain control over how her scars are understood. In Greek mythology, Cassandra is a prophetess who can see and predict the future but is cursed to have no one believe her. Like the mythic Cassandra, Cassandra Morgeson can express herself but is unable to control how others interpret her. She has knowledge and can change herself but cannot necessarily impart that knowledge to others. Ultimately, although Cassandra rhetorically owns her scars and transforms their *personal* significance, she has no more control over their public interpretation than Oatman did over her facial tattoos. Stoddard's terse style reflects her awareness of this ambiguity, as does the uncertain ending of her novel.

The conclusion of *The Morgesons* is an uneasy compromise between Cassandra's sexual, economic, and moral freedom, and the bleak future that seems to be in store for her and her family. Although Cassandra has inherited the Morgeson home and married Desmond Somers, with whom she has a relationship based on equality and mutual respect, she still seems to have much unfulfilled potential. She, like other women of the period, inhabits the domestic sphere, albeit unwillingly. Her sister has married Ben Somers only to have him die as a result of his alcohol abuse and leave her with a baby who appears to be mentally disabled. Cassandra and Desmond must care for both Veronica and the child, as Veronica is "[n]either a child nor an experienced adult" herself (Ryan 139). Cassandra and Desmond, on the other hand, do not have children, perhaps because they are wary of the Somers family curse of alcoholism, perhaps because they have little hope or vision for the future beyond the hard-won success of their own relationship.

As Lawrence Buell and Sandra Zagarell, editors of the most recent reprint of *The Morgesons*, note, "Since there is no sign that [Cassandra] has affected the larger social order with which she has been in conflict, the reader is left with the uneasy sense that the 'possession' she has achieved is both very private and ironically circumscribed" (xix). "Indeed," Ryan adds, "Stoddard's resolution seems to insist upon compromise" (145). Any other conclusion, however, would not have been appropriate for *The Morgesons*; as Stoddard noted just before the novel was published, "I endeavored to make a plain transcript of human life—a portion as it were of the great panorama without taking on a moral here or an explanation there. . . . Indications are that it will be misunderstood" ("Letters" 337). Insisting on a "plain transcript," Stoddard refused her readers the religious and moral constructs sometimes relied on by nineteenth-century American writers to mitigate the endings of their fictional texts, in which women characters, relegated to the domestic sphere, live lives of complete service to others. This rejection of conventional religion and morality also allowed Stoddard to reshape the understanding of the marked female body. In *The Morgesons*, the scarred and tattooed bodies of women like Cassandra are no longer a punish-ment, an indication of moral character, or even a burden to be borne reluctantly, but are instead an empowering image that could enable women to claim their own bodies and the experiences they represent. This is perhaps the one issue on which Stoddard refused to compromise.

CHAPTER FOUR

"The Skin of an American Slave"

The Mark of African American Manhood
in Abolitionist Literature

When the Civil War began in April 1861, African American men attempted in vain to volunteer for military service. As historian Jim Cullen writes, "The efforts of abolitionists to the contrary, secession, not slavery, was the pretext for the outbreak of hostilities, and the Lincoln administration assiduously courted slaveholding states still in the Union by avoiding any appearance of restructuring existing race relations" (78). For all their differences, most northern and southern white men agreed that this was, indeed, a white man's war and objected to the idea that black men, slave or free, should occupy a role formerly reserved only for white male citizens. Yet military necessity would accomplish what abolitionist politics could not. The Emancipation Proclamation, effective January 1, 1863, freed all slaves in states still in rebellion against the federal government; it also provided for the lawful enlistment of African American men in the Union army.[1] Eventually, 179,000 black men would serve in the army, the majority of whom came from Confederate and border states (Berlin et al. 206). Black soldiers would play major roles in a number of battles, including those at Port Hudson and Milliken's Bend, Louisiana, and Fort Wagner, South Carolina.

Abolitionists, black and white, and most African Americans were well aware that the enlistment of black men into the Union army would challenge fundamental notions of race, masculinity, and citizenship and would have a significant impact on the treatment of African Americans during and after the Civil War. On July 4, 1863, seven months after the Emancipation Proclamation took effect, *Harper's Weekly* responded to this controversial development with a drawing illustrating the transformation of one black man from slave to contraband and finally to Union soldier.[2] Gordon, the "typical negro" featured in the drawing, is portrayed in three poses, from left to right. The first panel, labeled "GORDON AS HE ENTERED OUR LINES," shows the subject sitting in a chair with his legs crossed. His feet are bare and his clothes tattered. In the second panel, "GORDON UNDER MEDICAL INSPECTION," Gordon wears only his pants and sits with his scarred back to the audience, his face turned just enough to reveal his profile (see figure 12). He stands upright in the third panel, wearing a uniform and holding a rifle in front of him; the panel is labeled "GORDON IN HIS UNIFORM AS A U.S. SOLDIER." The purpose of the illustration appears to be to demonstrate Gordon's ability to transform himself—or to be transformed—into a man and a soldier. Curiously enough, however, the final panel is not the most conspicuous in the series. Rather, the second panel, depicting Gordon's scars, is the largest and presumably the first to attract the reader's eye. Despite the label, which asserts that this image is drawn from Gordon's medical examination while in the Union camp, the illustration and the scars it highlights were more likely to remind readers that Gordon had been a slave, and a harshly treated slave at that.[3] The accompanying text also emphasizes "the degree of brutality which slavery has developed among . . . whites," rather than the significance of Gordon's military service ("Typical Negro" 429).[4] While his skin color suggests that Gordon was a slave, the scars are presented in the drawing as proof of that fact. Gordon is ultimately labeled a slave *because of his scars*, no matter what the smaller representations of him as contraband and Union soldier do to dispel that label.

In this sense, Gordon's scars contain the same kind of signifying power as Olive Oatman's tattoos. Caught between two (or more) states of being, both Oatman and Gordon fascinate audiences because their liminality is inscribed on their bodies. Although the dominant culture attempts (sometimes quite successfully) to dictate the ways in which these marks are read, the scar and the tattoo contain the potential for multiple meanings depending on the observer's individual politics, prejudices, and personality. In Gordon's case, for example, a northern abolitionist might read his scars quite differently from a racist Federal soldier who believed he was fighting for the restoration of the Union rather than the abolition of slavery. Context is everything, which is why the similarities and differences between the white, female figures discussed in previous chapters and characters of color, such as Gordon, cannot be elided. It is crucial to recognize the particular expendability of the black body in nineteenth-century America and thus its intense vulnerability to marking. However, the employment of the "conquering gaze" and the strategies for resistance discussed in earlier chapters (such as the "oppositional gaze") resonate throughout the rest of this study as well. As with many of the white women featured in previous chapters, Gordon attempts to return the gaze of his audience but is not successful in the most prominent panel, that which displays his scars. As contraband and soldier, Gor-

Figure 12. "A Typical Negro." *Harper's Monthly*, July 4, 1863.

don is represented as facing forward, yet it appears as if the display of his scars physically and ideologically prevents a simultaneous exchange of the gaze. The sidelong glance that Gordon is allowed here effectively transfers the powers of observation to his audience, denying this black man the agency of the returned gaze that would indicate reciprocity between him and his (presumably white) audience.[5]

This depiction of Gordon accents the conflicts inherent in the visual and literary use of the scar in representations of African American men, both before and during the Civil War.[6] Although "GORDON IN HIS UNIFORM AS A U.S.

SOLDIER" marks a new opportunity for African American men, the spectacle of Gordon's scarred back is representative of a long tradition in abolitionist literature. As this chapter demonstrates, throughout the antebellum period abolitionist texts had relied on the rhetorical power of the scarred slave body to remind white audiences of the brutality of slavery and encourage them to participate in the eradication of the institution. The marked body also frequently served as a catalyst of and tool for a renegotiation of black male identity and agency. Writers were careful, however, when discussing the role of violence in such a renegotiation and for the most part avoided discussing slave rebellions or African American participation in armed conflict. The issue of violence as a response to the institution of slavery became more difficult to ignore in the midst of the Civil War, in which white men's bodies were mutilated and scarred and black men's bodies were required—and frequently eagerly volunteered—to fill the depleted ranks of the Union army.[7] Written and set during the war, Louisa May Alcott's "My Contraband" (1863) examines the role of the marked body in discussions of African American male agency and the subsequent redefinition of black masculinity through violence. As Alcott's story reveals, however, abolitionist writers attempting to rewrite black male subjectivity during the war often became mired in the antebellum rhetoric of the scar, which threatened to limit African American men to submissive roles and outdated notions of black masculinity intended to counter white audiences' fears of the black soldier. This widespread cultural struggle over the meaning of manhood did not end with the Emancipation Proclamation or the surrender of Confederate troops at Appomattox Courthouse; the marked black body and its relationship to African American manhood continued to be renegotiated throughout the century.

Abolitionist Politics and the Marked Black Body

Depictions of the black body in abolitionist literature highlighting slave owners' brutal treatment of slaves generally fall into two categories: the scene of punishment and the body marked as a result of punishment. Critics such as Karen Halttunen and Marianne Noble have focused primarily on the scene of punishment, which is featured prominently in many abolitionist texts.[8] Fugitive slave narratives, for example, often detail the brutality of slavery, commonly describing the tortures inflicted on slaves, usually after failed escape attempts and even, perhaps more horrifyingly, for minor offenses. In *An Appeal in Favor of That Class of Americans Called Africans*, Lydia Maria Child cites from a letter written by a clergyman in which he describes the punishment inflicted on a seventeen-year-old boy who had broken an expensive pitcher:

It was night, and the slaves were all at home. The master had them collected into the most roomy negro-house, and a rousing fire made. . . . The door was fastened, that none of the negroes, either through fear or sympathy, should attempt to escape; he then told them that the design of this meeting was to teach them to remain at home and obey his orders. All things being now in train, George was called up, and by the assistance of his younger brother, laid on a broach bench or block. The master then cut off his ankles with a broad axe. In vain the unhappy victim screamed. Not a hand among so many dared to interfere. Having cast the feet into the fire he lectured the negroes at some length. He then proceeded to cut off his limbs below the knees. The sufferer besought him to begin with his head. It was all in vain—the master went on thus, until trunk, arms, and head, were all in the fire. (25–26)

Similar descriptions of gruesome punishments were used in abolitionist speeches in which speakers "strove to make their language as vivid as possible, fostering in audiences the feeling that a direct line of physical sensation linked them to the slave. Readers and listeners could then judge the morality of slavery by their own subjective responses to the physical and moral degradation inherent in the system" (Clark 481). Visual images depict the scene of punishment just as powerfully, as demonstrated by illustrations for the *American Anti-Slavery Almanac of 1840* in which slaves are shown being burned, whipped, chased by dogs, branded, and even dismembered. Jean Fagan Yellin cites a resolution passed in 1837 at the First Anti-Slavery Convention of American Women advocating the use of such visual images in the abolitionist cause "so that the speechless agony of the fettered slave may unceasingly appeal to the heart of the patriot, the philanthropist, and the Christian" (qtd. in Yellin 5). As this resolution reveals, white abolitionists were clearly aware that firsthand testimony and images of physical cruelty to slaves forced audiences to react with emotion rather than simply intellect. Yet as Yellin points out, this attempt to represent the "speechless agony" of the slave was problematic: "Did the freeborn white abolitionist feminists see their task as speaking for the 'voiceless' slave? Did they see it as enabling the slave to sound her own voice on the platform and in print?" (25). As the slave narratives of women such as Harriet Jacobs reveal, although black women would "sound [their] own voice[s]" in time, this often took place *despite* (rather than because of) the work of white abolitionists.[9]

The questions Yellin asks are especially relevant to the second method of depicting the black body in abolitionist literature: the textual or visual representation of the body marked as a result of punishment. In the hands of both white and black abolitionists, the scar was undoubtedly a powerful tool. On a practical level, the scar made the brutality of slavery more apparent to audiences. As theorist Elaine Scarry points out, unless pain is accompanied by "visible body damage," it is unreal to others (56). However, once this pain is made visible to others, it has the potential to inspire action: "To be oneself in pain is to be more acutely aware of having a body, as so also to see from the outside the wound in another person is to become more intensely aware of human embodiedness" (199). The actual scene of punishment is not necessary for such awareness to occur; in fact, the scar may function most effectively when its origins are left unclear. By refusing audiences the precise details of physical torture, the mere description of the scar forces them to "construct the images of torture in their minds" (Noble 136). Thus scars have a symbolic potential absent in the scene of punishment, allowing readers and authors to exercise their own imaginations and become actively involved in the text (sometimes the scar as described in abolitionist literature and sometimes the actual scar as text) in front of them. Perhaps most importantly, the scene of punishment sometimes results in the death of the slave, whereas the marked body implies a living person with needs and desires, a survivor who must be acknowledged and responded to. Although death was in fact a powerful sentimental tool, it also made sympathy the only possible response to the deceased, who could perhaps have benefited more from material goods and services that would have allowed him or her to survive. As Susan Sontag points out, sympathy also limits the observers' sense of their own complicity in the institutions and power relationships that cause suffering, in this case slavery. "So far as we feel sympathy," Sontag writes, "we feel we are not accomplices to what caused the suffering. Our sympathy proclaims our in- nocence as well as our impotence. To that extent, it can be (for all our good intentions) an impertinent—if not an inappropriate—response" (102).

One method of highlighting the marked body was to reprint runaway slave advertisements from southern newspapers and then to ask why, if the institution of slavery was as benevolent and paternalistic as its defenders claimed, slaves were so often marked with scars? Theodore Weld, editor of *American Slavery as It Is: Testimony of a Thousand Witnesses* (1839), asserted that "slaves are whipped with such inhuman severity, as to lacerate and mangle their flesh in the most shocking manner, leaving permanent scars and ridges." To support this accu- sation, he included in the book "testimony, for the most part . . . that of the slaveholders themselves, and in their own chosen words. A large portion of it will be taken from the advertisements, which they have published in their own newspapers, describing by the scars on their bodies made by the whip, their own runaway slaves" (62). Additional advertisements were then cited to demonstrate the ways in which slaves were branded, maimed, and shot by slave owners and then identified by the resulting scars. Such tactics were surely ef- fective, using the marked black body to prove to readers the cruelty of white slave owners and their willingness to publicize the evidence of such treatment to reclaim their runaway slaves. Yet the layers of mediation here motivate Yellin and other critics to question white abolitionists' claims to speak for slaves or to allow them to speak for themselves. In the case of *American Slavery as It Is*, for example, the slave's body "speaks" only through the mediation of two distinct groups of white people: first, the slave owners who publish the runaway slave advertisements, and second, the abolitionists who create a sort of pastiche from these advertisements, thus subverting, to some extent, their original meaning.

The slave narratives of black men can be similarly problematic, especially given the frequent involvement of white abolitionists in their publication, but these texts can still be fruitfully mined for what they reveal about black self-representation and ownership of the marked body. It is especially important to examine these narratives prior to any discussion of white-authored abolitionist texts since the characters and circumstances in abolitionist fiction were often directly borrowed from slave narratives. Although this borrowing might indicate a rather honorable desire to represent the institution of slavery and slaves themselves accurately, it can also call into question the white abolitionist's faith in the slave's ability to speak for himself or herself as effectively. I will return to the question of revisions later in this chapter; for now, I wish only to point out the way in which the expectations of white abolitionists certainly played a role in the conventional use of the scene of punishment and the scar in slave narratives. Many slave narrators, like Moses Grandy, use the scene of punishment to highlight the brutality of slave owners as well as the lasting physical pain caused by such men. In his *Narrative of the Life of Moses Grandy*, the author calls his master "a severe man." "Because I could not learn his way of hilling corn," Grandy writes, "he flogged me naked with a severe whip made of a very tough sapling; this lapped round me at each stroke, the point of it at last entered my belly and broke off, leaving an inch and a-half outside. . . . The wound festered, and discharged very much at the time, and hurt me for years after" (160). As powerful as this description is, such pain is, perhaps, more effectively represented by the visible scar. As in *American Slavery as It Is*, the scarred back in the slave narrative is a testament to brutal treatment. Runaway slave Charles Ball reported to his collaborator, Isaac Fisher, "[W]here the master happens to be a bad man, or a drunkard, the back of the unhappy . . . slave is seamed with scars from his neck to his hips" (285). Ball himself is said to have shown his scars to a sympathetic planter to demonstrate his mistress's cruelty and justify his escape (436). In some respects, then, the conventional use of the scene of punishment and the scar in slave narratives seem no different from that of other abolitionist publications described earlier in this chapter. The slave narrative often perpetuated the white abolitionist's focus on the marked slave body as a plea for sympathy. Because the accounts of both Grandy and Ball are also mediated in various ways by white abolitionists, they require us to be mindful of the ways in which such collaboration may have alternately empowered and silenced illiterate or newly literate former slaves.[10]

However, in claiming authorship, these narrators also claimed ownership of the body, and the two acts are frequently represented as one and the same. Both narrative and marked body serve as mutually reinforcing testimonies to the slave's experiences. For example, Frederick Douglass clearly associates his narrative with the marks on his body when he claims, "My feet have been so cracked with the frost, that the pen with which I am writing might be laid in the gashes" (549). Douglass's feet, which have been marked by his physical journey to freedom, in a sense hold the pen (and therefore the authority) that completes that journey by assisting Douglass in the articulation and publication of his narrative. Both methods of marking have been painful, but both have freed him to reclaim his own body as well as his own pain. Similarly, in the preface to *Twenty-Two Years a Slave and Forty Years a Freeman* (1857), Austin Steward boldly announces, "The author . . . sends out this history—presenting as it were his *own* body, with the marks and scars of the tender mercies of slave drivers upon it, and asking that these may plead in the name of Justice, Humanity, and Mercy, that those who have the power, may have the magnanimity to strike off the chains from the enslaved, and bid him stand up, a Freeman and a Brother" (xl). Thus Steward's scars are offered up as evidence to support his narrative or as an even more trustworthy form of narrative themselves. This presentation of the body as text is certainly conventional and can be said to reduce the black subject to nothing more than text, a "voiceless slave" whose only function is to serve as spectacle. Indeed, Steward's body had been used in this way before, when his master published a slave advertisement describing Steward as having "a large scar on the calf of one of his legs, occasioned by a wound, the skin and flesh having been torn by the hook of an ox chain" (Hodges xvii). Yet the fact remains that Douglass and Steward offer their *own* bodies up as text, something they could not do unless they were already in possession of them. It is only in following Steward's lead, for example, that the white author of a recommendatory letter published with Steward's *Twenty-Two Years a Slave* pronounces, "Every tongue which speaks for Freedom, which has once been held by the awful gag of Slavery, is trumpet-tongued—and he who pleads against this monstrous oppression, if he can say, 'here are the scars,' can do much" (xxxvii).

Moses Roper's *Narrative of the Adventures and Escape of Moses Roper, from American Slavery* (published in London in 1837 and Philadelphia in 1838) is a striking and extensive example of the black slave narrator's use of the body. This text is particularly important in that, according to William L. Andrews, it "was the prototype for the classic American slave narratives of the 1840s as authored by internationally renowned fugitives such as Frederick Douglass,

William Wells Brown, Henry Bibb, and James W. C. Pennington. Less self-revealing and rhetorically contentious than its more famous successors, Roper's *Narrative* set a template, nevertheless, on which its literary descendants could build and capitalize in later years" (7). Throughout his narrative, Roper refers continuously to brutal punishments inflicted on slave bodies, his own included. Such scenes drive him to attempt to run away repeatedly, and rather than being hindered by his appearance, such escape attempts are greatly assisted by his light skin, the result of mixed parentage. As Ian Frederick Finseth points out, Roper's skin thus defies efforts to "read" him as black and therefore a slave: "In a society whose dominant racial ideology and system of labor depended on the legibility of the 'black' body, Roper quickly recognizes the advantages of illegibility" (49). Thus Roper is able to pass and therefore elude the authorities who are confident of their ability to recognize and control "blackness."

In his text, however, Roper presents his body as legible text, both because of his skin color and because of the marks left on his flesh by the punishments received while enslaved. The whiteness of Roper's skin forces the facts of his parentage on his audience, continually raising the issue of the rape of black female slaves by white owners as well as slave owner's neglect of their slave children. For this purpose, Roper reminds his readers of his parentage more than once, doing so, significantly, at both the beginning and the end of his narrative. He opens the narrative with a striking story in which his father's wife attempts to kill Moses because he represents the sexual encounter between the master and a slave. Moses is saved by his grandmother, but both he and his mother are soon sold (41). Close to the end of his narrative, Roper insists again on the recognition of his heritage, abruptly reminding his readers, "I am part African, as well as Indian and white, my father being a white man, Henry Roper, Esq., Caswell county, North Carolina, U. S., a very wealthy slave-holder, who sold me when quite a child, for the strong resemblance I bore to him" (67). The testimony of Roper's flesh goes further in references to the marks left on his body by the harsh punishments inflicted on him, usually in response to his escape attempts. For example, after being captured and refusing to tell his master who had helped him remove his irons, his fingers and toes are squeezed and beaten until the nails fall off. "The marks of this treatment still remain upon me," Roper claims, "my nails never having grown perfect since" (57). After describing another brutal punishment, he adds, "This may appear incredible, but the marks which they left at present remain on my body, a standing testimony to the truth of this statement of his severity" (45). Roper thus offers his body to the audience but also provides them with his narrative to guide them in their reading of this text.

Although Roper clearly intends his body to "speak" to the severity of slavery, he refuses to allow his audience to read him as mere victim. His brilliant manipulation of circumstances and careful use of his own body is demonstrated, for example, when he tells a story in which he presents as evidence of his whiteness a written call to military duty. He explains, "The law is, that no slave or colored person performs this, but every person in America of the age of twenty-one is called upon to perform military duty, once or twice in the year, or pay a fine" (70). Thus the call that is issued because Roper *appears* white is used to reinforce that whiteness and safeguard his freedom. Perhaps more ironically, however, the replication of this document in Roper's narrative "conjure[s] up the image of an armed African American fugitive" almost thirty years prior to the beginning of the Civil War (Finseth 29). This image alternately suggests the potential patriotism of African Americans *and* the danger they might present to others if their concerns are not attended to. The combination of Roper's persistence, fierce sense of self-ownership, white skin, and access to firearms via the military presents a vital threat indeed to slave owners and sympathizers of slavery alike.

Another slave narrator, William Grimes, is much less subtle in presenting his marked body to his audience as testimony to the brutality of slavery and the failure of the American government. After telling the tale of his life in slavery, Grimes announces, "If it were not for the stripes on my back which were made while I was a slave, I would in my will, leave my skin a legacy to the government, desiring that it might be taken off and made into parchment, and then bind the constitution of glorious happy *and free* America. Let the skin of an American slave, bind the charter of American Liberty" (232). Grimes highlights the contradiction between his "stripes" and the notion of a "free America" as articulated in the Constitution. His legacy, which his disfiguring scars allegedly prevent him from enacting, is to remind his readers of the price African Americans have paid in flesh for the freedom of white Americans. Yet his flesh, described as "stripe[d]," also recalls the U.S. flag, ironically equating the body of the black slave with another important symbol of American independence and unity. Grimes not only refuses to be banished from the United States but also figures his own body as a central component of a reconsideration of American freedom.

The conventional use of the scar, then, did not preclude a more complicated reading stressing self-ownership and assertion rather than victimhood. Yet as these fugitive slave narratives demonstrate, some notion of the relationship between black slave and white audience influenced depictions of the marked black body. Whether the mark was intended as a plea for sympathy, evidence supporting a slave's verbal or written testimony, or a challenge to the U.S. government, it was also a negotiation of the respective roles that blacks and whites would play in the eradication of slavery and the reconstruction of black subjectivity.

As Carolyn Sorisio explains, "[S]peaking knowledge from the body carried with it certain risks—always came the possibility that your presence merely reified existing structures" (7). Slave narrators were sometimes required to place the needs of the abolitionist movement and the slaves they claimed to represent ahead of their own, thus relinquishing some measure of control over their own texts and bodies. Many such narratives went on to serve as models for and subjects of fiction by white abolitionist writers. The limited potential of the scar in these fictional texts is best demonstrated in that archetype of abolitionist fiction, Harriet Beecher Stowe's *Uncle Tom's Cabin* (1852).

"Ineffaceable Marks of the System"

In 1853, a year after the publication of *Uncle Tom's Cabin*, Stowe published *A Key to Uncle Tom's Cabin*, a compendium of information intended to corroborate the representation of slavery in the novel. She begins her chapter on George Harris by reporting that his character "has been represented as overdrawn, both as respects personal qualities and general intelligence. It has been said, too, that so many afflictive incidents happening to slaves are improbable, and present a distorted view of the institution" (13). Stowe insists that her portrayal of George has been drawn from "the continual living testimony" of fugitive slaves, including that of slave narrators Lewis Clark, Josiah Henson, and Frederick Douglass (19). Aware that the words of these fugitives are doubted or maligned in anti-abolitionist circles, she insists that her own faith in the honesty of slave narrators is based on their bodily presence, which cannot, apparently, be falsified: "But we shall be told the slaves are all a lying race, and that these are lies which they tell us. There are some things, however, about these slaves, which cannot lie. Those deep lines of patient sorrow upon the face; that attitude of crouching and humble subjection; that sad, habitual expression of hope deferred, in the eye, would tell their story, if the slave never spoke" (20). Stowe thus represents herself as a skillful reader of the slave body, an interpreter, perhaps, who occupies a privileged position between the victimized slave and the (presumably) white reader. What Stowe neglects to mention in her catalog of the bodily text, however, is the scars themselves, so central to her own depiction of the runaway male slave. As in the slave narratives on which she relied for the character of George Harris, the voice of the runaway slave in *Uncle Tom's Cabin* is often supported and even supplanted by the scars on his body. In fact, Stowe's depiction of the marked black body—female as well as male—is central to what Jane Tompkins first acknowledged as the sentimental power of this novel.[11] Although scars and the punishments that cause them are not something with which most of Stowe's readers would have been familiar, they did serve as an important first step in establishing relationships between black and white characters, frequently provoking responses that might otherwise have remained unspoken.

Such "visible body damage" often serves as a sentimental litmus test revealing more about the white characters in the novel than the black. For example, in Stowe's representation of the relationship between Miss Ophelia, the northern cousin of a southern slaveholder, and Topsy, a young female slave, she demonstrates the correct response to the marked black body and is thus advising readers in their own reactions to both her novel and the larger institution of slavery. When Ophelia sees, "on the back and shoulders of the child, great welts and calloused spots, ineffaceable marks of the system under which she had grown up thus far, her heart became pitiful within her" (209). Ophelia had initially resisted her responsibility for Topsy, who had been purchased from "a couple of drunken creatures" by Ophelia's brother, St. Clare (208). Although she had considered herself ideologically opposed to slavery, she found it difficult to bring herself to touch black people or even to recognize their humanity. The sight of Topsy's scars, however, prompts Ophelia to discover her own role as benefactress in Topsy's spiritual and moral regeneration. Although she has yet to fully accept Topsy as a human child in need of maternal love and guidance, the witnessing of Topsy's scars is the beginning of this process. Ophelia's pity for Topsy is offered as a model for readers who may share Ophelia's abstract politics as well as her denial of the humanity of African Americans. Topsy is the ideal recipient of this pity because although she is generally naughty and badly behaved, she is not violent or rebellious. She shows no anger toward her former masters and even tells Ophelia to whip her as they once did: "Laws, Missis, I's used to whippin'; I spects it's good for me" (217).

The portrayal of George Harris evokes different responses from characters in the novel and presumably from readers themselves. In one scene, George, who has passed as a white man and run away from his master, takes a room in a small Kentucky inn. Before he enters the inn, however, other customers discuss a handbill advertising his escape and offering four hundred dollars for his return, dead or alive. Central to the advertisement is the physical description of George: "Ran away from the subscriber, my mulatto boy, George. Said George six feet in height, a very light mulatto, brown curly hair; is very intelligent, speaks handsomely, can read and write; will probably try to pass for a white man; is deeply scarred on his back and shoulders; has been branded in his right hand with the letter H" (91). The description of George emphasizes his mixed blood and his subsequent ability to pass. Yet the handbill also takes note of the scars and brands inflicted on him by his master, marks intended to remove any privileges or advantages granted him by his skin color. As in the slave advertisements included in Weld's *American Slavery as It Is*, the scars and brands mark George as "black"—and therefore a slave—even if his skin color indicates otherwise.

The spectators at the inn, however, interpret the marked body of this slave in a number of ways, thereby emphasizing the gendered differences between this scene and that involving Ophelia and Topsy. Not only are the characters in this second scene male, but their interaction takes place outside the sentiment-inducing domestic sphere. Unlike Ophelia, these men do not actually witness the scars of the slave, and their responses to the textual scars do not evolve into practical action. Yet even in this Kentucky inn—which by its very nature is almost a mockery of a home—scars have the power to inspire sympathy and incite resistance to the institution of slavery. For example, one observer comments, "Any man that owns a boy like that, and can't find any better way of treating him, *deserves* to lose him. Such papers as these is a shame to Kentucky" (91). Although slavery as an institution is not rejected here, harsh treatment of slaves is. The same speaker goes even further, threatening to take action on George's behalf. After learning that George's master, Mr. Harris, holds the patent to a machine invented by George, he remarks on the irony of Harris making money from the patent and then branding George's hand. He asserts, "If I had a fair chance, I'd mark him, I reckon, so that he'd carry it *one* while" (92). In this hypothetical reversal of the existing situation, the white man is marked as if he were the slave, and his carrying of the mark is presumed to symbolize his humiliation and loss of power. The patent and the brand are also equated and thus shown to be inauthentic marks of ownership—in both cases, the ownership of stolen property. The first speaker's subversive proposal is silenced, however, by "a coarse-looking fellow," who claims that "[t]hese yer knowin' boys is allers aggravatin' and sarcy . . . that's why they gets cut up and marked so. If they behaved themselves, they wouldn't" (92). This speaker sees the scars as an indication of George's character rather than that of Mr. Harris. According to him, George's scars are a clear sign of his misbehavior and thus his inadequacy as a slave. Yet they are also a sign of his value as a slave: George himself acknowledges that the brand, in particular, was an effort to prevent him from running away.

Although he is "deeply scarred on his back and shoulders," the brand on his hand particularly galls George, who sees in it an insult as well as an attempt to subdue his spirit. The brand is the "most recent proof of Mr. Harris' regard," he tells his former employer, Mr. Wilson. "A fortnight ago, he took it into his head to give it to me, because he said he believed I should try to get away one of these days" (99). More conspicuous than the marks on his shoulders and back, George's brand is intended to advertise Mr. Harris's ownership of George. Yet the brand is also significant in that it indicates George's last name as well as that of his owner. Slaves were frequently given their owner's surname, symbolizing not their kinship to their owner (although this was often the case) but their status as property. George retains Mr. Harris's last name even after having escaped from slavery. Rather than change his name and defy the mark in his hand, George accepts the *H* and the name that it signifies as part of his identity as a free man.

In this partial acceptance of the brand, Stowe's portrayal evades one crucial but controversial interpretation of the marked slave body. The notion of the mark as a symbol of and justification for violent slave rebellion was one that made nineteenth-century white Americans extremely uncomfortable, no matter what their political affiliation or position on slavery. The fear of slaves rebelling in response to their brutal treatment by slave owners was pervasive in the antebellum United States, particularly in the South, and Stowe's avoidance of this topic was shared by many political activists. Even among male slave narrators, very few articulated the desire for violent rebellion or admitted to considering this option while in captivity.[12] Moses Roper's allusion to his opportunity to perform military duty (and therefore to have access to firearms) and Frederick Douglass's legendary battle with Mr. Covey represent the extent of slave narrators' leeway on the subject of violence and rebellion against whites. Abolitionists were frequently blamed for such uprisings and were careful to insist, as did Lydia Maria Child, "that slavery causes insurrections, while emancipation prevents them" (*Appeal in Favor* 80). Such statements condemned the institution of slavery, but most abolitionists were also careful to condemn violence in any form. Child insisted that the Anti-Slavery Society "do[es] not wish to see any coercive or dangerous measures pursued" and that "almost every individual among them, is a strong friend to Peace Societies" (*Appeal in Favor* 134). William Lloyd Garrison, a prominent abolitionist leader and editor of the weekly abolitionist newspaper, *The Liberator*, denounced the use of violence by blacks and whites alike, claiming that moral suasion was the proper way to go about abolishing slavery (Foner 7). As Philip Lapsansky notes, the "most frequently stated motive" of anti-abolitionists "for stifling abolitionist discussion was that such discussion could encourage slave revolts. As part of their effort to defuse fears of violence, the antislavery movement didn't produce representations of black violence, self-assertion, or control" (213–14). Although opinions on nonviolence did not split cleanly along racial lines, black abolitionists were generally more "uncomfortable with this commitment" to "Garrison's inflexibly nonviolent posture" (Wolff 603). David Walker's 1829 *Appeal to the Colored Citizens of the World* (1829), for example, represents a much more militant stance in its assertion that African Americans should take violent action if necessary to bring about the liberation of all slaves. For the most part, the prospect of slave rebellion posed a moral difficulty for abolitionists who desired above all to see the end of the institution of slavery but had problems conceiving exactly what part slaves themselves should have in the movement. Although *Uncle Tom's Cabin*, the single most influential book to come out of the abolitionist movement, avoids the issue of slave rebellion entirely, this "nonnarratable plot," as David Leverenz observes, "provide[s] a covert charge to the drama" of the novel and to George Harris's character in particular (123).

George is not by any means a subdued or servile slave; he tells his wife, Eliza, "Mas'r will find out that I'm one that whipping won't tame" (15). He even implies that he will respond violently to such treatment if he is pushed hard enough: "He says that though I don't say anything, he sees I've got the devil in me, and he means to bring it out; and one of these days it will come out in a way that he won't like, or I'm mistaken!" (14). Rather than waiting to be goaded into violence, George decides to escape and seek freedom for himself and his family. In Stowe's representation of George's branded hand, she avoids the issue of slave rebellion by placing the threat of vengeance in the mouth of a white man who claims that he would mark George's master if given the chance. Stowe also attempts to ease her reader's anxieties about slave rebellion with her insistence that George inherits his "high, indomitable spirit" from his white father rather than his black mother (94). As Leverenz notes, "attributing George's aggressive spirit to white maleness" eliminates "the threat of a strong black man" (123). At the end of the novel, when George and his family go to Liberia as part of a colonization project, he claims that the only way the African race will conquer is through "that sublime doctrine of love and forgiveness." He attributes his own shortcomings in this respect to the fact that "full half the blood in my veins is the hot and hasty Saxon" (376). The threat of rebellion or revenge in *Uncle Tom's Cabin* is carefully defused by insisting on such "natural" differences between the races and by transforming George from an angry slave into a peaceful missionary, safely transplanted to Africa, where he will now identify with the "affectionate, magnanimous, and forgiving" African race (376). Thus he does not represent the direct challenge to the U.S. government or its people that William Grimes and Frederick Douglass do. As represented by Stowe, the antebellum United States has no place for George Harris, whose experiences and body are a harsh reminder of the debt owed him; he is, therefore, marked as unassimilable and banished.

Black Manhood and the Persistence of the Scar

Despite their nonviolent posture, several abolitionists did recognize the potential for violence—either rebellion or war—if the issue of slavery was not attended to by the U.S. government. In her *Appeal in Favor of That Class of Ameri-*

cans Called Africans, Child herself wrote, "I believe revenge is always wicked; but I say, what the laws of every country acknowledge, that great provocations are a palliation of great crimes" (184). Although a number of slave rebellions received national attention throughout the antebellum period, the prediction of a violent response to the institution of slavery was ultimately fulfilled with the advent of the Civil War. The part that African Americans could play in this response was initially quite limited. For the first two years of the war, the federal government insisted that union, rather than slavery, was the cause for which thousands of northern soldiers were dying. Action regarding slaves first came about as the result of encounters between Union troops and southern slaves in occupied areas: many slaves escaped to Federal lines in the hope that they would be protected from their former masters. In August 1861, the U.S. Congress passed the First Confiscation Act, which "provided that a master who permitted his slave to labor in any Confederate service forfeited his claim to the slave" (Berlin et al. 192). Escaped slaves, called "contrabands," were then allowed and were sometimes forced to contribute their labor to the Union army. Many of these contrabands became soldiers after the Emancipation Proclamation provided for the lawful enlistment of African American men.

Americans had long regarded military service as proof of manhood as well as a requirement for citizenship, and African American men recognized the Civil War as their opportunity to claim a position of equality in American society.[13] Some African American activists like Douglass represented military service as a sanctioned form of slave rebellion: while traveling throughout the North encouraging black men to enlist, Douglass urged his recruits to "[r]emember Denmark Vesey . . . remember Nathaniel Turner" (qtd. in Foner 139). Indeed, late in 1862, Jefferson Davis declared that any black soldier captured by the Confederate army would be tried for insurrection. When citizens complained that such an accusation, punishable by death, would deprive them of valuable slaves, the Confederate Congress compromised, insisting that white officers of black regiments would be put to death for inciting slave rebellion, while black soldiers would be enslaved (Glatthaar 201). Perhaps with this in mind, Douglass and others were sometimes less eager to point out the parallels between rebellion and military service, emphasizing a black soldier's duty to the Union rather than revenge. For example, in a piece for his newspaper, *Douglass's Monthly*, Douglass claimed that African American soldiers were fighting "for principle, and not from passion" (qtd. in Cullen 81).

Set just after the Emancipation Proclamation and before the First Confiscation Act, Louisa May Alcott's "My Contraband" (1863) explores the racial politics surrounding black enlistment in the Union army. Although the opportunities open to African American men had changed drastically since the publication of *Uncle Tom's Cabin*, Alcott continues to use the marked black body to evoke sympathy in other characters and, presumably, her audience. Yet the marked body of Robert, a contraband slave turned soldier, also figures prominently in Alcott's attempt to renegotiate black male identity and agency in the midst of the Civil War. These two projects ultimately work against each other, and as a result, Alcott's first objective is far more successful than her second.

In "My Contraband," Faith Dane, a nurse in a Union hospital, develops a relationship with Robert, the wounded contraband who is assigned to her as a servant when she is asked to tend to a Rebel captain. As the captain hovers between life and death, Dane learns that he is Robert's half brother and has kidnapped, raped, and possibly murdered Robert's wife, Lucy. Insisting on revenge, Robert locks the doors to the patient's room, throws his water and medicine out the window, and intends to let him die. Yet Dane manages to convince Robert to let the captain live, telling him, "There is a better way of righting wrong than violence;—let me help you find it" (77). Robert leaves the hospital to settle in Massachusetts but eventually enlists in the Union army. Dane meets him again in another hospital, where he is dying from a wound received from his half brother, the Rebel captain, on the battlefield at Fort Wagner.

His mortal wound is only the last in a series that textually define Robert, dictating the way in which he and his body are read by Faith Dane and, by extension, Alcott's audience. The doctor who assigns Robert to Dane describes him as "that fine mulatto fellow who was found burying his rebel master after the fight, and, being badly cut over the head, our boys brought him along" (69–70). This wound plays an important part in Dane's initial response to Robert. As she approaches him for the first time, she has only a partial view of his face and is struck by his beauty as well as his melancholic attitude. An urge "to know and comfort him" impels her to touch him on the shoulder; when he turns to her, however, she is shocked at his physical appearance as well as the roles immediately assumed by each of them:

> Not only did the manhood seem to die out of him, but the comeliness that first attracted me; for, as he turned, I saw the ghastly wound that had laid open cheek and forehead. Being partly healed, it was no longer bandaged, but held together with strips of that transparent plaster which I never see without a shiver. . . . Part of his black hair had been shorn away, and one eye was nearly closed; pain so distorted, and the cruel saber-cut so marred that portion of his face, that, when I saw it, I felt as if a fine medal had been suddenly reversed, showing me a far more striking type of human suffering and wrong than Michael Angelo's bronze prisoner. By one of those inexplicable processes that often teach us how little we understand ourselves, my purpose was suddenly changed; and, though I went in to offer comfort as a friend, I merely gave an order as a mistress. (71)

Robert's wound, which conveys the truth of "human suffering and wrong" more effectively than the most powerful artistry, frustrates Dane's intentions and confuses her desire to categorize Robert as either man or slave. Rather than treating him as "a friend," as she had planned, she assumes the role of mistress, ordering him to open a window. Nurse Dane, a self-proclaimed abolitionist, translates Robert's wound/scar into a sign of his subservience, which simultaneously places her in a position of power. She quickly recovers from this urge, however, and thanks Robert for his assistance, congratulating him on obtaining his freedom.

As Betsy Klimasmith notes, "The mere presence of Robert's wound . . . emphasizes that he may not be easily classified" (125). Robert's divided nature—half black and half white, half slave and half freedman—is symbolized by his face, wounded and disfigured on one side, unmarred and handsome on the other. He is described as a liminal being, one who "belong[s] to neither race," because of his mixed-race heritage and his light skin (Alcott, "My Contraband" 72). Dr. Franck tells Dane that "the white blood makes him rather high and haughty about some things. He was in a bad way when he came in, but vowed he'd die in the street rather than turn in with the black fellows below" (70). Such a "haughty" rejection of his African American heritage is symbolized not just by Robert's wound but by the closing of one of his eyes. With his vision impaired in this way, this liminal being is unable to see clearly his place in American society. Robert does not consider himself a black man—in fact, he appears to see himself, with his one functioning eye, as a white man—but knows that his blood and his experiences as a slave mark him as black.

The partially healed wound also indicates the transitional stage Robert occupies, one reminiscent of Gordon and other African American men whose progress from slave to contraband to soldier was recorded in drawings published in northern newspapers and magazines. Indeed, there is some uncertainty about the wound itself and the circumstances in which it was inflicted. Did Union soldiers strike Robert as he served his Rebel master on the battlefield? Did Confederate soldiers inflict the wound? Or did Robert's master do it, perhaps in response to Robert's desire to take refuge behind Federal lines? These questions are left unanswered, thereby disrupting the otherwise strict moral distinctions in this story. Obtained on the battlefield, Robert's wound has the potential to signify his status as a free man, fighting to defend himself, his family, his country. Yet Dane does not react to him as she would to a white man with a war wound.

Alcott had already addressed the issue of the war wound in *Hospital Sketches* (1863), which is in part a reconstruction of white masculinity during the Civil War in response to the fragmentation and subsequent marking of the white

male body. Here Nurse Periwinkle, Alcott's fictional counterpart, helps her patients come to terms with their newly marked bodies, assuring them that their
wounds are evidence of their masculinity. One soldier, for example, worries
about how a particular young woman will respond to the "thunderin' scar" on
his cheek. Periwinkle "assure[s] him that if Josephine was a girl of sense, she
would admire the honorable scar, as a lasting proof that he had faced the en-
emy, for all women thought a wound the best decoration a brave soldier could
wear" (24). Similarly, a "little Sergeant" "with one leg gone, and the right arm
so shattered that it must evidently follow," works with Periwinkle to rehabilitate
his sense of self, physically and spiritually (38, 30).[14] Yet despite the grave nature
of his wounds and his extensive amputations, the soldier is able to make light
of them, at least in the presence of his nurse. "I've been in six scrimmages, and
never got a scratch till this last one," he tells her, "but it's done the business
pretty thoroughly for me, I should say. Lord! what a scramble there'll be for
arms and legs, when we old boys come out of our graves, on the Judgement Day:
wonder if we shall get our own again? If we do, my leg will have to tramp from
Fredericksburg, my arm from here, I suppose, and meet my body, wherever it
may be." Periwinkle reports, "The fancy seemed to tickle him mightily, for he
laughed blithely, and so did I" (31). The sergeant evidently does not worry about
the effect of his multiple amputations on his own relationship either; he is later
shown writing a letter to "My Dearest Jane," and Periwinkle reflects that he had
obviously "been more successful in the service of Commander-in-Chief Cupid
than that of Gen. Mars" (38).

Although amputation might initially be thought to provide a more difficult
challenge than scarring to the patient as well as to the nurse, Lisa A. Long's
research confirms Alcott's depiction of the two situations: "Certainly, their
wounded bodies did not represent the physical self-portrait to which injured
soldiers had been accustomed before the war. In many cases patients preferred
amputation to deformity, perhaps believing that in excising the offensive, dehumanizing marks of war, they would be able to regain some semblance of
their antebellum selves" (36). Depictions of wounded soldiers published in
popular magazines and newspapers also focused primarily on the amputee,
thus rehabilitating the soldier and romanticizing his reintegration into society.
In Winslow Homer's "Our Watering-Places—The Empty Sleeve at Newport"
(*Harper's Weekly*, August 26, 1865) for example, a young man wearing a Union
cap is shown riding in a phaeton with an attractive young woman. Presumably
because of the "empty sleeve," which is pinned to his coat, the woman holds
the horses' reins in her gloved hands. While her control of the carriage might
be an uncomfortable reminder to readers of women's increased public presence
during the war, the depiction of the amputee is a positive one, emphasizing his

return to romance and public life. Yet another Homer illustration similarly depicts the amputee's successful rehabilitation without the awkward reminder of altered gender politics. "Thanksgiving Day—The Church Porch" (*Frank Leslie's Illustrated Newspaper*, December 23, 1865) shows a crowd of people leaving a church. At least three soldiers accompany women out of the church, and one of these soldiers is on crutches, his leg amputated at the knee. Although his companion has her arm around him and looks at him with concern, his uniform and his presence among other veterans confirms his masculinity despite (or perhaps because of) the amputation.

According to both Homer and Alcott, the marked body of the white soldier has the potential to be reconfigured as a testimony to both the experience of fighting in battle and the personal characteristics that are said to develop as a result of such experience—strength, honor, bravery. Perhaps the more drastically "marked" the soldier's body, the better—hence the positive depictions of amputees. Above all, the wounded soldier is not a victim. The marked body of the slave, on the other hand, could arouse sympathy but not necessarily respect. Rather than seeing the limitations of whiteness or even southern society in the marked bodies of slaves, white observers saw the preconceived limitations of black men themselves and their inability to live up to ideals of (white) American manhood. As Frederick Douglass explained, "[H]uman nature is so constituted that it cannot honor a helpless man, although it can pity him; and even that it cannot do long, if the signs of power do not arise" (qtd. in O. Patterson 13).

Nurse Dane does in fact attempt to honor Robert's manhood, speaking directly to him for example, and addressing him as subject rather than object. Later both she and Dr. Franck offer material assistance to Robert in the form of money, a safe destination, and letters of introduction and recommendation. Yet again, however, Dane falls into the role of mistress just when she thinks she is being most respectful of him. Robert is introduced to her as "Bob," but Dane insists that her "pet whim" is to "teach the men self-respect by treating them respectfully. Tom, Dick, and Harry would pass, when lads rejoiced in those familiar abbreviations; but to address men old enough to be my father in that style did not suit my old-fashioned ideas of propriety" (72–73). Robert tells her that he has no "other name"; he explains, "[W]e has our master's names or do without. Mine's dead, and I won't have anything of his 'bout me" (73). Dane decides that she will call him Robert and reflects on the significance of this scene: "Through all the tame obedience years of servitude had taught him, I could see that the proud spirit his father gave him was not yet subdued, for the look and gesture with which he repudiated his master's name were a more effective declaration of independence than any Fourth-of-July orator could have prepared"

(73). Bob's repudiation of his last name is indeed a subtle act of rebellion—one that Stowe's George Harris eschews—that indicates the rejection of his master as well as his own status as a slave. Yet Dane chooses to replace his first name with a more formal one despite the fact that Robert is as a matter of fact *not* "old enough to be [her] father." The imposition of the name Robert could be interpreted as an act of ownership, as is also indicated by the title of the story: "*My Contraband.*" Just as disturbing here is Dane's insistence on Robert's pride being inherited from his white father rather than from any of his black antecedents. This gesture recalls Stowe's description of George Harris in *Uncle Tom's Cabin*, published eleven years earlier, and ignores the fact that Robert would have been named Bob while a slave on his father's plantation and would once have been given his father's surname not as a symbol of kinship but as a symbol of ownership. Dane does not acknowledge that Robert's relationship with his father cannot be romanticized any more than his relationship with his half brother. Robert's flesh reveals the futility of such romanticizing not only because of the color of his skin but also because of the scars he carries on his back.

Although the wound on Robert's face frustrates Dane's desire to label him either "slave" or "free," the sight of his scarred back enables her to place him into a category with which she is comfortable as an abolitionist and a woman. "Yer thought I was a white man once," Robert tells her and then dramatically reveals his scars: "With a sudden wrench he tore the shirt from neck to waist, and on his strong, brown shoulders showed me furrows deeply ploughed, wounds which, though healed, were ghastlier to me than any in that house" (78). It is not Robert's "brown shoulders" that prove him to be a black man—or rather, *not* to be a white man. His scars, not his skin color, are incontrovertible evidence that he has been a slave and is, at least in the eyes of the world, a black man. These scars confirm the truth of the tale Robert is telling Faith Dane, yet they also indicate the importance of this moment in the story. Will the scars and the memories they provoke incite murderous rebellion? Or will the scars evoke pity in the female abolitionist, making the outcome of the situation her responsibility rather than the slave's? Whose agency are the scars intended to foreground? Despite her assurance that "he was no longer slave or contraband," only the recipient of "an infinite compassion," Dane's pity gives her the upper hand, allowing her to take control of the situation and remove the captain from physical danger and Robert from what she perceives as spiritual danger.[15] As she searches for a way to accomplish this task, Dane despairs at the futility of appealing to Robert's sense of "self-control," "the beauty of forgiveness," "justice, or the mercy that should temper that stern virtue," or "brotherly love" (80). All characteristics of white bourgeois masculinity, these have been denied Robert as the son of a southern gentleman raised as a black slave. Instead, Dane convinces Robert that only if he lets the captain live will he be reunited with Lucy; the next day Robert leaves the hospital.

Dane and Robert meet again after the battle at Fort Wagner, where Robert is mortally wounded by the brother he had earlier allowed to live. Robert's mortal wound is the final frame in his symbolic transformation from slave to soldier, yet this wound will never heal and become a scar like those on his back and face. The wound received at Fort Wagner is more destructive than the others. Because the black soldier was allowed a measure of manhood denied the black male slave, however, Robert's war wound confers a different identity and arouses a different response from the observer. Robert's military service, like that of many other African American men, confirms his manhood "before many eyes that would not see, rings in many ears that would not hear, wins many hearts that would not hitherto believe" (83). Cullen notes that African American soldiers believed they were proving their manhood by demonstrating their responsibility to nation, race, and family (85). While Robert's loyalty to his wife, Lucy, had never been called into question, his service in battle with a black regiment could be interpreted as a demonstration of his newfound commitment to nation and race. According to this paradigm, Robert's initiation into bourgeois manhood, begun when he is dissuaded from killing his brother at the hospital, is complete by the time of his death at the end of the story. "I'd 'a' done it,—but it's better so," he tells Dane with his dying breath, "I'm satisfied" (86). Alcott reassures her readers that, like the wounded soldiers represented in *Hospital Sketches* and Winslow Homer's magazine illustrations, Robert is ultimately rewarded with "wife and home, eternal liberty and God" (86). The only difference is that Robert's rewards come to him in the afterlife rather than the phaeton or the "church porch."

Robert's death complicates the happy ending of "My Contraband," and the marks on his body present even more problems. Just as the scars on Robert's back were a continual reminder of his status as a slave even while he was a contraband, his facial scars mark Robert as a contraband while he lies dying of wounds received while fighting as a soldier. Indeed, Dane recognizes Robert in the hospital because of the "deep scar on his cheek," as well as the fact that the card above his bed reads "Robert Dane." Using the nurse's last name as his own could indicate respect and gratitude as well as simple necessity. Yet it could also imply ownership, a relationship that Dane has already romanticized in her (mis)understanding of Robert and his father. "Robert Dane" remains Faith Dane's contraband. Despite his efforts to transform himself, he is haunted by his past and by the body on which his history is inscribed. This body has become a text for others to interpret, a text over which Robert himself has no control. At the end of the story, he is completely without voice. "I turned again," Dane explains, "and Robert's eyes met mine. . . . He knew me, yet gave no greeting; was glad to see a woman's face, yet had no smile wherewith to welcome it; felt that he was dying, yet uttered no farewell" (84). Mark Patterson points out that "Robert Dane lies passive and almost entirely silent, while Nurse Dane and others speak for him" (161). Yet, as it has throughout the story, Robert's body also "speak[s] for him," telling a story that Dane presumes to interpret for her audience.

Robert's transformation from slave to contraband to soldier is further complicated by the discomfort with which many Americans regarded the possibility of blacks taking violent action against whites. Union strategists recognized that the very personal involvement of black soldiers in the issues being fought over would give the Union an edge unsurpassed even by the southerners' commitment to secession and desire to force Union invaders off their land (Glatthaar 9). Yet whites were concerned that such violence would become indiscriminate. Supporters of African American enlistment emphasized the self-control of black regiments, especially compared to the passionate Confederate soldiers who declared they would immediately execute any black soldiers taken captive in battle. However threatening the black soldier may have seemed to many whites, he also represented a containment of the anger and resentment that many feared would erupt in slave rebellion. Robert's attempt to murder his half brother is indicative of such a fear insofar as he does so to avenge his wife's rape and murder. Yet this threat is defused in several ways in "My Contraband," thereby reassuring audiences that Robert is not dangerous and that he and others like him can be used to strengthen Union forces and win the war.

When found by Union troops, Robert is burying the body of his master, presumably the man to whom his half brother sold him after beating him. As Dane approaches Robert for the first time, she imagines—without any real provocation—that he is mourning the loss of this master. Furthermore, Robert's anger toward his half brother is revealed to be justified by the violence done to his wife; the narrator insists that "no white man" could have felt more strongly or more sensitively about the wrongs inflicted on him. Therefore, Robert is represented as a faithful slave when treated kindly and a vengeful slave only when wronged and abused. His response to his wife's rape and murder is particularly understandable to a white audience that places men in the role of protector to women. Dane is also able to talk Robert out of murdering the captain, assuring him that violence is not the answer to his dilemma. Although she does not encourage Robert to fight in the war, it is apparent that *this* type of violence is acceptable to her; thus a distinction is made in "My Contraband" between the violence of the vengeful slave and the violence of the slave turned soldier. As Elizabeth Young points out, "[T]he translation of Robert's violent impulses into his bravery as a soldier controls the specter of armed black violence within the structured confines of the army" (97). Indeed, although the two types of "revenge" might not seem so different, nineteenth-century notions of manhood would have positioned them as polar opposites, one the result of uncontrollable passion and anger, the other the result of rational self-discipline and duty.[16]

Even as a soldier, however, Robert is denied the opportunity to avenge himself upon his half brother in a socially sanctioned way: although he attacks him on the battlefield, he does not succeed in killing him. A dark-skinned, free-born black man from Boston who survives to tell Dane the tale manages "to pitch that Reb into the fort as dead as Moses, git hold of Dane, an' bring him off" (85). And although Robert's desire for revenge would appear to be manifested in the zeal with which he attacks "Marster Ned" on the battlefield, this evidence is contradicted by a letter written to Dane just prior to his enlistment. "I thank yer, Missis," he writes, "an' if they let us, I'll fight fer yer till I'm killed, which I hope will be 'fore long" (83). Rather than enlisting to get revenge on his half brother or the South or even to demonstrate his loyalty to the Union, Robert desires to fight for Nurse Dane; he apparently regards her as having been the agent of his liberation even though he had already escaped slavery by the time he met her. He also hopes that the fighting will place him in a position in which he will be killed. Living only to die, Robert enlists as a form of suicide.

Despite his enlistment with a black regiment and the Boston soldier's assurance that "we boys always stan' by one another," Robert never comes to accept his identity as a black man (84). He is never motivated by what Sarah Elbert calls a "determin[ation] to rise with his race rather than in spite of it" (xliii). The Boston soldier tells Dane, "I never saw him till I joined the regiment, an' no one 'peared to have got much out of him. He was a shut-up sort of feller, an' didn't seem to care for anything but gettin' at the Rebs" (84). Thus the black regiment becomes simply an avenue through which Robert can fulfill his death wish. His final wound, therefore, allows him the satisfaction that he could not find in his pursuit of revenge or in his life as a black man.

Although Robert's options appear to be more numerous than those of other black men of the time, his potential is contained by the end of the story, and he is left only with spiritual redemption. With Robert, Lucy, and Ned all dead, nothing need be done for or to Robert. Unable to identify with black men and unaccepted by white men, he is thwarted in his quest for agency and identity. Writing eleven years after *Uncle Tom's Cabin*, Alcott is similarly unable to articulate a more effective way in which to negotiate the transition from slavery to free black manhood despite the paradigms set by the authors of slave narratives. Unlike Austin Steward, Moses Roper, and William Grimes, both George Harris and Robert are denuded of their anger and removed from the American scene, either through immigration or death. Like Gordon, the slave whose transformation was represented in *Harper's Weekly*, Robert and many black men like him were ultimately reduced to nothing more than their scars.

Marks of Recognition and Reunion

The power of sympathy as a tool for the abolitionist movement should not be underestimated, yet its limitations must be recognized as well. The rhetorical use of scars in abolitionist literature proved to be a limited tactic that did not allow for a progressive redefinition of black manhood during the Civil War period. Nineteenth-century American audiences were trained by abolitionist rhetoric to respond to scars with sympathy rather than respect or admiration for the person who could survive such dehumanizing abuse. Lydia Maria Child responded to this dilemma immediately following the war in *A Romance of the Republic* (1867), making an effort to alter the discourse of the marked black body by replacing the scar with the tattoo. Although Child's use of the tattoo does emphasize familial connection rather than the physical abuse highlighted by the textual scar, her critique falls short of actually locating a place for the marked black body within American society and culture. More than twenty-five years after the conclusion of the Civil War and the publication of Child's novel, however, Frances Ellen Watkins Harper reengaged this discourse in *Iola Leroy, or Shadows Uplifted* (1892), returning to the Civil War and politicizing the marked body by positioning it within the black community itself, where it would be read as a symbol of familial identity and reunion. These two novels, along with Alcott's "My Contraband," indicate the central importance of the Civil War in progressive racial politics during and after the war. Although it was not the conclusive factor in black male citizenship many had hoped for, it did provide the foundation for a reconsideration of masculinity within both the African American community and the larger United States.

A Romance of the Republic was written and published in response to what Child saw as the diminishing interest of white Americans in Reconstruction. She later explained her motivation to a friend: "[H]aving fought against Slavery, till the monster is legally dead, I was desirous to do what I could to undermine Prejudice" (qtd. in Nelson vii). The novel focuses on the lives of two sisters who have been raised in antebellum New Orleans as white women but discover after the death of their father that they are octoroons. To avoid their being sold as slaves, the elder sister, Rosa, agrees to what she believes is a marriage to Mr. Fitzgerald, a scoundrel who actually purchases the sisters as slaves. He removes them to his plantation, ostensibly to hide them from their father's creditors, but actually to reserve both women for his personal pleasure. When Fitzgerald marries a white woman, Rosa realizes that her marriage is a sham. Both she and Lily, Fitzgerald's legal wife, soon give birth to sons, and in a frenzy of grief and desperation, Rosa switches the infants in order for her child to be raised as a white gentleman. Lily's son (whom Rosa pretends is hers) is left behind in the care of a nurse while Rosa is rushed to the North before Fitzgerald can sell her to cover his own debts. In her absence, the baby and his nurse are kidnapped and sold. Years later, when Rosa and the nurse are reunited, she is told that prior to being captured, the baby had been tattooed in an effort to assure his identity if he were enslaved. The idea came to the nurse when a sea captain visited the family with whom she was staying: "[H]e was marking an anchor on his own arm with a needle and some sort of black stuff; and he said 't would never come out. I thought if they should carry off yer picaninny, it would be more easy to find him again if he was marked. I told the captain I had heard ye call him Gerald; and he said he would mark G. F. on his arm" (371–72). Unlike the brand on George Harris's hand or the scars on Robert's back, the tattoo on the infant's arm is not inflicted as a punishment. Even though he is too young to choose it for himself, the mark is intended to protect the child, to make him recoverable if he is kidnapped and sold into slavery. Although Lily's biological son is later searched for and discovered by Rosa's family, the tattoo plays only a small role in identifying him; his resemblance to both his father and his half brother are indisputable proof of the relationship and make the tattoo almost irrelevant in that respect.[17]

The tattoo proves useful in giving the young man a sense of identity apart from that of a slave, as is revealed when the half brothers are reunited while both are fighting for white Union regiments early in the Civil War. The former slave explains his escape attempt to Gerald Fitzgerald, the biological son of Rosa who has been raised as a white man. Gerald describes their encounter in a letter to Rosa, with whom he has been reunited: "After a while, he escaped in a woman's dress, contrived to open a communication with [his wife] Hen, and succeeded in carrying her off to New York. There he changed his woman's dress, and his slave name of Bob Bruteman, and called himself George Falkner. When I asked him why chose that name, he rolled up his sleeve and showed me G. F. marked on his arm. He said he didn't know who put them there, but he supposed they were the initials of his name" (407). Here the tattoo reminds the slave that he is human, that he has an identity and a name other than that given him by the slaveholder. Even though he is assigned the name Bob Bruteman, he is always aware that he is not a "brute" but a "man." He may not know his actual name, but renaming himself gives him control over his own identity.

Yet "George Falkner's" mark is problematic in ways similar to that of George Harris; although the tattoo is an indication of his actual name—Gerald Fitzgerald—it also indicates the complications of his parentage: he is named after his father, who once owned both him (as long as he was considered "black") and Rosa, his supposed mother. George's true identity is eventually revealed to him, and he decides "that he should prefer to be called by his father's name; for he thought he should feel more like a man to bear a name to which he knew that he had a right" (438). According to southern custom and law, George both is and is not entitled to his father's name: as a white man, he is legally a Fitzgerald, but as a slave (and therefore "black"), he is not to be acknowledged as a member of the family. The name is in fact the only thing that George receives from his father's family; although they are aware of his existence, they refuse to accept as kin a man raised as a slave and married to a black woman.

Although Rosa's family is racially mixed and politically progressive, George is nonetheless unable to find acceptance there or even in the larger context of the United States. George is employed by Rosa's husband, but although she is responsible for his enslavement, he is not given a place in her family or her affections. Nor is he told the true story about Rosa's actions; her husband simply tells him, "You are unmixed white; but you were left in the care of a negro nurse, and one of your father's creditor's seized you both, and sold you into slavery" (437). Finally, reminiscent of Stowe's dismissal of George Harris to Liberia at the end of Uncle Tom's Cabin, George Falkner and his wife sail to France after the war. He is told, "[E]ducate yourself, your wife, and your children, with a view to the station you will have it in your power to acquire" (436). Despite having a body marked by love rather than punishment, and despite being a "true" white man, George is not allowed to acquire this "station" in the United States.

By marking George Falkner with a tattoo instead of a scar, Child represents the body of the slave as the site of familial connection and individual identity rather than (or in addition to) brutality and dehumanization. However he interprets it, George's tattoo is a symbol of the family and the identity he has lost; his awareness of these things is enough to give him a sense of self denied many slaves. Yet George's status as "unmixed white" makes it impossible to draw connections between his marked body and the redefinition of black manhood. In fact, Child is much less concerned with black manhood or womanhood in this novel than she is with the intermixing of the races. Rosa's family and that of her sister are represented as having light skin with perhaps some African American features; their servants, on the other hand, are more obviously "black." George's wife is not in fact "black," but neither is she light skinned; despite Child's apparent willingness to examine the issue of interracial relationships, the experiment of the Falkners' marriage must take place abroad. Child sidesteps the issue of the marked black body in two ways in this novel: first, by marking the body with a tattoo rather than a scar, and second, by marking the "white" slave body rather than the "black" slave body. She thereby avoids the tendency to see the marked man as less than a man, though George's fate at the end of the novel—banished from his country and denied any sense of family by those who are responsible for his enslavement—recalls the fates of George Harris and Robert Dane and calls the effectiveness of the tattoo in this context into question.

Written during a period in which both northerners and southerners were quietly erasing African American participation in the Civil War from the historical record, *Iola Leroy* reconstructs the memory of the war in racial and gendered terms. Harper had been a well-known writer and antislavery activist at midcentury, and by the time her novel was published in 1892, she was acknowledged as one of the most significant African American public figures of the nineteenth century. As a black woman with enormous cultural influence, Harper's contribution to the discourses of black manhood and the marked black body offers a valuable contrast to the texts written before and during the war by white women authors—including *Uncle Tom's Cabin* and "My Contraband." Although hindsight provided her with a perspective denied the other writers discussed here, Harper's distinctive position as an African American woman also allowed her to reconfigure the complicated politics evident in white women's representations of the black male body.

Like *A Romance of the Republic*, *Iola Leroy* also emphasizes familial relationships and their dependence on the marked body in an institution that separates mothers and children as well as brothers and sisters. The Civil War functions in this text to bring families together again by allowing slaves to escape their masters and become mobile, encountering people and experiences that they would not have encountered while enslaved. The war also offers black men the opportunity to fight for their own freedom, an experience that Harper explicitly associates with the act of rebellion. Robert, a slave and uncle to the heroine of the novel, had always secretly harbored a desire to be free but was cautious in his preparations.

> He had heard of terrible vengeance being heaped upon the heads of some who had sought their freedom and failed in the attempt. . . . It would have been madness and folly for him to have attempted an insurrection against slavery, with the words of McClellan ringing in his ears: 'If you rise, I shall put you down with an iron hand,' and with the home guards ready to quench his aspirations for freedom with bayonets and blood. What could a set of unarmed and undisciplined men do against the fearful odds which beset their path?
>
> Robert waited eagerly and hopefully his chance to join the Union army, and was ready and willing to do anything required of him by which he could earn his freedom and prove his manhood. (35–36)[18]

Fighting in the war provided slaves with the most immediate access to respect and recognition from themselves as well as others. The impact of such service is revealed when Robert returns to visit his former mistress: "He was not the light-hearted, careless, mischief-loving Robby of former days, but a handsome man, with heavy moustaches, dark, earnest eyes, and proud military bearing" (150–51).

Combat is not the only avenue to manhood, however, in *Iola Leroy*. Robert's friend, Tom Anderson, is unable to serve as a soldier "on account of physical defects," yet he is acknowledged as one of the bravest and most useful men in the Union camp: "When tents were to be pitched, none were more ready to help than he. When burdens were to be borne, none were more willing to bend beneath them than Tom Anderson. When the battle-field was to be searched for the wounded and dying, no hand was more tender in its ministrations of kindness than his. As a general factotum in the army, he was ever ready and willing to serve anywhere and at any time, and to gather information from every possible source which could be of any service to the Union army" (40). As Elizabeth Young points out, such varied depictions of black men "chart inseparable commitments to blackness and manhood as well as to the Union cause" (208).

Black men are also not restricted to working for or with the military. Dr. Latimer, who has white skin but "belongs to that negro race both by blood and choice," dedicates himself to the African American race, serving as a physician to the black community (238). He is represented as an ideal man, one worthy of marrying Iola Leroy and joining her in "labor[ing] for those who had passed from the old oligarchy of slavery into the new commonwealth of freedom" (271). Dr. Latimer is indeed Iola's "ideal of a high, heroic manhood" (265). Twenty-five years removed from the Civil War, Harper is able to envision military service as a possible rather than necessary component of black manhood. Perhaps because of this broad definition of manhood, she is similarly able to transform the mark into a symbol of community and reunification rather than one of physical strength and bravery under fire.

According to Harper, the institution of slavery is the direct cause of the Civil War. If America is configured as a physical body, slavery is the "national wound . . . too deep to be lightly healed" (*Iola Leroy* 132). The author had used a similar metaphor in her poem "Eliza Harris" (1853), based on the character of George Harris's wife in *Uncle Tom's Cabin*:

> But she's free—yes, free from the land where the slave
> From the hand of oppression must rest in the grave;

Where bondage and torture, where scourges and chains,
Have plac'd on our banner indelible stains. (6)

Reminiscent of William Grimes's wish to "bind the charter of American Liberty" with "the skin of an American slave," Harper's poem also imagines the treasured American flag tainted by the physical wounds of slavery. *Iola Leroy* demonstrates that black men and women knew all too well what the war was about and sacrificed their own lives to heal the "national wound." For example, in *Iola Leroy*, Aunt Linda, an illiterate slave, recognizes slavery as the cause of the conflict and tells Robert, "But, somehow, Robby, I raley b'lieves dat we cullud folks is mixed up in dis fight" (12). Even the white officers of the black regiment in which Robert enlists acknowledge that the silence surrounding the issue of slavery has hindered Union war efforts: "At the beginning of this war we were not permeated with justice, and so were not ripe for victory" (132).

Yet while the wound of slavery separated families, the wounds of battle function in this novel to reunite them. When Robert is shot in battle, he is taken to the hospital where Iola serves as nurse. After recognizing a hymn that Iola had learned from her mother, he realizes that they might be related. Bodily marks solidify their family connection, which may have otherwise been too tenuous to pursue. Robert remembers that his sister, Iola's mother, "used to have a mole on her cheek, which mother used to tell her was her beauty spot," but is unable to recognize her in a picture in Iola's locket (141). Conveniently, Iola recalls that her mother had told her of a "red spot on [her brother's] temple" (149). The corresponding spot proves their kinship and allows them to unite in their search for the rest of the family. Iola's brother Harry is similarly reunited with his mother in a hospital after being wounded on the battlefield. Harry, who has been raised as a white man and only became familiar with his racial heritage after his father's death, had enlisted in a black regiment despite the recruiting officer's insistence that he can and should pass in a white regiment. "I am a colored man," Harry insists, "and unless I can be assigned to a colored regiment I am not willing to enter the army" (127). After being wounded, Harry awakes to find his mother volunteering in the hospital, and the two are reunited. "My dear son," Mrs. Leroy tells Harry, "I am deeply sorry that you are wounded, but I am glad that the fortunes of war have brought us together" (192). Eventually, the entire family unit is reunited and even expanded when Iola marries Dr. Latimer and Harry marries the dark-skinned Lucille Delany.

Unlike Child, Harper refuses to revise the discourse of the marked black body without reconsidering black manhood and its place within the larger community. Black manhood is vulnerable in *Iola Leroy*, but it is also protected by the familial unit, in which men can be healed. The physician, Dr. Latimer, and the nurse, Iola Leroy, signify the importance of emotional and physical healing, and their marriage suggests the healthful future awaiting the community in which they live and work. It is the strength of the community that enables these figures to remain in the United States and resist colonization or missionary work. "[W]hile I am in favor of missionary work," one character insists, "there is need here for the best heart and brain to work in unison for justice and righteousness" (247). The scars of this community are not disfiguring reminders of slavery but symbols of the healing powers of family and a commitment to African American racial uplift. By allowing for the development and maintenance of such a community in *Iola Leroy*, Harper is able to accomplish what other authors are not, perhaps because Harper had the benefit of hindsight, writing more than thirty years after the end of the war. Perhaps her own experiences as a black woman contributed to her vision. After all, as Claudia Tate points out, Harper "embraced the rhetoric of manhood as an emancipatory discourse to be mediated by both men and women." Her "use of the trope of manhood seems an expression of the collective political ambition of black people—both male and female—as citizens rather than a trope specifically referring to the patriarchal aspirations of enfranchised men" (132). Defining manhood, then, had much larger implications for Harper than it did, for example, for Alcott, whose "black" man vehemently denies his own blackness and whose bodily marks speak to his conflicted sense of identity. The scar, the tattoo, the birthmark, the war wound—these physical and metaphorical legacies of slavery and the Civil War could not simply be buried and forgotten. Rather, they had to be confronted and reconfigured in order for the black community to heal and progress.

CHAPTER FIVE

"Raising the Stigma"

African American Women

and the Corporeal Legacy of Slavery

In the preface to her novel, *Contending Forces: A Romance Illustrative of Negro Life North and South* (1900), Pauline Hopkins claims that she writes in order to "raise the stigma of degradation from [her] race" (13). The use of the word "stigma" here in Hopkins's declaration of her commitment to racial uplift is anything but incidental. As I demonstrated in chapter 4, the physical stigmata of slavery resulting from brutal abuse and debilitating labor were used not only to attract support for the abolitionist cause in antebellum America but also, paradoxically, to support racist beliefs about the physical, mental, and emotional inferiority of blacks. Slaves marked with scars could be seen as victims in need of assistance but rarely as people capable of agency themselves. Because scars or brands evoked pity but were rarely seen as marks of power, they could be seen in the postemancipation era as representing the "degradation" of slavery and as being somehow shameful.

At first glance, Hopkins's intention seems to be to *remove* or even to erase the stigma, the mark of shame, from the collective flesh of her race. Yet in "raising the stigma" she also *recalls* it for her turn-of-the-century readers, forcing them to confront the marked black body and its legacy; in doing so, she negates the shame associated with such marks for African Americans and places the responsibility for the marked body squarely on the white community. The word "raise" is subversively ambiguous when seen in this light. To raise a mark on the skin can be to cause it, yet "raising" can also suggest the suspension of the mark's validity—in this case, its significance as a symbol of "degradation." Additional definitions of the word "raise" are also appropriate once traditional meanings of the mark are invalidated: to raise the mark, for example, is to give it voice, perhaps even to stir up or incite rebellion based on what such a voice has to say. Hopkins seems aware of these multiple interpretations. It is only by "raising the stigma" in all these ways, however paradoxical they might seem, that the mark can be redeemed and African Americans empowered.

Hopkins is particularly interested in the relationship between African American women and the marked body. Indeed, throughout the first chapters of *Contending Forces* Hopkins looks to history to explore black women's embodied subjectivity before returning to the contemporary period to examine the ways in which black women in the post-Reconstruction years deal with this legacy. Hopkins does not, as so many critics have claimed, focus solely on rape and its impact on black women, although this issue is central to *Contending Forces*.[1] Rather, Hopkins anticipates Hortense Spillers's argument about the importance of physical and sexual violence in the history of the black female slave. In her article "Mama's Baby, Papa's Maybe: An American Grammar Book," Spillers notes the failure of many critics to recognize that the female slave "is not only the target of rape—in one sense, an interiorized violation of body and mind—but also the topic of specifically *externalized* acts of torture and prostration that we imagine as the peculiar province of *male* brutality and torture inflicted by other males." She goes on to claim that such scenes emphasize the fact that black "female flesh" is "unprotected" within the institution of slavery and ultimately "ungendered" by the violence inherent to the institution (68).

This chapter traces Hopkins's effort to "raise the stigma" by depicting the black female body in terms consistent with and in anticipation of Spillers's theory about physical violence. Beginning with abolitionist fiction by Lydia Maria Child and Harriet Beecher Stowe, I examine the contradictory legacy of the black female body. Hopkins responds to this legacy using the rhetoric of the stigma or the marked body in considering the intertwined but distinctly different natures of physical and sexual violence in *Contending Forces*, ultimately claiming that both contribute to black women's embodied subjectivity. In doing so, she radically critiques and revises the portrayal of the black woman in abolitionist fiction, making embodiment rather than transcendence of the body key to African American survival. Ultimately, by using the rhetoric of Christianity, Hopkins transforms her heroine, Sappho Clark, into a magnificent female Christ figure who *bridges* the corporeal and the spiritual rather than transcending one for the other.

In this sense, I return, then, to the subject of the first chapter: the cultural (re)negotiation and reintegration of the marked woman's body. Yet while Olive Oatman's voice and therefore her interpretation of her own tattoos is submerged beneath multiple narrative and performative layers, Hopkins "raises" her own voice and that of her heroine, insisting that African American women must tell their own stories.

The "Unprotected Flesh" of the Female Slave

I begin where Hopkins herself does—with the black woman's experience of violence and slavery in the antebellum period. In *"Doers of the Word": African American Women Speakers and Writers in the North (1830–1880)*, Carla L. Peterson notes the conceptualization of the nineteenth-century black woman in bodily terms, "in contrast to middle-class white women whose femininity, as defined by the cult of true womanhood, cohered around notions of the self-effacing body." In chapters 2 and 3, I demonstrated how such an ideal influenced and complicated representations of the marked white woman. As Peterson points out, however, it is crucial to recognize the impact of this ideal on African American women as well. Whether slave or free, "the black woman's body," Peterson insists, "was always envisioned as public and exposed" (20). Denied the protection of home and family as well as the culturally condoned femininity of their white counterparts, black women were perceived solely as laboring bodies, available for public use and public viewing. This perception facilitated the enslavement and exploitation of black women. It also made the abuse of female slaves possible in that a public, laboring body was the antithesis of white womanhood and its collective "self-effacing body." The black female body could be forced to work and physically abused because it was not gendered according to the codes of true (white) womanhood. Paradoxically, as Spillers points out, such labor and punishment effectively "ungendered" the body even further, creating a malignant cycle that left no room for the humanity or femininity of the black woman.

The physical abuse and subsequent scarring of female slaves in antebellum America has been carefully documented by late-twentieth-century historians such as Dorothy Sterling, Jacqueline Jones, and Brenda E. Stevenson.[2] According to Jones, "in the severity of punishment meted out to slaves, little distinction was made between the sexes. Black women attained parity with black men in terms of their productive abilities in the cotton fields; as a result they often received a proportionate share of the whippings" (19). Working in the homes of their masters and mistresses did not exempt female slaves from physical abuse; their proximity to whites often made them more vulnerable to suspicion and jealousy, particularly if a white woman became aware of her husband's sexual interest in a black woman. While the weapon of choice for masters and overseers was the whip, mistresses were known for punishing what they regarded as disloyalty or disobedience by "attack[ing] with any weapon available—knitting needles, tongs, a fork, butcher knife, ironing board, or pan of boiling water. In the heat of the moment, white women devised barbaric forms of punishment that resulted in the mutilation or permanent scarring of the female servants"

(25–26). As Stevenson notes, "public, sadistic maltreatment" of female slaves was intended "to shame them, to strip black women, both privately and pub-licly, of their humanity, femininity, and power (sexual, emotional, and moral) that they held within their families and communities" (194). In other words, such abuse was meant to reduce black women to the physical body at the same time it robbed them of control and ownership of their own corporeality.

As was the case with male slaves, abolitionists sought to highlight the atrocity of the abuse of black women by speaking about it in lectures and depicting it in literature. One such representation is an illustration from George Bourne's *Picture of Slavery in the United States of America* (see figure 13).[3] Here an African American woman, presumably a slave, is tied to a fence, while a white man be-hind her wields a whip with which he is preparing to strike her. Although this scene is shocking enough, additional details compound its horror. First, an-other man, who appears to be voyeuristically witnessing the punishment, can be seen in the near distance. Is he the owner of the slave and the whip-wielding man merely an overseer? Is he a passerby simply taking pleasure in the black woman's humiliation? Or is he the abolitionist himself, witnessing the scene that he will then report back to his fellows in the North? No clues are given as to his identity, yet his voyeurism recalls the background observers in the tattooing scenes discussed in chapter 1. There is no doubt that by watching this scene he is taking part in it, claiming a share in the system (perhaps unwillingly) that al-lows the physical punishment of African American women. Another disturbing element of the background of the illustration is the roof of a home, complete with chimney, visible through the branches of a tree. This home might have re-minded readers that such violence did not take place only in out of the way, un-civilized, undomesticated places; the beating of this woman takes place literally in someone's backyard. The final rhetorical stroke of this seemingly uncompli-cated illustration is Bourne's title: "Flogging American Women." The title very clearly identifies this black woman as an American and therefore indicates the responsibility of every other American to help her and her fellow slaves rather than simply observe them as does the mysterious man in the background of the illustration. "Flogging American Women" also reminds readers that this is not an individual case—she is just one of many *women* who will be whipped and otherwise abused as long as slavery is tolerated in the United States.

In addition to highlighting the physical abuse of female slaves, abolitionists strove to remind their audiences that black women were not entirely defined by their bodies and the labor they performed *or* the punishments they received. Just like white women, they were mothers, daughters, and wives whose famil-ial relationships were insignificant only according to the institution of slavery. In the *Narrative of Sojourner Truth* (1850), for example, Truth and her white

Figure 13. "Flogging American Women." From George Bourne, *Picture of Slavery in the United States of America* (Middletown, Conn.: E. Hunt, 1834).

collaborator, Olive Gilbert, detail Truth's inability to care for her father in his old age because the two slaves have different owners (52). Similarly, when her five- or six-year-old son, Peter, is sold away from her and taken illegally to Alabama, Truth is unable to obtain assistance from her former mistress, who proclaims, "*Ugh!* a *fine* fuss to make about a little *nigger*! Why, haven't you as many of 'em left as you can see to and take care of?" (65). As Elizabeth B. Clark points out, motherhood played an especially important role in abolitionist rhetoric:

> The generic story of the male slave whipped touched a chord with audiences, but few men were likely to find themselves in similar situations. All mothers, though, slave and free, understood danger to their children; the store of harrowing maternal fears could accommodate multiple unlikely variations. Tracts and essays sought to rouse maternal instincts in defense of slave women and children. Mothers who failed to make the connection were admonished point-blank to imagine the sale or murder of their own children. (482–83)

No such admonishment is necessary in Truth's narrative of her reunion with Peter, who has been beaten mercilessly by his master: "She commenced as soon as practicable to examine the boy, and found, to her utter astonishment, that from the crown of his head to the sole of his foot, the callosities and indurations on his entire body were most frightful to behold. His back she described as being like her fingers, as she laid them side by side" (70). Thus physical abuse and motherhood are linked in Truth's inability to protect her son from violence. Perhaps even more unbearable than her inability to protect him is her inability to comfort him after the beatings. "Sometimes," he tells her, "I crawled under the stoop, mammy, the blood running all about me, and my back would stick to the boards; and sometimes Miss Eliza would come and grease my sores, when all were abed and asleep" (71).

Yet as Alison Piepmeier has most recently pointed out, Truth does not allow herself to be framed as a sentimental victim, a helpless black woman who must be saved by the abolitionist (93–94). Although she is assisted by abolitionists in her search for her son, for example, she aggressively pursues this assistance and furthers her search, stating her case boldly to her former mistress, the mother of the man who sold her son, a lawyer, and the Ulster County grand jury. Truth is similarly active when it comes to resisting female helplessness and the un-gendering of the black female slave in her *Narrative* and her public persona. In her "Speech Delivered to the Woman's Rights Convention in Akron, Ohio," in 1859, for example, Truth reminds her listeners that she can be *both* laboring body and mother when she announces, "Look at me! Look at my arm! . . . I have plowed, and planted, and gathered into barns, and no man could head me—and aren't I a woman? I could work as much and eat as much as a man (when I could get it), and bear the lash as well—and aren't I a woman? I have borne thirteen children and seen them almost all sold off into slavery, and when I cried out with a mother's grief, none but Jesus heard—and aren't I a woman?" (26).[4] Truth's claim is reminiscent of her master's claim that "*that* wench . . . is better to me than a *man*—for she will do a good family's washing in the night, and be ready in the morning to go into the field, where she will do as much at raking and binding as my best hands" (*Narrative* 58). Yet Truth's emphasis in the "Speech" on her own family, her own children, rather than on the family of her master (or that family's "washing") is telling. In the "Speech," she distinguishes between the labor that benefits her master (the plowing, planting, and gathering) and the labor that produces her own children, who are then sold away from her. She does not, however, reject the physical and emotional strength gained from all these experiences; this strength, she insists, belongs to her, not to her master or to any white person, and entitles her to both the "woman's rights" and "Negroes' rights" for which she speaks ("Speech" 26).

Truth's display of her own body demonstrates an awareness and subversion of what Nell Irvin Painter calls the "all-too-common exhibition of an undressed black body, with its resonance of the slave auction that undressed women for sale." By inviting her audience to look at her body and by baring her muscular arm and her breast on various occasions, Truth "became a triumph of embodied rhetoric" rather than a passive victim (*Sojourner Truth* 140). Yet paradoxically, some of the very texts that purported to work toward the abolition of slavery and racial prejudice were frequently the ones that perpetuated the image of the passive black female body. Hazel Carby's research has revealed a "conventional portrayal," directly contrasting Truth's performances, "of mothers, sisters, and daughters as victims, of either brutal beatings or sexual abuse" in slave narratives by men. Carby explains:

> The victim appeared not just in her own right as a figure of oppression but was linked to a threat to, or denial of, the manhood of the male slave. Black manhood, in other words, could not be achieved or maintained because of the inability of the slave to protect the black woman in the same manner that convention dictated the inviolability of the body of the white woman. The slave woman, as victim, became defined in terms of a physical exploitation resulting from the lack of the assets of white womanhood: no masculine protector or home or family, the locus of the flowering of white womanhood. (35)

Slave narratives such as that of Frederick Douglass frequently describe the beating of black women slaves to which black men feel impotent to respond. Writing about his childhood, for example, Douglass recalls, "I have often been awakened at the dawn of day by the most heart-rending shrieks of an own aunt of mine, whom [Master] used to tie up to a joist, and whip upon her naked back till she was literally covered with blood. . . . The louder she screamed, the harder he whipped; and where the blood ran fastest, there he whipped longest." For Douglass, seeing his aunt brutally whipped by his master "was the blood-stained gate, the entrance to the hell of slavery, through which I was about to pass" (539). Douglass's Aunt Hester is a victim whose abuse highlights her own lack of agency but also, more importantly, that of Douglass himself. As Jeannine DeLombard points out, this scene is crucial to Douglass' narrative because "not only does this scene introduce the young slave to the identification of blackness with abject corporeality under slavery, but it demonstrates how the feminization of blackness serves to ungender and thus to dehumanize the enslaved male body" (259). Thus the primary concern here is Douglass's gender, not that of his aunt.

The abolitionist legacy was crucial to Hopkins's commitment to racial uplift as well as to her depiction of the slaveholding South in the first part of *Contending Forces*. Will Smith, the hero of the second half of the novel, might be speaking for Hopkins herself when he says, "As the anti-slavery apostles went everywhere, preaching the word fifty years before emancipation, *so must we do today*" (272). According to Carby, "The history of abolition was a consistent reference point for Hopkins; the possibility of the revival of such a force for political change was the source of her political optimism" (121). Especially relevant in this regard is the work of Lydia Maria Child, for whom Hopkins had so much respect that she published a three-part biographical sketch and selection of her letters in the *Colored American Magazine* in 1903. In the first installment of this series, Hopkins "thank[s] God for the inspiration of [Child's] example, founded on the great law of love and the brotherhood of man" ("Reminiscences" 279–80). And in the last, she insists, "Were [Child] living to-day, her trenchent [*sic*] pen would do us yeoman's service in the vexed question of disfranchisement and equality for the Afro-American" (454).

Yet Hopkins also insisted on interrogating the shortcomings of the white abolitionist legacy, and she would have agreed with her contemporary Victoria Earle Matthews that African American women needed to reclaim their right to represent their own particular experiences of oppression. Just a few years prior to the publication of *Contending Forces*, Matthews delivered a speech in which she insisted, "It is not within the power of anyone who has stood outside of Afro-American life to adequately estimate the extent of the effacement and debasement, and, therefore, of the gracious awakening . . . of the womanhood of our land" (149). Standing outside, Matthews seems to argue, does not allow for the vision or the experience that would produce an accurate assessment or representation of "Afro-American life." Yet representations of the "effacement and debasement" of African American womanhood were central to abolitionist literature, particularly as written by white women, and were often politically effective. As one of Child's most powerful short stories demonstrates, however, abolitionist fiction frequently used the same narrative patterns that Carby identified in male slave narratives, thus limiting the agency and "the gracious awakening" of black women.

Child's "Slavery's Pleasant Homes: A Faithful Sketch" (1843) begins with an interesting departure from most antebellum domestic fiction. The black slave, Rosa, is constructed as the ideal woman, physically robust as well as morally pure. She is described as "a young girl, elegantly formed, and beautiful as a dark velvet carnation. The blush, so easily excited, shone through the transparent brown of her smooth cheek, like claret through a bottle in the sunshine" (238). Rosa's vitality is "a beautiful contrast" to her mistress, Marion, who "was a pretty waxen little plaything, as fragile and as delicate as the white Petunia blossom" (238). Child's characterizations of Rosa and Marion rely on the notion that black women, no matter how light their complexion, are physically stronger than white women. Yet Rosa is both beautiful *and* light skinned enough that the blush can be seen on her cheek. Also essential is the fact that Rosa *does* blush, as every virtuous young woman should, that slavery has not corrupted her and made her wise beyond her years. As Carolyn Sorisio explains, many nineteenth-century scientists thought that "maternal and sexual qualities were racially determined characteristics" (34). Proslavery physician and author John H. Van Evrie, for example, used sentimental rhetoric to insist that the white woman's "blush of maiden modesty" was a sign of her natural purity. He questioned the black woman's morality because of her supposed inability to blush: "Can any one suppose such a thing possible to a black face? . . . And if the latter cannot reflect these things in her face—if her features are utterly incapable of expressive emotions so elevated and beautiful, is it not certain that she is without them—that they have no existence in her inner being, are no portion of her moral nature?" (qtd. in Sorisio 34–35). Because Rosa's blush directly contradicts Van Evrie's argument, Child creates room for sympathetic identification with her African American character. The potential for exploitation, for corruption, is hinted at and perhaps foretold in Rosa's skin color, however, despite her blush. As Karen Sanchez-Eppler has noted of a similar character, "as the child of sexual exploitation, she has inherited the role of being exploited. Her body displays not only a history of past miscegenation but also a promise of future mixings" (34). Thus Rosa's body quickly emerges as a contradictory text within the opening paragraphs of "Slavery's Pleasant Homes."

When Marion marries the wealthy Frederic Dalcho, she brings Rosa with her to her new home. There Rosa meets George, "the handsome quadroon brother of Frederic Dalcho, and his favorite slave," with whom she falls in love and marries (239). Yet Frederic also notices Rosa and, despite her marriage to his half brother, forces her to succumb to a sexual relationship with him. Although Rosa is entirely the victim in this relationship, both Marion and George initially feel betrayed by and angry with her for her affair with Frederic and both physically abuse her. Marion, who has heard her husband's voice in Rosa's room in the middle of the night, pretends to be angry with Rosa over a poorly tied shoe and strikes her. Immediately after the blow, she apologizes; the two women admit their misery and cry in each other's arms, "but neither sought any further to learn the other's secrets" (240). Similarly, when Rosa looks to her husband George for sympathy, "he flung her from him, with so much force that she reeled against the wall. 'Oh, George,' said she, with bitter anguish, 'what *can* I do? I am his *slave*.' The justice of her plea, and the pathos of her tones, softened his heart. He placed her head on his shoulder, and said more kindly, 'Keep out of his way, dear Rosa; keep out of his way' " (240). Rejected by both her mistress and her husband, offered silence by one and useless advice by the other, Rosa attempts to avoid Frederic but is repeatedly beaten for her disobedience: "[O]ne severe flogging succeeded another, till the tenderly-nurtured slave fainted under the cruel infliction, which was rendered doubly dangerous by the delicate state of her health. Maternal pains came on prematurely, and she died a few hours after" (240–41).[5] In the remainder of the story, George kills his master, confesses the crime when another man is about to be hanged for it, and is put to death.

Child concludes by lamenting the way in which George's death is reported in the newspapers, both North and South: "Not one was found to tell how the slave's young wife had been torn from him by his own brother, and murdered with slow tortures. Not one recorded the heroism that would not purchase life by another's death. . . . His very *name* was left unmentioned; he was only Mr. Dalcho's *slave!*" (242). Child accurately points out the silences in newspaper accounts of slave rebellions, but it is important to note that "Slavery's Pleasant Homes" replicates the narrative pattern of male slave narratives in which women are portrayed unequivocally as victims. Therefore, although the story critiques the cultural silencing of Rosa's desires in favor of those of her master and her mistress, Child herself positions Rosa as the victim of Frederic, Marion, *and* George and as the inspiration for George's act of rebellion and the assertion of his manhood rather than as an agent in her own right.

Although it is impossible to see Rosa as anything other than a victim, it is important to recognize that she is victimized in multiple ways throughout the story. Rosa's vulnerability to sexual abuse is indeed central to the narrative. Her death, her marriage to a man she loves, and her resistance to committing adultery confirm her victim status as well as her virtuous character and position her as a "true woman" who would die rather than endure sexual abuse. Granted, such representations of African American women were uncommon in the antebellum period. As Frances Smith Foster explains, the black woman's "ability to survive degradation was her downfall. As victim she became the assailant, since her submission to repeated violations was not in line with the values of sentimental heroines who died rather than be abused. Her survival of these ordeals and continued participation in other aspects of slave life seemed to connote, if not outright licentiousness, at least a less sensitive and abused spirit than that of white heroines" (131). Even though Rosa has already been raped by Frederic, Child insists that she remains virtuous at (and because of) her death; unlike the seduction novel heroine of the late eighteenth and early nineteenth centuries, Rosa is an unwilling partner and her virtue therefore untainted. This radical argument was developed further in Harriet Jacobs's *Incidents in the Life of a Slave Girl* (1861), which Child edited. Yet because of the autobiographical nature of Jacobs's narrative, Jacobs's survival of her own sexual experience necessitates the survival of her character, Linda Brent. Fictional characters, such as Child's Rosa, were more likely to die after sexual activity, and that death carried significant symbolic potential.

Yet Rosa's physical vulnerability is at least as important as her sexual vulnerability. When Frederic cannot have Rosa, he whips her in an attempt to show her how "unprotected" she really is and to force her to turn to him in order to survive. It is by beating her—*not* by raping her—that he robs her of the husband and unborn child who have confirmed her womanhood. Marion and George cannot protect Rosa from Frederic's sexual *and* physical abuse, but they are also guilty of taking advantage of her vulnerability—her "unprotected female flesh"—to express their own jealousy as well as their frustration (ironically, at least in part, with their inability to protect her). These attacks reinforce and compound her vulnerability, leaving her completely exposed to Frederic's desires.

Despite her repeated beatings, however, Rosa does not survive to develop scars on her "beautiful," "transparent" skin; her scars, like the child within her, are only partly formed when she dies. To convince her readers of Rosa's virtue and femininity, Child doesn't allow her to survive the "ungendering" of her beating or her miscarriage. Rosa's death contradicts earlier descriptions of her physical vitality but also—and for Child, more importantly—emphasizes her spiritual and moral purity, essential elements of nineteenth-century true womanhood.[6] Like Hopkins, Child might have seen "Slavery's Pleasant Homes" as her attempt to "raise the stigma" of black womanhood, but she achieves this goal only by erasing the body of her heroine, both literally and figuratively. Unfortunately, evidence of Frederic Dalcho's crime—and the legacy of rape and sexual exploitation inherited by Rosa—dies with her. Marion remains the only witness to her husband's wrongdoings, and the likelihood of her testimony is indicated by her disappearance from the narrative immediately after the death of her husband.

This is not to suggest, however, that slave women never survive to bear scars in abolitionist fiction. Yet unlike the beautiful Rosa or even Stowe's own George Harris, the scarred female slaves in *Uncle Tom's Cabin* are grotesque figures whose very visible, very vulnerable bodies evoke a complex mixture of disgust and sympathy in the reader. Stowe must separate this representation from that of the beautiful mulatta, whose sexual abuse can apparently be transcended in a way that physical abuse cannot.

The most striking example of the marked black woman in *Uncle Tom's Cabin* is Prue, a slave who belongs to a neighbor of the St. Clares. Prue is described as a "tall, bony colored woman," who has "a peculiar scowling expression of countenance, and sullen, grumbling voice" (186). She acknowledges her grotesque appearance, calling herself "a poor, old, cut-up critter" and insisting that her unpleasant exterior reflects interior shortcomings as well: "I's ugly,—I's wicked,—I's gwine straight to torment" (186, 188). To her fellow slaves, Prue represents the horror, the complete abjection, to which any of them may be subject at any moment. Rather than feeling pity for her, however, several other slaves mock her and reprimand her for drinking despite her constant reiteration of the wish that she were dead and out of her misery (186). One slave, whose master is far kinder than Prue's, calls her a "[d]isgusting old beast," and insists "If I was her master, I'd cut her up worse than she is." "[Y]e couldn't do that ar, no ways," says Dinah, another slave. "Her back's a far sight now,—she can't never get a dress together over it" (187). Despite this knowledge, the "pert chambermaid," Jane, continues to be repulsed by Prue and proclaims that "such low creatures ought not to be allowed to go round to genteel families" (186–87). Prue's despondent responses to the theft of her children and the constant physical abuse to which she has been subjected have made her "disgusting" to both whites and blacks, who see her behavior as justification for further abuse rather than sympathy.

True to Spillers's theory about "unprotected female flesh," Prue has been "ungendered" by oppression, and her body becomes a grotesque parody of the ideal female body: she is prevented from assuming the role of mother to her children, and her body is literally covered with wounds and scars. The scars on Prue's back even prevent her from closing her dress over her shoulders, thereby limiting any claim she has to the requisite modesty of femininity. Ultimately, Prue is whipped to death; the woman who replaces Prue tells Dinah, "[S]he got drunk agin,—and they had her down cellar,—and thar they left her all day,—and I hearn 'em saying that the *flies had got to her,*—and *she's dead!*" (190). Even in death Prue is reduced to the grotesque—a mere piece of flesh on which insects feed. Although Prue's life and death are similar to that of Child's Rosa in important ways—the lack of protection for both her and her children, death from a series of violent floggings—sentimental identification with Prue is much more difficult than with Rosa. Unlike Rosa, Prue is not attractive or educated. She is simply described as "colored," and her ability or inability to blush is of little consequence. Most importantly, Prue survives a number of beatings prior to her death and develops emotional and physical scars that disfigure her and distort the ways in which others regard her and her experiences.

Other women characters in *Uncle Tom's Cabin* are able to escape and survive slavery—Eliza, Cassy, and Emmeline are all beautiful, light-skinned slaves who manage to outsmart their owners and gain their liberty. Yet although these characters are separated from their families and abused sexually, none of them is physically abused, and none bears scars similar to those of Prue. They not only survive but become newly domesticated, virtuous women upon escaping from slavery. Even Cassy, who has conspired to murder the white man who had forced her to become his mistress, becomes a new woman simply by being reunited with her family. At the end of the novel, the narrator explains, "And, indeed, in two or three days, such a change has passed over Cassy, that our readers would scarcely know her. The despairing, haggard expression of her face had given way to one of gentle trust. She seemed to sink, at once, into the bosom of the family, and to take the little ones into her heart as something for which it long had waited. . . . Cassy yielded at once, and with her whole soul, to every good influence, and became a devout and tender Christian" (373). The transformation of Cassy is physical as well as spiritual and emotional; as she regains her natural role as Christian matriarch, the "despairing, haggard expression of her face" disappears, and she becomes a new woman. Cassy's despair, which appears to be etched into her face, is nowhere near as permanent or as difficult to transcend as the inscription of scars on the body of a woman like Prue. The redemption of the grotesque black woman, then, was more difficult than that of the sexually abused mulatta and would remain an issue after the Civil War, particularly for African American women seeking to write the black female body out of the many stereotypes still binding it.

Grace Montfort and the Physical Inscription of Race

Although Hopkins admired the work of white abolitionist writers such as Child, she clearly agreed with Victoria Earle Matthews that only African Americans could produce an honest portrait of their own community. In the preface to *Contending Forces*, she insists, "*No one will do this for us; we must ourselves develop the men and women who will faithfully portray the inmost thoughts and feelings of the Negro with all the fire and romance that lie dormant in our history*, and, as yet, unrecognized by writers of the Anglo-Saxon race" (14, emphasis in original). Hopkins answers her own call to action in this novel by tracing the "growth and development" of the black woman throughout American history and separating her narrative into two parts: the first, which takes place in the antebellum South, and the second, set in the post-Reconstruction North. To fully understand the discussion of the embodied nature of black female subjectivity, one must address both sections of the novel.[7]

Although the main action of *Contending Forces* takes place at the end of the nineteenth century, the novel opens with "a retrospect of the past" on which the rest of the narrative depends (17). This retrospect features Charles Montfort, a British slaveholder living in Bermuda who transports his slaves to the American South after Great Britain's adoption of a bill of gradual emancipation. Montfort is represented as typical of white slave-owning men, "neither a cruel man, nor an avaricious one; but like all men in commercial life, or traders doing business in their own productions, he lost sight of the individual right or wrong of the matter, or we might say with more truth, that he perverted right to be what was conducive to his own interests" (22). The Montforts are initially embraced by the planter class in their new North Carolina home. Their idyllic existence is disrupted, however, by Hank Davis and Bill Sampson, lower-class white men who are jealous of the Montforts' good fortune, and the lustful Anson Pollock, an upper-class landowner who is "determin[ed] to possess the lovely Grace Montfort at all hazards" (45). Pollock and his accomplices spread rumors that Montfort intends to free his slaves and, perhaps a more unforgivable sin in the antebellum South, that his wife, Grace, has African blood in her veins. The latter rumor originates with Sampson, who observes the Montforts entering Pamlico Sound and tells Hank "that thet ar female's got a black streak in her somewhar" (41). The rumors about Grace's ancestry effectively cast doubt on her racial identity independent of any factual evidence. Sampson's self-professed ability to discern blackness in Grace's "creamy" skin ("of the tint of the camellia") is enough to render her vulnerable (40).

Even though "[e]veryone voted her the dearest and most beautiful woman they had ever known," Grace's presumed blackness renders her helpless when Pollock and his men unexpectedly invade her home and murder her husband (45). "Mrs. Montfort's arms were grasped by rude hands," Hopkins writes, "and she was forcibly drawn out upon the verandah, where in the sunlight of the beautiful morning she saw the body of her husband lying face downward. She was dimly conscious of hearing the cries of frightened slaves mingled with the screams of her children. Through it all she realized but two things—that the lifeless object lying there so still was the body of her husband, and that the sensual face of Anson Pollock, whom she had grown to loathe and fear, was gloating over her agony, devilish in its triumph" (67). Faced with the death of Charles and completely at the mercy of Pollock, Grace faints, reviving only when she is being bound to the whipping post in preparation for a flogging.

Hopkins's detailed description of this whipping has played a major role in critical readings of *Contending Forces* and is therefore worth quoting at length:

> [Grace] was bound to the whipping post as the victim to the stake, and lashed with rawhides alternately by the two strong, savage men. Hank Davis drew first blood. . . . With all his mighty strength he brought the lash down upon the frail and shrinking form. O God! Was there none to save her! The air whistled as the snaky leather thong curled and writhed in its rapid, vengeful descent. A shriek from the victim—a spurt of blood that spattered the torturer—a long, raw gash across a tender, white back. Hank gazed at the cut with critical satisfaction, as he compared its depth with the skin and blood that encased the long, tapering lash. It was now Bill's turn.
>
> "I'll go you one better," he said, as he sighted the distance and exact place to make his mark with mathematical precision. . . . Again the rawhide whistled through the air, falling across the other cut squarely in the center. Another shriek, a stifled sob, a long-drawn quivering sigh—then the deep stillness of unconsciousness. Again and again was the outrage repeated. Fainting fit followed fainting fit. The blood stood in a pool about her feet.
>
> When Hank Davis had satiated his vengeful thirst, he cut the ropes which bound her, and she sank upon the ground again—unconscious, bleeding, friendless, alone. (68–70)

As in "Slavery's Pleasant Homes," the beating of Hopkins's heroine signifies her lack of protection and her subsequent vulnerability to abuse. Grace's status within her community depends entirely on her husband, whose racial identity and wealth provide her with a claim to privileged white womanhood. When her husband becomes a "lifeless object," Grace, too, is objectified against her will. Bound to the whipping post, she is entirely a victim, like Rosa, ultimately speechless and powerless.

Following the lead of Carby, critics generally read Grace's whipping as a rape.[8] Carby writes:

> In a graphic and tortured two-page scene, Hopkins represented the brutal rape of Grace in the displaced form of a whipping by two of the vigilantes. Her clothes were ripped from her body, and she was "whipped" alternately "by the two strong,

savage men." Hopkins's metaphoric replacement of the "snaky, leather thong" for the phallus was a crude but effective device, and "the blood [which] stood in a pool about her feet" was the final evidence that the "outrage" that had been committed was rape. (132)

Carby's reading of this scene is important in that it highlights the sexual elements of flogging, particularly for black women; these elements were present in Child's "Slavery's Pleasant Homes," and Hopkins's language certainly suggests that she regards the whipping of the black female body as a form of sexual violation. Yet Carby's paradigm conflates physical and sexual abuse, which Spillers warns against, and ignores the particularity of physical abuse. Allison Berg, on the other hand, quite accurately calls this whipping "a slave-branding" and goes on to point out that Hank and Bill "lay claim to Grace by marking her with visible lines of blood. Her allegedly black blood externalized and literalized— the racial privilege suggested by her 'tender *white* back' overwritten by marks testifying to her racial difference—Grace becomes wholly identified with the 'contaminated' bloodline that both motivates and justifies their actions" (134). Grace's blood thus appears to confirm the truth of Sampson's initial vision of her, yet the real truth is that no other resolution to this scene is possible. Paradoxically, Grace is abused because she is black, but she is also black because she is abused—the actual color of her skin appears to be irrelevant. The cuts on her back, then, are examined with satisfaction as evidence of the reestablishment of order in Newbern, North Carolina—order disrupted by the arrival of the Montforts with their suspicious racial heritage and unorthodox beliefs about slavery. Grace's whipping results in the revelation of her blood, which marks her as black, while Hank and Bill's power over her reinforces their own identities as white men, no matter what their social status within the white community.

That Grace's whipping is depicted in an illustration confirms this point's importance to the novel; it is one of just eight illustrations in *Contending Forces* (see figure 14). The illustration appears as a frontispiece, directly opposite the title page and just following a photograph of Hopkins herself. Somewhat reminiscent of "Flogging American Women" from Bourne's *Picture of Slavery in the United States of America*, the drawing depicts Grace Montfort, Hank Davis, and Bill Sampson in the moment after Grace is cut down from the whipping post.[9] The two men stand over Grace, holding their whips, their faces shaded by broad-brimmed hats. One looks down at the whip in his hand, but the other looks directly at his victim. Grace lies on the ground facing away from the audience, her dress around her waist, her back striped by marks from the whips. Blood pools at her side. The most striking part of the illustration is the whiteness of Grace's skin, surpassed only by a white garment wrapped around her waist. Grace's skin, at least as white as that of her captors, is emphasized in contrast to the dark ground on which she lies as well as to her dark hair and clothing.

Following the lead of Berg, I suggest that the disfigurement of Grace's back and her position on the ground mark her as black and as a slave despite her fair skin. In this sense, she is similar to the contraband Gordon discussed in chapter 4 and Robert of "My Contraband." No matter what her racial identity and social status before she is violated by Pollock's flunkies, Grace effectively *becomes* black while she is tied to the whipping post. Although the rumors raise suspicions about Grace's racial heritage, it is only through the murder of her patriarchal protector and the utter disregard for her flesh that she is violently marked as black and regarded as such by her community. The "conquering gaze" of her abuser, represented in the illustration, confirms her racial identity as well as his own powers of vision. Grace's inability to employ an "oppositional gaze" is symbolized by the way she is positioned in the illustration; turned away from her persecutors as well as the audience, Grace is clearly bereft of any power, visual or otherwise.

Carby argues that Hopkins did not intend for her readers to know definitively whether or not Grace Montfort was actually a black woman: "The readers were left to guess her actual heritage; what was important was that the suspicion of black blood was enough cause for the ostracism of the whole family and Grace Montfort's transition from the pedestal of virtue to the illicit object of the sexual desire of a local landowner, Anson Pollock" (131). I agree with Carby that the social and physical marking of Grace as black is more important than her actual heritage.[10] Yet the hint of Grace's blackness should not be so quickly disregarded. Unlike most critics of *Contending Forces*, I do not see Grace as a completely unproblematic figure, reduced to an object through no fault of her own. Clearly no woman, white or black, deserves such treatment. As Hopkins makes clear in her novel, however, it is crucial that we recognize Grace's complicity in the very system that subjects her to abuse and eventually drives her to suicide.[11] Child's "Slavery's Pleasant Homes" highlighted the white woman's role in the institution of slavery, but Hopkins takes this one step further by effectively transforming the plantation mistress into a black woman and having her experience the physical and sexual abuse particular to black female slaves.

Hopkins is perhaps most explicit about the issue of complicity in and responsibility for the institution of slavery in her discussion of Grace's husband, Charles. She explains:

> Nature avenges herself upon us for every law violated in the mad rush for wealth
> or position or personal comfort where the rights of others of the human family

Figure 14. "He cut the ropes that bound her, and she sank upon the ground again."
From Pauline E. Hopkins, *Contending Forces: A Romance Illustrative of Negro Life
North and South* (Boston, Mass.: Colored Co-operative Publishing, 1900). Courtesy
of the Library of Congress.

are not respected. If Charles Montfort had been contented to accept the rulings of the English Parliament, and had allowed his human property to come under the new laws just made for its government, although poorer in the end, he would have spared himself and family all the horrors which were to follow his selfish flight to save that property. (65)

Yet while the decision to leave Bermuda with his slaves is Charles's, his wife makes the decision to accompany him; in the first chapter of the novel, Charles tells a friend that Grace "has had her choice, but prefers hardships with me to life without me" (29). Although the Montforts are represented as particularly generous slave owners who plan someday to free their slaves, they still have a whipping post on their plantation at least a year after assuming the property; this whipping post ironically becomes the scene of Grace's beating. In addition, Grace does not simply benefit from the labor of her husband's slaves. Her intimate connection to the institution is exemplified in her relationship with her "foster sister," Lucy, who was raised as Grace's slave despite Hopkins's assurance that "[t]heir relations had always been those of inseparable friends rather than of mistress and slave" (46). This assurance is belied by the fact that Grace calls Lucy by her first name only, whereas Lucy calls Grace "Miss Grace" (46). Married to a white slave owner and the owner of at least one slave herself, Grace, like Child's Marion, is undoubtedly complicit in the institution of slavery; she is the embodiment of true *white* womanhood, particularly as the stereotype necessitated a willful ignorance of political and social realities as well as women's collusion in them.

Given Hopkins's desire to turn the tables on white Americans, showing them their responsibility for the horrors of slavery, Grace's transformation into a black woman seems particularly fitting. As a black female slave, she must endure unwanted sexual attention, like Rosa; and like Sojourner Truth and Prue, she must be denied her children and her own role as mother. Indeed, the "mingl[ing]" of "the cries of frightened slaves" with "the screams of [Grace's] children," which she hears just before she is tied to the whipping post, can be read as the transformation of the Montfort sons into slaves themselves. (Both boys are sold into slavery after Grace's death.) Yet the cries of the slaves can also be seen as a mocking reminder of the violence done to slaves within the very institution that has sustained Grace as the epitome of true womanhood. Although Grace is admittedly a more sympathetic character than her husband, it is possible that Hopkins intends the whipping as a punishment for Grace's abuse of power rather than for her (supposed) black blood. Throughout this scene, Grace resists the enforced shift from white to black, mistress to slave, and ultimately kills herself rather than survive without the recognition of the society that has robbed her of her husband and her children as well as her status as privileged white woman. Unable to deal with the shifting identities produced by the open wounds on her back, Grace drowns herself, and her place as Pollock's mistress is filled by her slave, Lucy. Like Child's Rosa, Grace dies without giving herself the chance to develop scars, to survive atrocity and nurture herself and her children through the trials to come. Lucy, on the other hand, does not die until long after the Civil War; she lives to be at least one hundred years old and dies while living with her daughter and granddaughter in Bermuda. Just prior to her death, she provides crucial eyewitness testimony to the murder of Charles Montfort, thus ensuring that his descendants will inherit his fortune.

Sappho Clark and the Redemption of the Marked Body

It is possible to read Grace's death as similar to that of Rosa in "Slavery's Pleasant Homes." Following the lead of Frances Smith Foster, Venetria Patton notes, "By leaving Grace's ancestry ambiguous, Hopkins opens up the possibility that a black woman could not survive such a vicious attack. This would go against popular racist beliefs that justified the atrocities of slavery by the fact that the slaves could endure them" (112). Yet the remainder of Hopkins's novel, which takes place almost one hundred years later, confirms her investment in the survival of African American women and opens Grace's death—and the popular abolitionist trope of the dead mulatta—up to criticism.[12] This survival requires a redefinition of black womanhood in the late nineteenth century and a renegotiation of the connection between corporeality and identity. Mrs. Willis, Hopkins's representation of black women's commitment to racial uplift, refers to just such a renegotiation when she tells her female audience, "Thirty-five years of liberty have made us a new people. The marks of servitude and oppression are dropping slowly from us; let us hasten the transformation of the body by the nobility of the soul" (153).

The second part of Contending Forces is set in the late nineteenth century and recounts the post-Reconstruction experiences of the Montforts' descendents, the Smiths. Sappho Clark is a beautiful, mysterious young woman who boards with the Smiths. At first glance, Sappho seems to be anything but a marked woman; in fact, she hardly appears to be "marked" as an African American woman. A classic beauty, like Grace Montfort, she is "[t]all and fair, with hair of a golden cast, aquiline nose, rosebud mouth, soft brown eyes veiled by long, dark lashes which swept her cheek, just now covered with a delicate rose flush" (107). Yet Hopkins insists that Sappho is a "woman with a story written on her face" (89). Indeed, the young woman has a history of sexual abuse and a young child, both of which she attempts to hide from the Smith family in order to pass as unmarked. When Sappho and Will Smith fall in love, however, Sappho runs away rather than lie to him about her past and trick him into marriage with a "fallen woman," as she sees herself. As the story unfolds throughout the novel, readers learn along with the Smiths that Sappho is actually Mabelle Beaubean, a mixed-blood woman who was raised in a wealthy Louisiana home. Mabelle's white uncle had pretended friendship for her but eventually kidnapped the girl, raped her, and left her in a brothel in New Orleans. Rescued by a family friend, Mabelle was taken to a convent, where it was believed she died in childbirth.

Given that Hopkins's novel is written and set amidst an era of African American resistance to the politically motivated lynchings of black men (and some black women), Mabelle's rape must be read within this context. Had she been a white woman, her rape would have sparked a violent response against the black community and the man responsible. Although such violence would not have been sanctioned formally, it would have gone relatively unaddressed by any court or officer of the law. Yet no matter how light her skin, Mabelle is not a white woman; she is an African American woman and is, therefore, absent from the lynching paradigm that takes into account only the actions and reactions of three individuals: the white woman, the black man, and the white man. As Sandra Gunning observes, "[I]n white supremacist thinking black women are invisible and their experience of lynching and rape completely denied" (76).[13]

Yet it is not just in the white community that Mabelle's voice is silenced. Sappho's hidden past is first related in a meeting of the American Colored League, held to address the problem of lynching. Angered by earlier speakers' desires to placate white politicians, a delegate named Luke Sawyer stands up to testify to his own experiences with racial oppression and violence. Both of the stories he tells involve the physical and sexual abuse of black women as well as the silencing of these women by both the violence itself and the conventions of the lynching narrative that are ultimately—and ironically—quite similar to those of the male slave narrative. In the first story, Sawyer's family is murdered in the middle of the night by a group of vigilante white men; these men "whipped my mother and sister," Sawyer explains, "and otherwise abused them so that they died next day" (257). Sawyer's second story is that of Mabelle/Sappho, but the expectations for this story have already been established in the first. A raped black woman dies, end of story. Although the stories do focus on the violated woman and the crime that has been committed against her, the most sympathetic figure in the scene is Sawyer himself, denied the opportunity to protect the "female flesh" entrusted to him. When "in order to destroy [her] identity" "the good Sisters" of the convent give out the story that Mabelle has died, the rumor is not difficult to believe because it seems to be the only script available to the raped black woman (328–29). Because Sappho lives, she must find another framework for her story that will allow her to deal with what Lois Lamphere Brown has called the "emotional scars" of her sexual abuse (61).[14]

Brown follows Hopkins's lead in the use of this metaphor; Hopkins herself recognizes the parallels between Grace's whipping and Sappho's rape, tying the two together through the metaphor of scarring. At the end of the novel, she writes: "Innocent or guilty, our deeds done in the flesh pursue us with relentless vigor unto the end of life. Sometimes the rough winds of adversity are tempered to the shorn lamb who is not responsible for the acts which are forced upon him; God in infinite wisdom and justice remits the severity of our sufferings; but the tracings still remain upon the sands of life—we bind up the wounds—they heal, but the scars remain" (341). The scars that Sappho bears are those of Grace Montfort as well; whether physical or sexual or both, they are the mark of "sexual compromises, illicit desires, and dishonored family bonds" that form the particular burden of African American women during and after slavery (L. L. Brown 54). They are a symbol of black women's vulnerability to the abuse that marks them as less than woman, less than *human*, in a white patriarchal culture. They are also indicative of the physical and emotional tearing of children away from their mothers throughout *Contending Forces*. Although Sappho's scars are distinctly metaphorical, in making such a gesture—similar, perhaps, to Stoddard's metaphorical transformation of Cassandra Morgeson's scars into tattoos—Hopkins powerfully overturns the narrative violence of the denial or the removal of the mark detailed elsewhere in this study. Regarding scars as signs of healing, Hopkins textually inscribes them onto Sappho's body precisely because they symbolize the survival of trauma. As in Stoddard's novel *The Morgesons*, the scarred female body, rather than being an object of shame, is instead a source of pride and power that an individual woman can pass on to her community.

Unlike Grace and other fictional black women whose bodies are violated, Sappho lives to bear her scars; she survives the rape, the loss of her family, and the destruction of her identity by the well-meaning sisters of the convent. Indeed, in direct contrast to the nuns, Hopkins demonstrates that it is only through the revival of Sappho's identity as a black woman that she can be redeemed, and she frames Sappho's restoration using religious rhetoric. This framing effectively ties the two sections of *Contending Forces* together insofar as African American employment of Christian discourse is a reclamation of the very concepts that were frequently used to justify the existence of slavery. As Joycelyn Moody points out, "the proponents of slavery did not count on Africans in turn using Christianity to interpret the bondage in which they found themselves," or, for that matter, to interpret their own oppression in the postslavery United States (x).

Throughout *Contending Forces*, Sappho is compared to a number of religious figures: an "angel" (349), a "martyr" (358), and even Mary, the virgin mother of Christ (386–87). The most important of these associations, however, and the one most prevalent in the novel, is that of Sappho Clark with Jesus Christ. In a passage reminiscent of Hopkins's condemnation of Charles Montfort for disrespecting "the rights of others of the human family" (65), Sappho is absolved of responsibility for her rape and pregnancy and also positioned as a Christ figure: "We may right a wrong, but we cannot restore our victim to his primeval state of happiness. Something is lost that can never be regained. The wages of sin is death. Innocent or guilty, the laws of nature are immutable. So with shoulders bent and mis-shapen with heavy burdens, the Negro plods along bearing his cross—carrying *the sins of others*" (332, emphasis in original). Like Christ, "the Negro" in general and Sappho in particular are destined by society to pay for others' actions, despite their own innocence. Sappho's cross is not her own sin, as she has been led to believe, but the sins of others, those who have violated her mind and body. Hopkins confirms Sappho's absolution and redemption in the Easter reconciliation scene between Will and Sappho, which decidedly marks Sappho's affinity to Christ as the most important of the religious references in *Contending Forces* and also implies that Sappho is reborn through her love for Will. Indeed, after Will and Sappho are reunited and happily agree to marry, "Sappho was welcomed right royally by Doctor Lewis, Dora and her mother, as one risen from the dead" (394).

Sappho's status as risen Christ figure, however, does not negate the body or erase it as did Christ figures in abolitionist fiction, the most famous of which is Harriet Beecher Stowe's Uncle Tom. The emphasis in Hopkins's scenario is on resurrection and rebirth rather than suffering and death. Restitution for suffering at the hands of others is made on earth rather than in heaven, and Hopkins's Christ figure ends the novel as an embodied woman rather than as a transcendent spirit. Carby writes, "A desire for a pure black womanhood, an uncolonized black female body, was the false hope of Sappho's pretense. The only possible future for her black womanhood was through a confrontation with, not denial of, her history" (144). This history is both personal and collective—Mabelle's rape and subsequent silencing and the abuse of black women slaves as represented by Grace and Lucy. By confronting her history, Sappho is allowed to be both mother and wife. And as Kate McCullough notes, "Hopkins certainly represents Sappho as bearing erotic desire for Will, the hero marked by the narrative as Sappho's rightful husband. In the end Hopkins sanctions that desire by bringing the two together in marriage" (32–33).[15] Thus Sappho is rewarded for carrying the cross of others' sins—not just by the removal of the cross but by the fulfillment of her physical and emotional desires in marriage. As a black woman, Sappho continues to be vulnerable to the mark; yet married to Will and, more importantly, restored to the African American community, Sappho is no longer unprotected female flesh.

As risen Christ figure and a reincarnation of sorts of Grace Montfort, Sappho bears the scars, the stigmata, with which Grace was unable to live. Her scars testify both to her struggles and to her redemption—of her body, her sexuality, and her right to a loving relationship and a fulfilling life. Ultimately, they highlight the presence of the black women in the lynch narrative as well as the efforts of the black community to heal the wounds caused by physical and sexual violence. Grace's name points toward her womanly charm but also indicates that through divine assistance she is set aside for some holy purpose despite her own sin. Sappho as Christ figure is the embodiment of God's "grace," bringing together the divine and the mortal, the spiritual and corporeal, elements of Grace's own fragmented life.

Sappho as Christ figure allows me to come full circle to Hopkins's claim to "raise the stigma of degradation from [her] race" (13). Read in multiple ways— as a mark of shame, as a representation of the physical abuse of slaves, as a physical manifestation of the emulation of Christ and the forgiveness of Christianity, and as a call to action—the stigma is central to Hopkins's representation of the past, the present, and the future for African American women in *Contending Forces*. The scarred female body carried such weight for the African American woman, however, that even Hopkins can address it only metaphorically, and despite the use of the scar as metaphor, Sappho is still familiar as the sexually violated mulatta who is redeemed by love and family. Yet Hopkins comes closer than any of her predecessors to creating a black female heroine and a black community that learn how to survive and accommodate the scars of slavery and racial oppression. Unlike Child's Rosa, Sappho will survive to commit herself to her family and her race. The death of the marked black woman simply could not be an option outside abolitionist fiction if, as Hopkins's contemporary Anna Julia Cooper insisted, "Negro womanhood" was "an essential fundamental for the elevation of the race" at the turn of the twentieth century (68).

Epilogue

Tattooed Ladies

◯◯◯ Irene Woodward, the "tattooed lady" who appeared on stage just weeks after the debut of Nora Hildebrandt, told the *New York Times* that she had decided to exhibit herself after seeing Captain Costentenus, the man who claimed he had been forcibly tattooed by indigenous women while being held captive. While it is not clear exactly what it was about Costentenus's performance that inspired Woodward, it is likely that his one thousand dollar a week salary had something to do with it. As Margot Mifflin, author of *Bodies of Subversion: A Secret History of Women and Tattoo*, observes, "As the popularity of freak shows grew throughout the century, a combination of economic need and the growing post–[Civil W]ar influx of women into jobs outside the home emboldened them to pursue this tantalizingly lucrative livelihood" (12). Almost fifty years later, a young woman named Betty Broadbent was told that she could earn more money as a tattooed woman than she could as "Spidora—an illusionist whose head [was] projected, through mirrors, onto a stuffed spider's body to create the effect of a human-headed spider" (30). According to Mifflin, Broadbent "enjoyed a 40-year career during which she traveled with every major American circus, as well as independent shows in Australia and New Zealand" (30). She also competed in the first televised beauty contest, held at the 1939 World's Fair (30).

Describing her first job for Ringling Brothers, Broadbent explained that she would appear on stage in a floor-length robe that hid all her tattoos: "The platform lecturer would announce, 'And now, ladies and gentlemen, the lady who's different!' Up till then, nobody had the slightest idea what was different about me. I'd unzip my robe and I'd be wearing a costume underneath, sort of a long bathing suit that came four inches above my knees" (30). Thus Broadbent's performance, as well as those of other "freaks," relied on the exploitation of difference; audiences came prepared to gawk at the spectacle of the other from a safe distance. In reality, however, (and perhaps this contributed to the attraction) the bodies of tattooed ladies highlighted their similarities to *as well as* their differences from the women who observed them from the audience. As Mifflin points out, the desire for *more*—more money, more freedom of movement, more independence—represented by the tattooed lady was actually shared by many American women throughout the late-nineteenth century and into the twentieth. Although tattooed women may have seemed trapped by their excessively visible bodies, these very bodies gave them access to a world outside the home, free from poverty and many restrictions otherwise placed on women's lives. They "may have sacrificed social respectability for their vocation, but they were rewarded with travel, money, and public recognition, as well as an active social circle that, for those who were disowned by disapproving relatives, functioned as family" (Mifflin 32). Similarly, if on a much less dramatic scale, the average American woman enjoyed more rights and freedoms in the early twentieth century, including the right to vote; increased access to schools, trades and professions; and the choice of whether or not to marry. The tattooed lady both benefited from and represented these advances as well as the rather shocking proposition that a woman might own her own body—and then might choose to mark that body accordingly.

While economics certainly had the greatest influence on women's tattooing in the late-nineteenth and early-twentieth centuries, pleasure and a love of decoration also played a role. In the biography sold at her performances, Irene Woodward asserted that her own father had begun tattooing her when she was six. (In reality, she was tattooed by famed tattoo artist Samuel O'Reilly, the inventor of the electric tattoo machine, and his apprentice, Charlie Wagner.) Although it was not originally her choice to be tattooed, it was, according to her biography, her desire that he continue: "At first the father implanted a few stars in the child's fair skin. Then a picture was indelibly portrayed by the father's hand. In spite of the pain the girl was delighted, and coaxed her father to continue" (qtd. in Mifflin 20). This representation of the girl's enthusiasm for the tattooing project may have been artfully placed in her biography to tantalize her audience. Certainly, the similarity between it and the narrative of Nora Hildebrandt, said to be tattooed by *her* father, implies that audiences were titillated by the incestuous implications of these tales. In general, audiences appear to have been drawn to tattoo narratives featuring the transgression of societal boundaries—fathers tattooing daughters, people of color tattooing white men and women. Nevertheless, Woodward's biography is especially intriguing in that it acknowledges the element of pleasure in tattooing (as both the receiver and the exhibitor of the tattoo) as well as the tattoo's potential to represent transgressive desires.

It is difficult to know what personal significance tattoos had for women like Hildebrandt, Woodward, and Broadbent. Did Broadbent see her difference from the women of her audience as more than a matter of physical appearance? Did she feel that her tattoos marked something deeper, something more essential to her personality? Most likely we will never be entirely sure, although Broadbent's fond remembrances of her days as a performer indicate that she did not regret being tattooed (Mifflin 32). The era of the tattooed lady ended in the 1960s. As Mifflin explains, "By the '60s, medical progress had yielded cures for some of the conditions that were the bedrock of freak shows, and a better educated public was less inclined to laugh at and more willing to question such displays, making tattooed attractions superannuated at best, and reviled at worst" (47). At the same time, however, tattoos became more acceptable within the general population, sparking a fashion trend that waxed and waned and seems to have peaked in the first years of the twenty-first century. According to one study, prevalence rates for tattoos were estimated in 1998 at 10 to 20 percent of men and 7 percent of women with tattoos in the United States (qtd. in Hawkes 593). Another study estimates that "women currently acquire half of all tattoos, a rate that has quadrupled since the 1970s" (Hawkes 594).

Without the economic motivation, then, why do women choose to mark their own bodies in today's world? As Joan Jacobs Brumberg and others note, the "body project" is common to most late-twentieth and early-twenty-first century girls and women. But what prompts some to dye their hair, to diet, to get cosmetic surgery, or to wear distinctive clothing, and others to have their skin inscribed in ink? For many, tattooing, a traditionally male activity, allows them to step outside culturally prescribed norms of female beauty. As Victoria Pitts notes, "Women body modifiers have argued that modifying the body promotes symbolic rebellion, resistance, and self-transformation—that marking and transforming the body can symbolically 'reclaim' the body from its victimization and objectification in patriarchal culture" (49). Yet sociologist Michael Atkinson cautions against reading all "non-normative body projects such as tattooing" as a subversion of "hegemonic ideologies about femininity—especially images of the weak, sexually objectified, or otherwise submissive woman" (220). Depending on the size, design, and location of the tattoo, women's tattoos can just as easily be seen as an accommodation of cultural norms regarding female beauty and sexuality. As Atkinson notes, "[A]lthough women have historically shunned widespread participation in tattooing, newly established sensibilities about female sexuality have incorporated this body practice into the mix" (225). Thus, just as in the days of the first tattooed ladies, it is impossible to label the decision to be tattooed as one freely chosen by women. In fact, by tattooing themselves to obtain economic independence, Broadbent and her peers may have been making a bolder rebellion against women's place in American society than the young women of the late-twentieth century who sport butterflies and flowers on their ankles.

This recognition should not, however, dispel the assertion made by many studies of women's tattoos that "women, through marking their bodies with tattoos and through the narratives that they construct about them, are working to erase the oppressive marks of a patriarchal society and to replace them with marks of their own choosing" (DeMello, *Bodies of Inscription* 173). Atkinson himself argues that many women go so far as to "reveal their tattoos as a means of exhibiting gender wounds" that are often the result of physical and/or sexual assault or poor body image (228). Similarly, Mifflin explains that "[t]he term 'psychic armor' is sometimes used to describe tattoos acquired during periods of change" and cites the experience of a woman who was tattooed around her lower abdomen to symbolize her recovery from childhood sexual abuse (106, 115). Tattooing is also becoming an alternative to prostheses or breast reconstruction for some breast cancer survivors. By having a tattoo inked across her mastectomy scar, for example, Andree Connors not only reclaimed the mark as her own but also insisted on the visibility of her own body: "This [breast cancer] is an invisible epidemic: everybody looks 'normal' cause they're wearing prostheses. So the message does not get across to the world that we are being killed off by breast cancer" (qtd. in Mifflin 152).

Such use of the tattoo to make a political statement about the lives and bodies of women is becoming increasingly more common for women who are heavily tattooed as well as those who have just one or two carefully selected designs. Krystyne Kolorful, the woman who holds the Guinness record as the world's most tattooed woman, explains her tattoos "as a way of writing over the sense of physical violation" she experienced as a result of childhood sexual abuse (Mifflin 121). Yet she also interprets the marks as a feminist statement, a public flouting of beauty standards for women as well as a statement of her control over her own body. "Heavily tattooed women really confront people with their independence," she insists. "Even if you just get one, you're doing something that is so contradictory to the morals of our society. That's why women like me took it to the level that we did: we wanted to make a really big statement that this is my body and I'm doing with it what I choose" (qtd. in Mifflin 118). Another young woman who chose to have two pinup girls tattooed on her arm sees the display of her tattoos as a political act, one that will force men to rethink the cultural spectacle of the female body: "[T]hat is the reaction I want from men. I want a guy to look at me, look at my tattoos, and have everything he thinks about women screwed up" (qtd. in Atkinson 229).

Although methods of marking and societal attitudes toward body modification have changed significantly since 1900, the mark remains a powerful image and an important part of an individual's—and a culture's—self-definition. Scholars studying tattoos and scars in the late twentieth and early twenty-first centuries insist that the stories behind the marked body are as important as the mark itself. In an article on scars in the popular magazine *Psychology Today*, for example, the author notes that "even with unintended scars, their context plays a critical part in the emotional response of both bearer and viewer" (Austin 79). And in her book *Bodies of Inscription: A Cultural History of the Modern Tattoo Community*, Margo DeMello argues that it is through what she calls "tattoo narratives" that tattooed people "provide meaning for their tattoos, meanings that are especially necessary within a . . . context that traditionally has not viewed tattoos in a positive light" (152). As I have demonstrated throughout *Identifying Marks*, in nineteenth-century America people used "context" and "narrative" in similar ways, constructing a complex relationship between corporeality and identity, spectacle and audience, which has influenced the ways in which we understand the marked body today. It is crucial to note, however, that the tattoo narratives discussed here and elsewhere in this study also operate on the understanding that women's bodies are always already marked by the cultures in which they live, and that tattooing *can* allow women to assert their own agency and sense of ownership of their own bodies. As Pitts observes, "In marking their bodies, they appear to shift both their private self-identifications and their public identities, telling new stories to themselves and others about the meaning of their embodiment. . . . [T]he practices imply that their body-stories are in flux, opened to the possibilities of reinscription and renaming" (73).

While such body projects are alternately seen as triumphant and pathological (depending on the bearer of the mark, the observer, the scene in which the mark is viewed, and any number of other factors), they are a reminder of the ways in which women's bodies continue to be marked—by force and by choice—in the late-twentieth and early-twenty-first centuries. That women *are* marked is suggested by the women cited here; the question is whether they will also decide to mark themselves, to claim their own bodies as a way of denying the power their culture holds over them. The physical mark in this case is just as powerful as the emotional one, and the two are often intimately linked, as they were in Elizabeth Stoddard's *The Morgesons* and Pauline Hopkins's *Contending Forces*. Similarly, as in nineteenth-century texts, the mark and its varied interpretations are inflected by race, class, sexuality, and other factors that shape our identities.

The rhetoric of the mark persists in the work of contemporary writers (especially writers of color) who recognize its continued relevance. African American women novelists Octavia Butler, Sherley Anne Williams, Toni Morrison, and Phyllis Alesia Perry feature characters forced to confront their scarred bodies, reminders of the realities of slavery. For Morrison's Sethe, these scars ultimately mark her victory over oppression as well. The scars of Dessa Rose, the heroine of Williams's novel of the same name, symbolize her resistance to the expectation that the black woman's body be a public spectacle, a grotesque statement of her worth as a slave or a human being. Both Butler and Perry feature African American heroines living in the twentieth century whose bodies are mysteriously marked by the past, reminders of the legacy of slavery.[1]

The rhetorical power of the marked body is also skillfully employed to address the effect of racism in Lorna Dee Cervantes's "Poem for The Young White Man Who Asked Me How I, an Intelligent, Well-Read Person, Could Believe in the War between Races" (1981). After telling her listener that he may not "believe in revolution" because he is not the target of racist attacks (both physical and verbal), Cervantes explains,

> I'm marked by the color of my skin.
> The bullets are discrete and designed to kill slowly.
> They are aiming at my children.
> These are facts.
> Let me show you my wounds: my stumbling mind, my
> "excuse me" tongue, and this
> nagging preoccupation
> with the feeling of not being good enough.
>
> These bullets bury deeper than logic.
> Racism is not intellectual.
> I can not reason these scars away. (313)

Like Pauline Hopkins, Cervantes insists that the scars resulting from racism are not merely physical. They *might* be physical: earlier in the poem she refers to crosses burning, "goose-steppers round every corner," and "snipers in the schools" (312, 313). Yet the other manifestations of racism—what prejudice does to your mind, your voice, your self-esteem—are just as terrible and perhaps even more damaging. The "Young White Man" and other white readers may question Cervantes, may demand that she be rational, but as she points out, "Racism is not intellectual." It is for Cervantes to testify to the power of her "wounds" and the extent of the damage done to her body and mind.

The voices of those who are marked are often silenced in one way or another—made pathological, judged irrational, or even marked for death. Cervantes is told to be rational, to avoid having her emotions override her intellect. Women with tattoos, especially large and/or multiple tattoos, are often treated as unfeminine, unprofessional, and unnatural. Yet as a culture, perhaps we need to learn how to listen to the testimony of those who are marked in various ways. Knowing the history of cultural marking in the United States is certainly one step toward understanding the tattoo, the scar, and other marks, both forcible and chosen. A comprehensive reading of the marked body in the twentieth and early twenty-first centuries is beyond the scope of this study. This is not to say, however, that the history I have outlined here is not relevant to such a reading. To demonstrate how this reading might look and to call attention to the critical and political work yet to be done in this field, I conclude this study of the nineteenth century with two twenty-first-century case studies.

Two recent court cases demonstrate the complicated politics of early twenty-first century forcible marks and, appropriately, bring my study back full circle to issues of gender, violence, and vision. Both cases involve women suing their gynecologists for marking their bodies during intimate medical procedures. In the first, Dr. Allan Zarkin, a New York doctor who had just delivered a child by caesarean section, used his scalpel to carve his initials into the mother's abdomen an inch above her incision. The doctor, who had decided to initial his work because he had done such a "beautiful job," was sued by his patient in 2000. In describing her response to the experience, Liana Gedz, the patient, used the rhetoric of ownership and sexual abuse, insisting that the initials, three by one and a half inches, made her feel "like a branded animal," adding, "I feel like I was raped." Clearly, the patient perceives Zarkin's incision as a highly personal, even sexual invasion of her body and sense of self. Yet while Gedz's insistence that she feels like a "branded animal" implies that she reads the mark as a symbol of ownership, it is her husband's ownership of her body, in addition to (or rather than) her own that she is concerned with in another quoted statement: "I'm so embarrassed to get undressed in front of my husband because I have another man's initials on my stomach" ("Dr. Zorro"). Thus, as in many nineteenth-century texts, the mark symbolizes an experience that may obstruct a woman's primary heterosexual relationship, a relationship from which she derives much of her identity.

Although Zarkin's lawyer insisted that he suffered from an Alzheimer's-like disease that rendered him unaccountable for his actions, hospital staff members dubbed Zarkin "Dr. Zorro" soon after the incident, a reference to the legendary swashbuckler Zorro who marks his presence with a slashed Z. The nickname trivializes the incident, positioning Zarkin as a do-gooder who was perhaps a bit carried away in his passion for helping others. Yet comparing Zarkin to a swordfighter also highlights the deadliness of the blade that *he* carried—the scalpel—and its power to maim, mark, or kill. The nickname positions the incident within a martial context, perhaps reminiscent of Cassandra Morgeson's claim that she got her own scars "in battle." While Cassandra's comment highlights her own agency, the woman in this case was clearly at the mercy of her Aylmer-like physician, who sees the women he treats as somehow his own, worthy recipients of his mark.

A 2003 case raises similar issues while complicating our understanding of the mark and a woman's ownership of her body in a technologically advanced age. Just three years after the suit against Zarkin, a Kentucky physician was sued by a patient for branding her uterus with the initials of his alma mater ("UK") during a hysterectomy. The patient, Stephanie Means, claimed that she suffered emotional distress after viewing a videotape of the operation. "It was a mockery of my body," she told a reporter. "This was an organ that created my two beautiful children, and I wanted it discarded with respect. And it wasn't. It was used as a toy in the operating room, without my consent. So I felt as though I was an insignificant person" (Taylor and Kocher). Dr. Michael Guiler, the surgeon, responded to her complaint by explaining that such marks are routine in hysterectomies, giving doctors a "point of reference" during the operation. He insisted that the initials "were not intended to demean the patient in any way and were done only with the patient's safety in mind" (Garay). Nine other women later joined the suit, several of whom also insisted that the hysterectomies were actually medically unnecessary (Evans).

Both cases recall my focus throughout *Identifying Marks* on the ability of the supposedly noncorporeal white man to dominate, control, and frequently mark those subject to his power. As another physician involved in the Kentucky case noted, "Markings have been around forever to keep us out of trouble and . . . for navigational purposes" ("Nine Women"). While this comment was intended to explain the common practice of branding, burning, or stitching the uterus to keep one's orientation during surgery, it also highlights the way in which marked bodies allow the unmarked to "navigate" their way through the culture in which they live, retaining the "conquering gaze" to which I refer in the introduction. Whether the subjugated are tattooed "savages" or scarred slaves, their bodies are constant reminders to those employing the gaze of their own superiority as well as their own power to further mark and thus demarcate these bodies. Medical technology allows for the extension of such power in the early twenty-first century beyond the boundaries visible to the naked eye. In this sense, it makes markings such as Guiler's easier to get away with: if the surgeon himself had not provided the patient with a videotape of the procedure, Means would presumably never have known about the branding and would not, therefore, have been damaged by it.

Yet no matter how advanced technological methods are, Means insists that surgical patients have the right to "expect their doctor to treat them with respect. They don't expect to be tattooed or branded with the doctor's alma mater on a lark during surgery. That's not what you paid for" (Taylor and Kocher). Means and the other women suing the doctors claim that their bodies belong to them even when, as in the case of a hysterectomy, the uterus is being removed from the body. The patient insists that both her body and her uterus should have been treated "with respect." She uses the word "tattoo" to refer to her experience to imply that the mark and the damage resulting from it are somehow permanent. Yet in doing so, she also presumably refers to the nature of the mark itself—the initials of Guiler's alma mater, which took the place of the stitches or burn marks that are more common according to the chairwoman of the Kentucky chapter of the American College of Obstetricians and Gynecologists (Bracely). The initials indicate that the marks are more than a navigational tool for Guiler; they are, it would seem, more personal, closer to Dr. Zorro's "AZ" than is immediately apparent. Guiler's mark implied his own ownership of the procedure and perhaps even of the uterus itself; in skillfully and successfully removing it from the woman's body, he becomes its temporary owner until it is cast off as refuse. Yet Means refuses to accept the notion that she should not be indignant about the brand just because her uterus is no longer inside her body, insisting that both she and her uterus deserve respect. The mark on her uterus, she claims, has marked her, and therefore only she can testify to the damage caused by the experience. It is not up to Guiler to say what the marks have done to her or what she will do with them.

Has the marking of bodies become less prevalent in the twenty-first century? Probably not. Has it become less violent, less obvious? Do we live more in the age of discipline than in the age of punishment? Perhaps. Only one thing seems certain: as long as bodies are forcibly marked by those who assume themselves to be unmarked, there will be some effort to reclaim the self, to exercise one's own agency. Doctors and others who have the power to employ the conquering gaze have historically been able to navigate American culture using the marked bodies around them. Yet it is possible for the marked to use their tattoos and scars as navigational tools as well—a symbol of where they have been, where they are now, and, perhaps most importantly, where they are going.

NOTES

Introduction: "Carved in Flesh"

1. The discourse of disability can also be considered in this context since it functions here in much the same way as race and gender. Disabilities are often regarded as "natural" and wholly defining of one's personality and identity. A primary example of this type of character in nineteenth-century American literature is the hunchback Deb from Rebecca Harding Davis's novella *Life in the Iron Mills*. Yet as Thomson points out in *Extraordinary Bodies*, "disability is a representation, a cultural interpretation of physical transformation or configuration, and a comparison of bodies that structures social relations and institutions. Disability, then, is the attribution of corporeal deviance—not so much a property of bodies as a product of cultural rules about what bodies should be or do" (6). For more on disability as a social construct, see Stone; Bogdan; Hevey; Liachowitz; Davis; and Thomson, *Freakery*. I touch on the intersection between disability and gender in chapter 2.

2. This is not to say that Hester in any way takes pleasure in the wearing of the letter. In fact, the moments when she *does* seem to feel pleasure—interacting with her daughter, Pearl, and talking to Dimmesdale in the forest—are the moments when the letter particularly galls her. As the scene in the forest shows, Pearl also demands that her mother wear the letter when she does not wish to, thus enacting power over her that is eventually denied the magistrates themselves.

One. Capturing Identity in Ink: Tattooing and the White Captive

1. According to Mifflin, Martin Hildebrandt was a German immigrant who opened the first professional tattoo studio in New York in the 1840s. He made his living tattooing sailors, performers, and, during the Civil War, both Union and Confederate soldiers (10). See also Sanders.

2. For more on Buffalo Bill, see Kasson, *Buffalo Bill's Wild West*, especially chapter 5, "American Indian Performers in the Wild West."

3. For more on tattooed performers in the United States and abroad, see Bogdan 241–56 and Oettermann. For more on "tattooed ladies" and their performances in museums, freak shows, and circuses, see Mifflin 10–32.

4. See especially *Discipline and Punish* and *History of Sexuality*.

5. Morrison notes a similar dynamic in *Playing in the Dark*. She writes, "As a writer reading, I came to realize the obvious: the subject of the dream is the dreamer. The fabrication of an Africanist persona is reflexive; an extraordinary meditation on the self; a powerful exploration of the fears and desires that reside in the writerly conscious. It is an astonishing revelation of longing, of terror, of perplexity, of shame, of magnanimity. It requires hard work not to see this" (17).

6. Such distinctions make for fascinating conversations about *Typee*, both in schol-arship and in the classroom. But this conversation is not served by scholars who both dismiss the importance of genre and make Melville out to be the exception in his adapta-tion of multiple generic conventions in nineteenth-century America. One such scholar is John Bryant, who in his introduction to the Penguin edition of *Typee* insists, "This book is not a novel." He goes on to say that the text has characteristics of the novel, the autobiography, the travel book, and the anthropological study. He concludes, however, by claiming that "it is best to come to *Typee* divested of any preconceived expectations of form" and asserting that "[o]ne might as well call [*Typee*] just a piece of writing" (xi). This employment of multiple genres and generic conventions is actually quite common in the work of antebellum authors such as Caroline Kirkland, Fanny Fern, and Hannah Crafts. Many of their texts, however, have been dismissed as sophomoric and unsophis-ticated because of such complexities.

7. Many critics have commented on tattooing in *Typee*, citing it as one of the threats—the other being cannibalism—that prompt Tommo to leave Typee Valley. See Dryden; Abrams; and Ruland. For more recent analyses of tattooing in *Typee*, see Evelev and Ot-ter 9–49. Ultimately, I agree with Otter that tattooing, rather than cannibalism, is the primary impetus for Tommo's escape.

8. I am assuming that, given the importance of tattooing in the novel, Melville would have made explicit mention of any tattoos received on board ship. Although many sailors were tattooed during the time in which the novel is set, Tommo does not seem to be. Without any discussion of this in *Typee*, one can only assume that he rejects tattooing altogether because of the way in which it positions the body culturally. To be tattooed as a sailor would be to resign himself to a permanent and visible working-class status within the American social hierarchy.

9. In *Omoo*, the sequel to *Typee*, Melville details Tommo's encounter with a white man who has allowed himself to be tattooed in such a way. Lem Hardy is "a white man, in the South Sea girdle, and tattooed in the face. A broad blue band stretched across his face from ear to ear, and on his forehead was the taper figure of a blue shark, nothing but fins from head to tail." Although Tommo's individual reaction is unclear, he explains that "[s]ome of us gazed upon this man with a feeling akin to horror, no ways abated when informed that he had voluntarily submitted to this embellishment of his countenance" (27).

10. My discussion of Tommo is influenced by what Roediger calls the "critical studies of whiteness" (*Colored White* 15). Roediger has been one of the most important figures in this field of study; in an early book, *The Wages of Whiteness*, he insists that scholars address "the white problem—the question of how and why whites reach the conclusion that their whiteness is meaningful" (6). Other important figures in the field include Ig-natiev and Frankenberg. Frankenberg's assertion that "[n]aming 'whiteness' displaces it from the unmarked, unnamed status that is itself an effect of its dominance" prompts much of the work of this study (6).

11. My argument here is in direct contrast to Otter's claim that "the narrator [of *Typee*] connects masculinity and the ability to endure tattooing" (21).

12. In 1933 Parry noted that "[t]he very process of tattooing is essentially sexual. There are the long, sharp needles. There is the liquid poured into the pricked skin. There are the two participants of the act, one active, the other passive. There is the curious mixture of pleasure and pain" (1).

13. See Anderson for an extensive discussion of Melville's use of sources.

14. According to Washburn, the Brewsterites believed "that the [Mormon] church, as guided by its leaders following the departure from Nauvoo, Illinois, in 1846, had chosen the wrong refuge in the valley of the Great Salt Lake" (vi). Brewster would eventually be repudiated by the leaders of the church in Salt Lake City.

15. The Yavapais are misidentified in Stratton's text as Apaches.

16. For a more complete analysis of the way in which the narrative changed from the first to the third editions, see Derounian-Stodola, "Indian Captivity Narratives" and "Captive and Her Editor."

17. For more on captivity narratives, see Slotkin; Kolodny; Namias; Derounian-Stodola and Levernier; Ebersole; Castiglia; and Derounian-Stodola, *Women's Indian Captivity Narratives*. For the influence of the captivity narrative on American fiction, see Burnham.

18. All quotes are from the third edition of the narrative.

19. In a discussion of clothing in English and French colonial literature, Gordon Sayre notes that the wearing of fur "profoundly affected the confrontation of Europeans with the natives of northeastern North America. . . . [P]elts were not fully clothes to the explorer's eyes, as they simply covered one's skin with another's and seemed more like raw materials than finished garments. Because they were keen to obtain the beaver pelts that had been clothing, the *coureurs de bois* were inclined to view the Canadian human and beaver as two animals wearing the same skin" (154). A similar dynamic seems to be working in Stratton's narrative in that the Indians' clothing appears to reveal their true animalistic nature. This is reflected again in a passage in which Lorenzo is attacked by wolves, which he claims are "bent upon . . . completing the work left unfinished by their brothers, the Apaches" (103).

20. According to Derounian-Stodola, "Illustrations played a much more important role in the second and third editions of the Oatman publication than in the first. Between the first and third editions, for example, the number of engravings rose from twelve to sixteen, and the treatment of the subject generally became more sensational and sentimental. Moreover, the engravings in the first and second edition (done in San Francisco) are cruder than those in the third (New York) edition" ("Indian Captivity Narratives" 38). In all three editions, however, Olive and Mary Ann are depicted as wearing the bark skirt—and nothing else—after being taken captive.

21. Clothing is also an important factor in the forced assimilation of Indian children into white culture, as is revealed in the autobiographical writing of Zitkala-Ša (Gertrude Bonnin). She recounts the story of her arrival at the missionary school for Indian children: "We were placed in a line of girls who were marching into the dining room. These were Indian girls, in stiff shoes and closely clinging dresses. The small girls wore sleeved aprons and shingled hair. As I walked noiselessly in my soft moccasins, I felt like sinking

to the floor, for my blanket had been stripped from my shoulders. I looked hard at the Indian girls, who seemed not to care that they were even more immodestly dressed than I, in their tightly fitting clothes" (436). Soon after, Zitkala-Ša's own moccasins are taken from her and replaced by shoes, and her hair is "shingled like a coward's!" (437).

22. Derounian-Stodola's research shows that this is yet another example of Stratton's "prudishness" and his efforts to "sanitize the truth." In "The Captive and Her Editor," she writes, "In 1856, there were no officer's wives at Fort Yuma, but there were camp followers and at least one madam—the legendary Sarah Bowman, called 'The Great Western' owing to her size, who in addition to pimping also did laundry, nursed the sick and wounded, and kept a mess table. The captive and the camp follower: it sounds like a great story. Yet the reality may have been more down-to-earth. A kindly, capable woman then in her early forties, Bowman eased Oatman's physical, psychological, and cultural isolation, and like a surrogate mother caring for a daughter, in the limbo of Fort Yuma helped Olive begin to deal with the difficulties of making herself into a white woman" (179). There does not seem to be any evidence to support Derounian-Stodola's interpretation of the nature of the relationship between Bowman and Oatman, but Stratton's erasure of Bowman in favor of the fictive "wife of one of the officers" is certainly telling.

23. According to Derounian-Stodola, "Throughout the captivity literature, women are generally depicted as either helpless victims or provoked avengers." Although she goes on to acknowledge that "deeper analysis reveals aspects of victimization and survival . . . in both [types] of women," Olive Oatman and her sister are primarily framed as victims in *Captivity of the Oatman Girls* (Introduction xxi).

24. Palmer began work on *The White Captive* just two months after the first edition of Stratton's narrative was published in California. Although it is possible that Palmer read about Oatman's captivity in New York City newspapers before beginning work on the sculpture, the narrative itself was not published in New York until April 1858, and Oatman probably did not begin lecturing until May 1858. *The White Captive* was completed in August 1859. Although influence is probably impossible to prove, I do not agree with Palmer's biographer, who states that "the idea of captivity in the hands of the Indians was so common that there is no need to search for specific inspiration" (Webster 184). Oatman's tattoos clearly differentiate her narrative from others in the genre and may thus have had a distinct influence on Palmer's representation of captivity.

25. Kirk Savage points out a similar problem in sculptural representations of African Americans in the nineteenth century. He claims that, "[b]roadly speaking, classical sculpture still served as the benchmark of the sculptural and thereby defined what was not sculpture—most fundamentally, the body of the 'Negro,' the black antithesis of classical whiteness" (12). Savage goes on to say that "the equation of freedom with the ideals of art helps explain why slavery was so difficult to represent in art and why the representation of emancipation meant purifying the body of slavery's scars" (57). In other words, bodily marks—scars and, one might add, tattoos—disrupt the representation of the classical ideals of nineteenth-century sculpture.

Two. "Burning into the Bone": Romantic Love and the Marked Woman

1. As Looby notes in his analysis of Thompson's fiction, "Thompson specialized in the opposite of ideality, purity, and perfection: his novels are replete with the disgusting, the corrupt, and the damaged" (651). In this sense, *City Crimes* is a typical Thompson novel. For more on Thompson, see Reynolds, and Reynolds and Gladman. According to Reynolds and Gladman, characters such as Josephine Franklin and the Dead Man were the heart and soul of sensational fiction, a discourse that "entertained . . . readers with sensational accounts of sex and violence" and "subvert[ed] middle-class mores, unmask[ed] hypocrisy, and expose[d] the prevailing fluidity of American life" (xi). Thus the character of Josephine, for instance, provided male *and* female readers with somewhat explicit descriptions of sexual acts through which they could live vicariously while also knowingly condemning societal hypocrisy and perhaps even the limitations placed on women's sexual behavior in nineteenth-century America. Looby, on the other hand, argues that the restoration of order in Thompson's sensational novels complicates his claim to undermine the status quo. "In the guise of an unblinkered attention to awful social realities—and it should be noted that Thompson does, in fact, offer a remarkable mapping of a newly complex urban world of drastic spatial separations, class antagonisms, and rampant displacements of customary social statuses—Thompson presents enchanting visions of erotic and criminal excess that may arouse resentment, envy, and even a proto-political understanding of structured social inequity, public moral hypocrisy, and legal corruption. Yet eventually he circumscribes and diffuses that understanding by always concluding with narrative restorations of sentimental domestic norms and de facto endorsements of present social and political arrangements" (653–54). In direct response to Reynolds's championing of sensational fiction and Looby's critique, Keetley argues "that politically multivalent popular texts rarely serve only the purported interests of one group—either men or women—and that to fix popular literature at only one end of the political spectrum, as either undermining or confirming dominant culture, is necessarily reductive." In Keetley's analysis of pamphlet literature featuring "female fiends" who murder their husbands (among other crimes), she moves beyond such binaries to "address instead how judging its political end or its cultural work in the abstract is secondary to untangling its varied and competing meanings with a particularly compelling contemporary set of meanings" (350). In my own efforts to examine representations of the scarred woman in both sentimental and sensational fiction within the context of romantic love, I adopt Keetley's approach to popular texts and their meanings.

2. The Dead Man is also punished for his wrongdoing by the end of *City Crimes*. After a vigorous physical encounter, he is ultimately captured, tortured, and blown up by his enemies. Although this retributive act is violent and disgusting, it is sanctioned and even rewarded according to the melodramatic codes that drive sensational fiction. The mastermind behind the Dead Man's torture and death, a mysterious stranger known only as the Doctor, goes on to "become one of the most respectable physicians" in Boston and marries "an amiable lady" (309).

3. According to Lystra, the notion of romantic love began in the early nineteenth century but by 1830 was "fast becoming the necessary condition for marriage in the American middle class" (28). Lystra's fascinating study of romantic love focuses on the letters of more than one hundred nineteenth-century American men and women.

4. The reconceptualization of sentimentalism has been a central aspect of feminist studies of nineteenth-century American literature, beginning with Tompkins's *Sensational Designs*. See also Fisher; Samuels, *Culture of Sentiment*; and Dobson, "American Renaissance Revisioned" and "Reclaiming Sentimental Literature." For the impact of sentimental culture on the writings of women of color, see Tate; Wexler; and Peterson. For the sentimental depiction of disabled figures, see Thomson, "Crippled Girls and Lame Old Women" and *Extraordinary Bodies*; and Klages. For more traditional interpretations of sentimentality, see Pattee; H. R. Brown; Mott; Hart; Papashvily; and A. Douglas.

5. Wendell argues that "a feminist understanding of bodily suffering" must be developed, particularly one that acknowledges the positive aspects of transcendence for the ill and disabled in the late twentieth century. She writes, "I do not think that we need to subscribe to some kind of mind-body dualism to recognize that there are degrees to which consciousness and the sense of self may be tied to bodily sensations and limitations, or to see the value of practices, available to some people in some circumstances, that loosen the connection. Nor do I think we need to devalue the body or bodily experience to value the ability to gain some emotional or cognitive distance from them. On the contrary, to devalue the body for this reason would be foolish, since it is bodily changes and conditions that lead us to discover these strategies. . . . Thus, the body itself takes us into and then beyond its sufferings and limitations" (178). Wendell's argument adds an important perspective to recent feminist theories of the body. It also has some relevance to representations of disability and the transcendence of the body in nineteenth-century American literature, but it is important to note that, in many cases, it is the white, middle-class, able-bodied writer prescribing transcendence for someone whose body distinguishes him or her as different or "other." This is certainly true for *The Lamplighter* and also for many abolitionist texts of the same period. Wendell is making a case for the disabled person's right and ability to transcend his or her *own* body in order to lead a productive and satisfying emotional and intellectual life. To the extent that the disabled female body in these texts symbolizes white women's attitudes toward corporeality in the mid-nineteenth century, the benefits and limitations of transcendence will be considered later in this chapter.

6. It is important to note that in the course of the novel, Mr. Graham marries a widow he meets while on vacation. It is implied that theirs is not, however, a romantic match. Mrs. Graham is represented as a greedy, selfish woman, a poor partner for the man who has been accustomed to the subservience of his daughter for much of his life. Neither Mr. Graham nor his wife is truly in love with the other, which is why neither has the distinct sense of self (and subsequent self-knowledge) that Lystra insists is developed within the nineteenth-century courtship process.

7. As Klages points out, "sexuality becomes the limit of the blind person's ability to

participate fully in domestic life. . . . While reproductive sexuality can be figured as the product of the desire, not for selfish pleasure but for dependent objects on whom to practice maternal self-sacrifice, such sexuality is inaccessible to disabled people, who are culturally enjoined from reproducing their defect" (77). In such a paradigm, the fact that Emily Graham was not born blind would have little significance.

8. For Emily's blindness as punishment for incest, see Goshgarian 163–66 and Cherniavsky 86–87.

9. In *Confidence Men and Painted Women*, Halttunen insists that appearance was essential to the ways in which people judged and reacted to others in mid-nineteenth-century America. Advice writers of the period insisted "that all aspects of manner and appearance were visible outward signs of inner moral qualities" (40). This "sentimental typology of conduct" placed even more emphasis on appearance for women, for whom "[t]rue womanly beauty was not an accident of form" but "the outward expression of a virtuous mind and heart" (40, 71). And more important than any arrangement of hair or clothing was a woman's complexion, which was said to be permanently marked by bad temper (88).

10. See Noble 132–33 for her critique of Sanchez-Eppler's argument. Noble reviews the passage in Stowe's *Dred* that Sanchez-Eppler uses as evidence for her argument that "[i]n sentimental fiction bodily signs are adamantly and repeatedly presented as the preferred and most potent mechanisms both for communicating meaning and for marking the fact of its transmission" (Sanchez-Eppler 27). Noble claims that in her reading of this scene, "Sanchez-Eppler conflates two separate operations: trust in the advice given by one's own body and trust in the signs provided by the other's body. Nina is describing a gut feeling; however, such a response does not place implicit trust in the other's gut, but in one's own gut. Sanchez-Eppler describes a hermeneutic activity, a physiognomy of culturally determined—racially and sexually encoded—bodily meanings. . . . Nina is trying to make a point about different—female—ways of knowing that are superior to abstract thinking" (132). I agree with Noble that a "woman's way of knowing" is essential to the sentimental project. Yet Noble seems to ignore the preponderance of evidence in sentimental texts, some of which I include in this chapter, that outer appearance is indeed assumed to reflect inner qualities *of the person being observed as well as the observer* in the culture of sentiment. Halttunen's research on advice books supports this argument as well. A "woman's way of knowing" does not preclude "a physiognomy of culturally determined meanings." Sentimental authors insisted that women, with their intimate, care-giving, life-giving relationship to the body, were more adept at recognizing such bodily meanings than men.

11. Hawthorne makes this point in "The Minister's Black Veil" (1836), in which the minister's veil hints at the presence of the mark without ever revealing its reality. The mark exists symbolically in this story whether or not it is ever manifested on the minister's body.

12. In this sense, Spofford is very similar to her contemporary Elizabeth Stoddard. Smith and Weinauer have recently commented that "Stoddard's status as perpetual misfit provides a significant insight into the problematic process of canon formation and

reformation and, most disturbingly, shows how the act of critical revaluation and reconstruction may fall prey to the techniques of the exclusionary practices it exposes" (8). For more on Spofford, see my "Harriet Prescott Spofford."

13. Spofford explains that the Strathsay family live in "St. Anne's in the Provinces." Sainte-Anne, later known as Sainte Anne's Point, was renamed Fredericktown on February 22, 1785, after Prince Frederick Augustus, the second son of King George III. The city, the capital of New Brunswick, is now known as Fredericton. Spofford was born in Calais, Maine, located on the border of Maine and New Brunswick, and may have been familiar with the city and its history.

14. Oddly, although Alice's father and son are crucial to the frame of the story, Spofford does not name them.

15. Such experimentation actually became more likely within the paradigm of romantic love. As Lystra notes, "Some indeterminate level of sexual expression and satisfaction was acceptable in Victorian courtships when individuals were in love and the expectation of marriage was strong. Intercourse, however, was a physical boundary not to be crossed until after marriage." Yet romantic love included the potential for sexual activity insofar as "sexual expressions were read as symbolic communications of one's real and truest self, part of the hidden essence of the individual" (59).

16. Berger's observations on the difference between the "presence" of men and that of women is enlightening here. He writes, "A man's presence suggests what he is capable of doing to you or for you. His presence may be fabricated, in the sense that he pretends to be capable of what he is not. But the presence is always toward a power which he exercises on others. By contrast, a woman's presence expresses her own attitude to herself, and defines what can and cannot be done to her" (45–46).

Three. "Tattooed Still": The Inscription of Female Agency

1. Gilman explains that "[t]he name *aesthetic surgery* seems to be a label for those procedures which society at any given time sees as unnecessary, as nonmedical, as signs of vanity" (8). This definition is, of course, complicated by Wendell's notion of "social disabilities," introduced in chapter 2.

2. Gilman claims that "[m]ost of the patients on whom late nineteenth-century surgeons exhibited their procedures were men." The Woodbury Institute's advertisement seems to contradict this claim. Whether or not men were actually the primary consumers of aesthetic surgery, women were certainly essential to the rhetoric used to advertise such services.

3. See Gilman 16–17. According to Gilman, "Most of the modern procedures employed in aesthetic surgery date to the 1880s and 1890s" (3).

4. *The Morgesons* is, of course, important to nineteenth-century American literary history for other reasons. As Stern notes, "With *The Morgesons*, Stoddard allows us to reimagine a postsentimental genealogy for American women's fiction of the Civil War and post–Civil War eras" (108). This genealogy might include other authors such as Spofford, Rebecca Harding Davis, and Constance Fenimore Woolson. Stern claims quite

rightly that "critics . . . have failed to be mindful of the ways in which novels working in the absence of sentimental formulae, far from proving out of sync with, if not actually unassimilable to, the dominant terms of this mid-nineteenth-century discourse, may, in fact, engage in trenchant philosophical and political critiques of sentimentalism's very premises" (109). For recent attempts to rethink the careers and work of postbellum American women writers, see Boyd and Sofer. I borrow the term "oppositional gaze" from hooks's essay "The Oppositional Gaze."

5. Moore explains that Stoddard's "shipbuilding father, Wilson Barstow, was the younger brother of Dr. Gideon Barstow of Salem who had married Hawthorne's first cousin, Nancy Forrester, daughter of Simon Forrester and Rachel Hawthorne" (121–22).

6. See Buell 351–70 for a discussion of Hawthorne and Stoddard as practitioners of the "provincial gothic" in *The House of Seven Gables* (1851) and *The Morgesons*.

7. My use of the term and practice of "resistant reading" is inspired, of course, by Fetterley's classic *The Resistant Reader*.

8. Grosz suggests "that, in feminist terms at least, it is problematic to see the body as a blank, passive page, a neutral 'medium' or signifier for the inscription of a text. If the writing or inscription metaphor is to be of any use for feminism—and I believe that it can be extremely useful—the specific modes of materiality of the 'page'/body must be taken into account; one and the same message, inscribed on a male or a female body, does not always or even usually mean the same thing or result in the same text. The elision of the question of sexual (and racial) specificity of the inscribed surface occurs throughout the history of accounts of the body" (*Volatile Bodies* 156).

9. Shakinovsky takes the idea of Georgiana as text even further, arguing that "the shape of the mark invites a particular association with the world of writing, foregrounding its signifying quality. This, in conjunction with the notion that it is a 'bloody hand,' a 'crimson stain,' announces it as a kind of women's writing. The particular conjunction of femininity and assertiveness that is embodied in the mark appears to be precisely what Aylmer cannot tolerate" (272). In this sense, she insists, "the ambiguities of reading and writing" are intertwined with "the action of the story itself" (269).

10. This bodily commitment to seafaring is reflected in Stoddard's portrayal of a proud sailor who has "blue stars and [a] crescent moon pricked in India-ink on his right hand" in her second novel, *Two Men*, published in 1865 (123).

11. It is not known exactly why Stoddard, who lived in New York, wrote for a California newspaper. Matlack suggests that she did so to maintain close contact with her brother, who lived in California in the 1850s. Regardless of the reasons she wrote, Stoddard's column for the *Daily Alta* was very popular; it appeared for four years and was moved after the first year from the back pages of the paper to the front page of the Sunday edition (Weir, "Our Lady Correspondent" 74).

12. The articles appeared on January 11, March 24, April 7, and April 23. See Pettid for a more extensive list of books, manuscripts, and newspaper and magazine articles that refer to Oatman.

13. In her column on May 4, 1856, Stoddard refers to another article that she read in the *Daily Alta*. Although this reference does not prove that Stoddard read the re-

ports on Oatman, it does indicate that she received the paper and at least occasionally read it.

14. Ryan reads Veronica quite differently than I do here. She writes, "Veronica creates an illegible surface that thwarts the efforts of others to 'read' her; she creates illness and pain, through which she participates in her own version of self-development. If Cassandra is 'possessed' (as Aunt Mercy proclaims in the opening of the novel), then Veronica is the ultimate embodiment of *self*-possession. Her rejection of both exterior objects of desire and desire itself highlights her sense of power and autonomy" (138).

15. For another reading of Veronica, see Stern.

Four. *"The Skin of an American Slave": The Mark of African American Manhood in Abolitionist Literature*

1. Regiments of black troops had been formed in South Carolina, Kansas, and Louisiana prior to 1863 and some had even seen combat. President Abraham Lincoln and the federal government did not endorse such actions, insisting that the northern people in general were not ready to accept African American men as soldiers.

2. Such illustrations were common in northern periodicals such as *Harper's Weekly*. The sentiment expressed by these illustrations was more crudely articulated in the 1883 memoirs of Robert Cowden, colonel of the Fifty-ninth U.S. Colored Infantry, who described the transformation of the "plantation negro": "Yesterday a filthy, repulsive 'nigger,' to-day a neatly attired man; yesterday a slave, to-day a freeman, yesterday a civilian, to-day a soldier" (qtd. in McPherson 173).

3. The sketches of Gordon are often reprinted or discussed in historical studies of the period. My point about the significance of the second panel, which shows Gordon under medical inspection, is supported by the way in which the series is reprinted in McPherson's *Negro's Civil War*, where the second panel is placed first, presumably in an attempt to emphasize Gordon's transformation from slave to contraband to soldier.

4. *Harper's Weekly* offers a dramatic range of representations of African American men during the Civil War. In a six-month period prior to the publication of the illustration featuring Gordon, the magazine printed a variety of illustrations depicting brave black soldiers preparing for and participating in battle. "The Battle at Milliken's Bend," for example, was reproduced in the same issue of the magazine as the drawings of Gordon. Yet other drawings represented blacks with stereotypically large lips and tattered finery. "Cutting His Old Associates," published on January 17, 1863, showed such a black man speaking to a gathering of farm animals. "Ugh! Get out," he tells them. "I ain't one ob you no more. *I'se a Man, I is!*"

5. Sontag also focuses on the observer of images of suffering: "[T]he gruesome invites us to be either spectators or cowards, unable to look. Those with the stomach to look are playing a role authorized by many glorious depictions of suffering. Torment, a canonical subject in art, is often represented in painting as a spectacle, something being watched (or ignored) by other people. The implication is: no, it cannot be stopped—and the mingling of inattentive with attentive onlookers underscores this" (42).

6. The issue of scarred black women both resembles and differs from that of black men. Black women were depicted less often with scars, particularly in abolitionist fiction, although they were frequently described as being physically or sexually abused. Furthermore, with the enlistment of black men in the Union army, the issue of black manhood was a part of public discourse in a way that black womanhood was not. See chapter 5 for my discussion of African American women and the marked body.

7. Although slave labor was an important resource for the Confederacy, the notion of freeing slaves in exchange for their military service was not proposed until January 1864. This proposal was promptly rejected by the Confederate president, Jefferson Davis; yet by December other high-ranking officials in the South saw the need for such an act in order to avoid absolute defeat. Interestingly, some recognized that "the proposition to make soldiers of [their] slaves" would indeed confirm the slaves' manhood, thus causing ideological difficulties for the Confederacy. General Howell Cobb wrote, "You cannot make soldiers of slaves, nor slaves of soldiers. . . . The day you make soldiers of them is the beginning of the end of the revolution. If slaves will make good soldiers our whole theory of slaves is wrong" (qtd. in McPherson 248). With the support of Robert E. Lee, commander of the Army of Northern Virginia, Davis signed a "Negro Soldier Law" on March 13, 1864, which did make soldiers of slaves, albeit only with the consent of the slaves' owners and the individual states. Although a few companies of black soldiers were enrolled, the war was over before any regiments could be organized. See McPherson 245–48.

8. In "Humanitarianism and the Pornography of Pain in Anglo-American Culture," Halttunen calls this technique the "pornography of pain" and attributes its origins to the culture of sensibility in eighteenth-century England, "a new set of attitudes and emotional conventions at the heart of which was a sympathetic concern for the pain and suffering of other sentient beings" (303). The unacceptability of pain was, however, precisely what made it titillating for audiences. Halttunen demonstrates that whereas humanitarian reformers and pornographers of the same period may have had very different intentions, they shared a need to exploit the scene of punishment. Of the humanitarian reformers, she writes, "The treatment of scenarios of suffering, if not narrowly pornographic in nature, assumed that the spectacle of pain was a source of illicit excitement, prurience, and obscenity—the power to evoke revulsion and disgust" (325). See also Noble.

9. Hartman asks similar questions about "the spectacular character of [images of] black suffering." She writes, "At issue here is the precariousness of empathy and the uncertain line between witness and spectator. Only more obscene than the brutality unleashed at the whipping post is the demand that this suffering be materialized and evidenced by the display of the tortured body or endless recitations of the ghastly and the terrible. In light of this, how does one give expression to these outrages without exacerbating the indifference to suffering that is the consequence of the benumbing spectacle or contend with the narcissistic identification that obliterates the other or the prurience that too often is the response to such displays?" (4).

10. For example, Andreá N. Williams writes, "Seeing that [noted British abolitionist George] Thompson had influence over both the composition of the narrative and

the success of his English mission, Moses Grandy, as an unlettered former bondsman, may have felt constrained when detailing his life history to an unfamiliar white man on foreign soil. Under such circumstances, the former slave had every reason to represent himself as wholly dignified and reputable, excluding any details that might mar his carefully managed self-portrait" (137). She goes on to explain that "the composition history of the *Narrative of the Life of Moses Grandy* requires that readers treat this text with some care, minding both what it says and what it does not say, or, perhaps, what it says only by implication" (137–38).

11. See Tompkins 122–46.

12. Yuval Taylor's *I Was Born a Slave* includes William Parker's *Freedman's Story*, drafted in 1858 but not published until February and March of 1866, when it appeared in the *Atlantic Monthly* (significantly *after* the end of the Civil War). Parker's narrative describes the 1851 Christiana Riot, a violent encounter between black residents in Lancaster County, Pennsylvania, and Maryland slave hunters. Taylor writes, "Among slave narratives, Parker's is perhaps the strongest example of black self-determination and quasi-revolutionary activity. Whether engaging in verbal braggadocio or physical battle, Parker never backed down, and his bravado made him an irresistible force" (744).

13. For more on the experiences of African American men who served in the Civil War, see McPherson; Cullen; and Glatthaar.

14. My reference to rehabilitation owes much to Long's recent book, *Rehabilitating Bodies*. As Long explains, "Rehabilitative . . . means 'to reestablish on a firm or solid basis.' Thus Civil War writers and thinkers sought to secure bodies by making individuals and the events in which they participated predictable, unalterable, and static. . . . [F]ixed bodies could ensure definite stories, and rehabilitative Civil War texts offered the promise of the converse as well: fixed stories might produce definite bodies" (7). The sergeant's fantasy about the spiritual reunion of his body and his amputated limbs produces one such "definite body" out of the chaos of battle and physical pain.

15. Klimasmith insists that when Robert reveals his back to Nurse Dane, he counters her description of him as Spanish, "prevent[ing] her from assigning him an alternative national identity and denying his experience in slavery" (120). "Because he positions himself as the subject, Robert can claim his identity as both black and a man by forcing Nurse Dane to read his body correctly" (126). I think that Klimasmith's reading ignores several crucial points in the story. Robert himself is none too eager to identify himself as black; he segregates himself from the other contrabands, isolating himself in a liminal space between black and white and refusing to share that space with others. The scars do represent his experience as a slave, but that experience consisted of continual humiliation, thereby preventing him from being both a slave and a man as manhood was defined in nineteenth-century America.

16. W. E. B. DuBois would later note the irony of military service being used as proof of the manhood of black men; he wrote, "How extraordinary, and what a tribute to ignorance and religious hypocrisy, is the fact that in the minds of most people, even those of liberals, only murder makes men. The slave pleaded, he was humble; he protected the

women of the South, and the world ignored him. The slave killed white men; and behold, he was a man" (qtd. in Cullen 90–91).

17. The tattoo functions in a similar way in an earlier story by Child, "Willie Wharton," which was published in the *Atlantic Monthly* in March 1863. Here Willie's tattoo of a prairie dog helps his white family identify him after he has lived with and married into an Indian tribe.

18. General George B. McClellan vehemently resisted the abolitionist implications of the Civil War and "strove to preserve his reputation as the slaveholder's friend" (Berlin et al. 32). In a letter written to Lincoln in 1862, he insisted that "[n]either confiscation of property, political executions of persons, territorial organization of States, or forcible abolition of slavery, should be contemplated for a moment" (qtd. in Berlin et al. 33).

Five. *"Raising the Stigma": African American Women and the Corporeal Legacy of Slavery*

1. McCullough writes, "Using rape in place of 'passing' as a figure for relations between the races, Hopkins self-consciously underscores the ways in which the white American imagination had linked sexuality to racial identity and had, moreover, figured a racial 'threat' in sexual terms. Thus, she both addresses and redresses the discursive terms used to construct African American womanhood and in so doing exhibits not a post-Reconstruction African American drive toward assimilation but an emphasis on the historical construction of race relations and how they are sexually configured" (25). McCullough's argument, as well as those of many other critics who work from Carby's stunning analysis of Grace Montfort's "rape" in her *Reconstructing Womanhood*, is very insightful, and in no way do I intend to claim that rape is not of crucial importance in *Contending Forces*. I am merely suggesting that the critical focus on rape has blinded us to other aspects of this text for too long.

2. See Jones 11–43; Sterling 5–69; and Stevenson 194–96. See also Painter, "Soul Murder and Slavery," for a consideration of the psychological effects of physical and sexual abuse.

3. According to Mayer, George Bourne was a mentor of sorts for William Lloyd Garrison. When struggling with the issues of colonization and gradualism, Garrison read a tract written by Bourne in 1816, *The Book and Slavery Irreconcilable*, which convinced him of the sinfulness of slavery (69).

4. I quote from Karlyn Kohrs Campbell's edited version of Truth's "Speech." For a discussion of the difference between this text and the Frances Gage version, supposedly recorded at the convention, see Logan 18–21. For more on Frances Gage and her reconstruction of this speech, see Painter, *Sojourner Truth* 164–78. Painter believes that Gage actually inserts the mention of women's reproductive work after Truth's claim to have done men's fieldwork as a slave. Truth's loss of her children was not mentioned in the account of her speech published immediately after the convention.

5. Child does not describe exactly how Rosa was beaten or how far along she was in her pregnancy. Such explicit details would have been regarded as inappropriate, even in

abolitionist fiction. Historian Jacqueline Jones, however, explains that pregnant women were frequently beaten. To protect the fetus—which represented a future slave and potential economic value—and to facilitate the abuse of the mother, a hole was dug in the ground in which the woman would lie face down. "Slave women's roles as workers and as childbearers came together in these trenches, these graves for the living, in southern cottonfields. The uniformity of procedure suggests that the terrorizing of pregnant women was not uncommon" (20).

6. The pervasiveness of this argument is revealed in a scene from the slave narrative, *Twelve Years a Slave: Narrative of Solomon Northrup, a Citizen of New-York, Kidnapped in Washington City in 1841, and Rescued in 1853, from a Cotton Plantation Near the Red River in Louisiana.* According to Yuval Taylor, this narrative, which was published in 1853, was one of the most popular and fastest-selling slave narratives (160). Northrup recounts being forced to whip a slave named Patsey, who is frequently beaten by her mistress because she is jealous of Patsey's sexual relationship with her husband, and by her master because he is attempting to prove to his wife that he does not care for the slave woman. When Northrup refuses to whip Patsey anymore, the master takes over. After the beating, which Patsey survives, Northrup reflects, "A blessed thing it would have been for her—days and weeks and months of misery it would have saved her—had she never lifted up her head in life again. Indeed, from that time forward she was not what she had been" (199). Therefore, even this slave narrator attempts to fit slave women into the paradigm of true womanhood, in which death is preferable to survival for a sexually violated woman.

7. Many articles on *Contending Forces* give the first section of the book only a cursory reading, focusing instead on the second. See McCullough and L. L. Brown especially. Notable exceptions are Carby; Patton; and Berg. Given Hopkins's sense of the interconnectedness of the present and the past, it makes sense to look at both parts of the novel.

8. See, for instance, Tate; Patton; and L. L. Brown.

9. The illustrations in *Contending Forces* are by R. Emmett Owen (1878–1957), a prolific artist whose illustrations appeared in magazines such as *Scribner's, Cosmopolitan,* and *Harper's Bazaar,* as well as many popular novels. Owen is also well known for his Impressionist paintings of New England. His carefully shaded illustrations work extremely well with Hopkins's dominant themes of race, blood, and skin color and deserve more attention than they have heretofore received.

10. Hopkins does, however, strongly suggest that both Charles and Grace Montfort may have descended from slaves. In writing about Bermuda, she says, "In many cases African blood had become diluted from amalgamation with the higher race, and many of these 'colored' people became rich planters or business men (themselves owning slaves) through the favors heaped upon them by their white parents. This being the case, there might even have been a strain of African blood polluting the fair stream of Montfort's vitality, or even his wife's, which fact would not have caused him an instant's uneasiness" (22–23).

11. For more on plantation mistresses and their involvement in the institution of slavery, see Clinton; Fox-Genovese; and Stevenson.

12. Berg notes that Grace's death is a reflection of her problematic adherence to the codes of True Womanhood: "[H]er suicide testifies to her purity (and thus her 'whiteness'), proving her constitutionally unable to withstand assaults on her virtue. Yet paradoxically, this virtue, the *sine qua non* of femininity, prevents her from performing woman's highest function, that of the mother" (142).

13. For more on Hopkins's critique of lynching in *Contending Forces*, see Carby 137–44. For more on lynching in general, see Wiegman 81–113; T. Harris; Tolnay and Beck; Gunning; and Piepmeier 129–71.

14. Other critics also discuss Sappho's experiences in terms of scarring without analyzing the metaphor and the way in which it connects her story with that of Grace Montfort. Tate, for example, writes of the rape of Sappho: "She survives this encounter with racism, but she bears its scars. However, it is precisely her scarred womanhood that motivates her heroic self-transformation and thereby revises notions of female virtue beyond the scope of [Francis Ellen Watkins Harper's] *Iola Leroy*" (148).

15. Lois Lamphere Brown disagrees with this reading of Sappho as a passionate, embodied woman at the end of *Contending Forces*: "Sappho's proximity to the nun's holiness, chastity, and institutionalized purity seems to be the only effective antidote to slavery's desecration of women of color. When Sappho marries Smith and leaves New Orleans, her reinstated virtue is maintained, since she and Smith become ready-made parents without having sexual relations. Indeed, her son Alphonse is presented as such an angelic figure of whiteness that he seems to reiterate the image of his mother's restored purity" (63).

Epilogue: Tattooed Ladies

1. See Butler; S. A. Williams; Morrison, *Beloved*; and Perry.

WORKS CITED

Abrams, Robert E. "*Typee* and *Omoo*: Herman Melville and the Ungraspable Phantom of Identity." *Critical Essays on Herman Melville's Typee*. Boston: G. K. Hall, 1982. 201–10.

Alcott, Louisa May. *Hospital Sketches*. 1863. *Alternative Alcott*. Ed. Elaine Showalter. New Brunswick, N.J.: Rutgers University Press, 1988. 3–73.

——. "My Contraband." 1863. *Louisa May Alcott and Race, Sex, and Slavery*. Ed. Sarah Elbert. Boston: Northeastern University Press, 1997. 69–86.

Amstutz, Margaret A. "Elizabeth Stoddard as Returned Californian: A Reading of the *Daily Alta California* Columns." *American Culture, Canons and the Case of Elizabeth Stoddard*. Ed. Robert McClure Smith and Ellen Weinauer. Tuscaloosa: University of Alabama Press, 2003. 65–82.

Anderson, Charles Roberts. *Melville in the South Seas*. 1939. New York: Dover, 1966.

Andrews, William L., ed. *North Carolina Slave Narratives: The Lives of Moses Roper, Lunsford Lane, Moses Grandy, and Thomas H. Jones*. Chapel Hill: University of North Carolina Press, 2003.

Atkinson, Michael. "Pretty in Ink: Conformity, Resistance, and Negotiation in Women's Tattooing." *Sex Roles* 47 (Sept. 2002): 219–35.

Austin, Elizabeth. "Marks of Mystery." *Psychology Today* (July–Aug. 1999): 46–82.

Ball, Charles. *Slavery in the United States: A Narrative of the Life and Adventures of Charles Ball, a Black Man Who Lived Forty Years in Maryland, South Carolina, and Georgia as a Slave*. 1836. Y. Taylor 263–486.

Berg, Allison. "Reconstructing Motherhood: Pauline Hopkins' *Contending Forces*." *Studies in American Fiction* 24.2 (Autumn 1996): 131–50.

Berger, John. *Ways of Seeing*. New York: Penguin Books, 1972.

Berlin, Ira, Barbara J. Fields, Steven F. Miller, Joseph P. Reidy, and Leslie S. Rowland. *Slaves No More: Three Essays on Emancipation and the Civil War*. New York: Cambridge University Press, 1992.

Blanchard, Marc. "Post-Bourgeois Tattoo: Reflections on Skin-Writing in Late-Capitalistic Societies." *Visualizing Theory: Selected Essays From V. A. R. 1990–1994*. New York: Routledge, 1995. 287–300.

Bogdan, Robert. *Freak Show: Presenting Human Oddities for Amusement and Profit*. Chicago: University of Chicago Press, 1988.

Boyd, Anne E. *Writing for Immortality: Women Writers and the Emergence of High Literary Culture in America*. Baltimore: Johns Hopkins University Press, 2004.

Bracely, Dawn Marie. "Surgical Branding Shows Disrespect for Patient." *Buffalo News* 16 Feb. 2003. E1. 568 words. 24 Jan. 2005. http://web.lexis-nexis.com.

Brown, Charles Brockden. *Edgar Huntly: Or, Memoirs of a Sleep-Walker*. 1799. New York: Penguin Books, 1988.

Brown, Herbert Ross. *The Sentimental Novel in America, 1789–1860.* Durham, N.C.: Duke University Press, 1940.

Brown, Lois Lamphere. " 'To Allow No Tragic End': Defensive Postures in Pauline Hopkins' *Contending Forces.*" *The Unruly Voice: Rediscovering Pauline Hopkins.* Ed. John Cullen Gruesser. Urbana: University of Illinois Press, 1996. 50–70.

Brumberg, Joan Jacobs. *The Body Project: An Intimate History of American Girls.* New York: Vintage Books, 1997.

Bryant, John. Introduction. *Typee: A Peep at Polynesian Life.* By Herman Melville. New York: Penguin Books, 1996. ix–xxx.

Buell, Lawrence. *New England Literary Culture: From Revolution through Renaissance.* New York: Cambridge University Press, 1986.

Buell, Lawrence, and Sandra A. Zagarell. "Biographical and Critical Introduction." *The Morgesons and Other Writings, Published and Unpublished.* Philadelphia: University of Pennsylvania Press, 1984. xi–xxv.

Burnham, Michelle. *Captivity and Sentiment: Cultural Exchange in American Literature, 1682–1861.* Hanover, N.H.: University Press of New England, 1997.

Butler, Octavia. *Kindred.* 1979. Boston: Beacon, 1988.

Carby, Hazel V. *Reconstructing Womanhood: The Emergence of the Afro-American Woman Novelist.* New York: Oxford University Press, 1987.

Castiglia, Christopher. *Bound and Determined: Captivity, Culture-Crossing, and White Womanhood from Mary Rowlandson to Patty Hearst.* Chicago: University of Chicago Press, 1996.

Cervantes, Lorna Dee. "Poem for the Young White Man Who Asked Me How I, An Intelligent, Well-Read Person, Could Believe in the War between the Races." *No More Masks: An Anthology of Twentieth-Century American Women Poets, Newly Revised and Expanded.* New York: HarperPerennial, 1993. 312–13.

Cherniavsky, Eva. *That Pale Mother Rising: Sentimental Discourses and the Imitation of Motherhood in 19th-Century America.* Bloomington: Indiana University Press, 1995.

Child, Lydia Maria. *An Appeal in Favor of That Class of Americans Called Africans.* 1833. Ed. Carolyn L. Karcher. Amherst: University of Massachusetts Press, 1996.

———. *A Romance of the Republic.* 1867. Ed. Dana D. Nelson. Lexington: University Press of Kentucky, 1997.

———. "Slavery's Pleasant Homes. A Faithful Sketch." 1843. *A Lydia Maria Child Reader.* Ed. Carolyn L. Karcher. Durham, N.C.: Duke University Press, 1997. 238–42.

———. "Willie Wharton." 1863. *A Lydia Maria Child Reader.* Ed. Carolyn L. Karcher. Durham, N.C.: Duke University Press, 1997. 47–78.

Clark, Elizabeth B. " 'The Sacred Rights of the Weak': Pain, Sympathy, and the Culture of Individual Rights in Antebellum America." *Journal of American History* 82.2 (Sept. 1995): 463–93.

Clinton, Catherine. *The Plantation Mistress: Woman's World in the Old South.* New York: Pantheon, 1982.

Cogan, Francis B. *All-American Girl: The Ideal of Real Womanhood in Mid-Nineteenth-Century America.* Athens: University of Georgia Press, 1989.

Cooper, Anna Julia Heywood. "Womanhood a Vital Element in the Regeneration and Progress of a Race." 1886. Logan 53–74.

Cooper, James Fenimore. *The Last of the Mohicans.* 1826. New York: Penguin Books, 1986.

Cullen, Jim. " 'I'se a Man Now': Gender and African American Men." *Divided Houses: Gender and the Civil War.* Ed. Catherine Clinton and Nina Silber. New York: Oxford University Press, 1992. 76–91.

Cummins, Maria Susanna. *The Lamplighter.* 1854. Ed. Nina Baym. New Brunswick, N.J.: Rutgers University Press, 1988.

"Cutting His Old Associates." Cartoon. *Harper's Weekly* 17 Jan. 1863: 48.

Davis, Lennard. *Enforcing Normalcy: Disability, Deafness, and the Body.* New York: Verso, 1995.

DeLombard, Jeannine. " 'Eye-Witness to the Cruelty': Southern Violence and Northern Testimony in Frederick Douglass's 1845 *Narrative.*" *American Literature* 73.2 (June 2001): 245–75.

DeMello, Margot. *Bodies of Inscription: A Cultural History of the Modern Tattoo Community.* Durham, N.C.: Duke University Press, 2000.

———. "The Carnivalesque Body: Women and Tattoos." *Pierced Hearts and True Love: A Century of Drawings for Tattoos.* Organized by the Drawing Center and Don Ed Hardy. New York: The Drawing Center and Hardy Marks Publications, 1995. 73–79.

Dennet, Andrea Stulman. *Weird and Wonderful: The Dime Museum in America.* New York: New York University Press, 1997.

Derounian-Stodola, Kathryn Zabelle. "The Captive and Her Editor: The Ciphering of Olive Oatman and Royal B. Stratton." *Prospects: An Annual of American Studies* 23 (1998): 171–92.

———. "The Indian Captivity Narratives of Mary Rowlandson and Olive Oatman: Case Studies in the Continuity, Evolution, and Exploitation of Literary Discourse." *Studies in the Literary Imagination* 27 (1994): 33–46.

———. Introduction. Derounian-Stodola, *Women's Indian Captivity Narratives,* xi–xxviii.

———, ed. *Women's Indian Captivity Narratives.* New York: Penguin Books, 1998.

Derounian-Stodola, Kathryn Zabelle, and James Arthur Levernier. *The Indian Captivity Narrative.* New York: Twayne, 1993.

Doane, Mary Ann. "Film and the Masquerade: Theorizing the Female Spectator." *Writing on the Body: Female Embodiment and Feminist Theory.* Ed. Katie Conboy, Nadia Medina, and Sarah Stanbury. New York: Columbia University Press, 1997. 176–94.

Dobson, Joanne. "The American Renaissance Reconsidered." *The (Other) American Tradition: Nineteenth-Century Women Writers.* Ed. Joyce W. Warren. New Brunswick, N.J.: Rutgers University Press, 1993. 164–82.

———. "Reclaiming Sentimental Literature." *American Literature* 69.2 (June 1997): 263–88.

Douglas, Ann. *The Feminization of American Culture.* New York: Avon, 1978.

Douglass, Frederick. *Narrative of the Life of Frederick Douglass, An American Slave.* 1845. Y. Taylor 528–99.

" 'Dr. Zorro' Leaves Mark on Patient's Abdomen." *Lincoln Journal Star* 22 Jan. 2000.

Dryden, Edgar. "Portraits of the Artist as a Young Man." *Critical Essays on Herman Melville's* Typee. Boston: G. K. Hall, 1982. 173–82.

Ebersole, Gary. *Captured by Texts: Puritan to Postmodern Images of Indian Captivity.* Charlottesville: University Press of Virginia, 1995.

Elbert, Sarah. Introduction. *Louisa May Alcott on Race, Sex, and Slavery.* Boston: Northeastern University Press, 1997. ix–lx.

Evans, Murray. "Surgeon Who Branded Uteri during Hysterectomies Target of Three Lawsuits." Associated Press 29 Aug. 2003. 396 words. 24 Jan. 2005. http://web.lexis-nexis.com.

Evelev, John. " 'Made in the Marquesas': *Typee,* Tattooing and Melville's Critique of the Literary Marketplace." *Arizona Quarterly* 48.4 (Winter 1992): 19–45.

Fetterley, Judith. *The Resisting Reader: A Feminist Approach to American Fiction.* Bloomington: Indiana University Press, 1978.

Finseth, Ian Frederick. Introduction. *The Narrative of the Adventures and Escape of Moses Roper.* Andrews 23–34.

Fisher, Philip. *Hard Facts: Setting and Form in the American Novel.* New York: Oxford University Press, 1985.

"Five Years among Wild Savages." Undated broadside. Everett D. Graff Collection. Newberry Library, Chicago.

Foner, Eric, ed. *Nat Turner.* Englewood Cliffs, N.J.: Prentice-Hall, 1971.

Foster, Frances Smith. *Witnessing Slavery: The Development of the Ante-bellum Slave Narrative.* Westport, Conn.: Greenwood, 1979.

Foucault, Michel. *Discipline and Punish: The Birth of the Prison.* 1975. New York: Vintage Books, 1995.

———. *The History of Sexuality: An Introduction.* 1976. New York: Vintage Books, 1990.

Fox-Genovese, Elizabeth. *Within the Plantation Household: Black and White Women of the Old South.* Chapel Hill: University of North Carolina Press, 1988.

Frankenberg, Ruth. *White Women, Race Matters: The Social Construction of Race.* Minneapolis: University of Minnesota Press, 1994.

Garay, Annabelle. "A Brand on an Organ Stirs Up Controversy." Associated Press 29 Jan. 2003. 245 words. 24 Jan. 24, 2005. http://web.lexis-nexis.com.

Gell, Alfred. *Wrapping in Images: Tattooing in Polynesia.* New York: Oxford University Press, 1993.

Gilman, Sander. *Making the Body Beautiful: A Cultural History of Aesthetic Surgery.* Princeton, N.J.: Princeton University Press, 1999.

Glatthaar, Joseph T. *Forged in Battle: The Civil War Alliance of Black Soldiers and White Officers.* New York: Macmillan, 1990.

Goshgarian, G. M. *To Kiss the Chastening Rod: Domestic Fiction and Sexual Ideology in the American Renaissance*. Ithaca, N.Y.: Cornell University Press, 1992.

Grandy, Moses. *Narrative of the Life of Moses Grandy*. Ed. Andrea N. Williams. Andrews 157–86.

Grimes, William. *Life of William Grimes, The Runaway Slave*. 1825. Y. Taylor 184–233.

Grosz, Elizabeth. "Intolerable Ambiguity: Freaks as/at the Limit." Thomson, *Freakery* 55–66.

———. *Volatile Bodies: Toward a Corporeal Feminism*. Bloomington: Indiana University Press, 1994.

Gunning, Sandra. *Rape, Race, and Lynching: The Red Record of American Literature, 1890–1913*. New York: Oxford University Press, 1996.

Halttunen, Karen. *Confidence Men and Painted Women: A Study of Middle-Class Culture in America, 1830–1870*. New Haven, Conn.: Yale University Press, 1982.

———. "Humanitarianism and the Pornography of Pain in Anglo-American Culture." *American Historical Review* 100.2 (Apr. 1995): 303–34.

———. *Murder Most Foul: The Killer and the American Gothic Imagination*. Cambridge, Mass.: Harvard University Press, 1998.

Haraway, Donna. "The Persistence of Vision." *Writing on the Body: Female Embodiment and Feminist Theory*. Ed. Katie Conroy, Nadia Medina, and Sarah Stanbury. New York: Columbia University Press, 1993. 283–95.

Harding, Brian. Explanatory notes. Hawthorne, *Scarlet Letter* 265–93.

Harper, Frances Ellen Watkins. *A Brighter Coming Day: A Frances Ellen Harper Reader*. Ed. Frances Smith Foster. New York: Feminist Press, 1990.

———. "Eliza Harris." *Complete Poems of Frances E. W. Harper*. Ed. Maryemma Graham. New York: Oxford University Press, 1988. 6.

———. *Iola Leroy, or Shadows Uplifted*. 1892. New York: Oxford University Press, 1988.

Harris, Susan K. *19th-Century American Women's Novels: Interpretive Strategies*. New York: Cambridge University Press, 1990.

Harris, Trudier. *Exorcising Blackness: Historical and Literary Lynching and Burning Rituals*. Bloomington: Indiana University Press, 1984.

Hart, James D. *The Popular Book: A History of America's Literary Taste*. New York: Oxford University Press, 1950.

Hartman, Saidiya. *Scenes of Subjection: Terror, Slavery, and Self-Making in Nineteenth-Century America*. New York: Oxford University Press, 1997.

Hawkes, Daina, Charlene Y. Senn, and Chantal Thorn. "Factors That Influence Attitudes toward Women with Tattoos." *Sex Roles* 50 (May 2004): 593–604.

Hawthorne, Nathaniel. "The Birthmark." *Young Goodman Brown and Other Tales*. Ed. Brian Harding. New York: Oxford University Press, 1987. 175–92.

———. "The Minister's Black Veil." *Young Goodman Brown and Other Tales*. Ed. Brian Harding. New York: Oxford University Press, 1987. 144–57.

———. *The Scarlet Letter.* 1850. Ed. Brian Harding. New York: Oxford University Press, 1990.

Hevey, David. *The Creatures Time Forgot: Photography and Disability Imagery.* London: Routledge, 1992.

Hodges, Graham Russell. Introduction. *Twenty-Two Years a Slave and Forty Years a Freeman.* By Austin Steward. Syracuse, N.Y.: Syracuse University Press, 2002. vi–xxxii.

Holden, Horace. *A Narrative of the Shipwreck, Captivity & Sufferings of Horace Holden and Benj. H. Nute.* 1836. Fairfield, Wash.: Ye Galleon, 1975.

hooks, bell. "The Oppositional Gaze: Black Female Spectators." 1992. *The Feminism and Visual Culture Reader.* Ed. Amelia Jones. London: Routledge, 2003. 94–105.

Hopkins, Pauline E. *Contending Forces: A Romance Illustrative of Negro Life North and South.* 1900. Ed. Richard Yarborough. New York: Oxford University Press, 1988.

———. "Reminiscences of the Life and Times of Lydia Maria Child." Parts 1–3. *Colored American Magazine* Feb. 1903: 279–84; Mar. 1903: 353–57; May/June 1903: 399–400.

Ignatiev, Noel. *How the Irish Became White.* New York: Routledge, 1995.

Jacobs, Harriet. *Incidents in the Life of a Slave Girl.* 1861. Cambridge, Mass.: Harvard University Press, 1987.

John H. Woodbury Dermatological Institute. Advertisement. *Leslie's Weekly* 26 May 1898: 344.

Johnson, Nan. *Gender and Rhetorical Space in American Life, 1866–1910.* Carbondale: Southern Illinois University Press, 2002.

Jones, Jacqueline. *Labor of Love, Labor of Sorrow: Black Women, Work, and the Family, from Slavery to the Present.* 1985. New York: Vintage, 1995.

Kasson, Joy S. *Buffalo Bill's Wild West: Celebrity, Memory, and Popular History.* New York: Hill and Wang, 2000.

———. *Marble Queens and Captives: Women in Nineteenth-Century American Sculpture.* New Haven, Conn.: Yale University Press, 1990.

Keetley, Dawn. "Victim and Victimizer: Female Fiends and Unease over Marriage in Antebellum Sensational Fiction." *American Quarterly* 51.2 (June 1999): 344–84.

Klages, Mary. *Woeful Afflictions: Disability and Sentimentality in Victorian America.* Philadelphia: University of Pennsylvania Press, 1999.

Klimasmith, Betsy. "Slave, Master, Mistress, Slave: Genre and Interracial Desire in Louisa May Alcott's Fiction." *ATQ* 11.2 (1997): 115–35.

Kolodny, Annette. *The Land before Her: Fantasy and Experience of the American Frontiers, 1630–1860.* Chapel Hill: University of North Carolina Press, 1984.

Kroeber, A. L. "Olive Oatman's Return." *Kroeber Anthropological Society Papers* 4 (1951): 1–18.

Kroeber, A. L., and Clifton B. Kroeber. "Olive Oatman's First Account of Her Captivity among the Mohave." *California Historical Society Quarterly* 41 (1962): 309–17.

Lapsansky, Phillip. "Graphic Discord: Abolitionist and Antiabolitionist Images." *The*

Abolitionist Sisterhood. Ed. Jean Fagan Yellin and John C. Van Horne. Ithaca, N.Y.: Cornell University Press, 1994. 201–30.

Leverenz, David. "Alive with Contradictions: Close Reading, Liberal Pluralism, and Nonnarratable Plots in *Uncle Tom's Cabin.*" *Approaches to Teaching Stowe's Uncle Tom's Cabin.* Ed. Elizabeth Ammons and Susan Belasco. New York: MLA, 2000. 120–31.

Liachowitz, Claire H. *Disability as a Social Construct: Legislative Roots.* Philadelphia: Pennsylvania University Press, 1988.

Lloyd-Smith, Allan Gardner. *Eve Tempted: Writing and Sexuality in Hawthorne's Fiction.* Totowa, N.J.: Barnes and Noble, 1984.

Logan, Shirley Wilson, ed. *With Pen and Voice: A Critical Anthology of Nineteenth-Century African American Women.* Carbondale: Southern Illinois University Press, 1995.

Long, Lisa A. *Rehabilitating Bodies: Health, History, and the American Civil War.* Philadelphia: University of Pennsylvania Press, 2004.

Looby, Christopher. "George Thompson's 'Romance of the Real': Transgression and Taboo in American Sensation Fiction." *American Literature* 65.4 (Dec. 1993): 651–72.

Lystra, Karen. *Searching the Heart: Women, Men, and Romantic Love in Nineteenth-Century America.* New York: Oxford University Press, 1989.

Mascia-Lees, Frances E., and Patricia Sharpe. "The Marked and the Un(re)Marked: Tattoo and Gender in Theory and Narrative." *Tattoo, Torture, Mutilation, and Adornment: The Denaturalization of the Body in Culture and Text.* Ed. Frances E. Mascia-Lees and Patricia Sharpe. Albany: State University of New York Press, 1992. 145–69.

Matlack, James Hendrickson. "The Literary Career of Elizabeth Barstow Stoddard." Diss. Yale University, 1968. Ann Arbor: UMI, 1968.

Matthews, Victoria Earle. "The Awakening of the Afro-American Woman." 1897. Logan 149–55.

Mayer, Henry. *All On Fire: William Lloyd Garrison and the Abolition of Slavery.* New York: St. Martin's, 1998.

McCullough, Kate. "Slavery, Sexuality, and Genre: Pauline Hopkins and the Representation of Female Desire." *The Unruly Voice: Rediscovering Pauline Hopkins.* Ed. John Cullen Gruesser. Urbana: University of Illinois Press, 1996. 21–49.

McPherson, James M. *The Negro's Civil War.* 1965. New York: Ballantine, 1991.

Melville, Herman. *Moby-Dick.* 1851. Ed. Herschel Parker and Harrison Hayford. New York: W. W. Norton, 2002.

———. *Omoo: A Narrative of Adventures in the South Seas.* 1847. Evanston, Ill.: Northwestern University Press and Newberry Library, 1968.

———. *Typee: A Peep at Polynesian Life.* 1846. Evanston, Ill.: Northwestern University Press and Newberry Library, 1968.

Mifflin, Margot. *Bodies of Subversion: A Secret History of Women and Tattoo.* New York: Juno Books, 1997.

Moody, Joycelyn. *Sentimental Confessions: Spiritual Narratives of Nineteenth-Century African American Women.* Athens: University of Georgia Press, 2001.

Moore, Margaret B. "Elizabeth Barstow Stoddard's 'Immortal Feather.' " *Hawthorne and Women: Engendering and Expanding the Hawthorne Tradition.* Ed. John L. Idol Jr. and Melinda M. Ponder. Boston: University of Massachusetts Press, 1999. 121–30.

Morrison, Toni. *Beloved.* New York: Penguin Books, 2000.

———. *Playing in the Dark: Whiteness and the Literary Imagination.* Cambridge, Mass.: Harvard University Press, 1992.

Mott, Frank Luther. *Golden Multitudes: The Story of Best Sellers in the United States.* New York: Macmillan, 1947.

Mulvey, Laura. "Visual Pleasure and Narrative Cinema." 1975. *The Feminism and Visual Culture Reader.* Ed. Amelia Jones. New York: Routledge, 2003. 44–53.

Namias, June. *White Captives: Gender and Ethnicity on the American Frontier.* Chapel Hill: University of North Carolina Press, 1993.

Nelson, Dana D. Introduction. Child, *Romance of the Republic* v–xxii.

Newman, Simon. "Reading the Bodies of Early American Seafarers." *William and Mary Quarterly* 40.1 (Jan. 1998): 59–82.

"Nine Women Want to Join Lawsuit against Surgeon over Branding." Associated Press 20 Feb. 2003. 719 words. 24 Jan. 2005. http://web.lexis-nexis.com.

Noble, Marianne. *The Masochistic Pleasures of Sentimental Literature.* Princeton, N.J.: Princeton University Press, 2000.

Northrup, Solomon. *Twelve Years a Slave: Narrative of Solomon Northrup, a Citizen of New-York, Kidnapped in Washington City in 1841, and Rescued in 1853, from a Cotton Plantation near the Red River, in Louisiana.* 1853. Ed. Sue Eakin and Joseph Logsdon. Baton Rouge: Louisiana State University Press, 1968.

Oettermann, Stephan. "On Display: Tattooed Entertainers in America and Germany." *Written on the Body: The Tattoo in European and American History.* Ed. Jane Caplan. Princeton, N.J.: Princeton University Press, 2000. 193–211.

Otter, Samuel. *Melville's Anatomies.* Berkeley: University of California Press, 1999.

Painter, Nell Irvin. *Sojourner Truth: A Life, a Symbol.* New York: W. W. Norton, 1996.

———. "Soul Murder and Slavery: Toward a Fully Loaded Cost Accounting." *U.S. History as Women's History: New Feminist Essays.* Ed. Linda K. Kerber, Alice Kessler-Harris, and Kathryn Kish Sklar. Chapel Hill: University of North Carolina Press, 1995. 125–46.

Papashvily, Helen. *All the Happy Endings.* New York: Harper, 1956.

Parker, Herschel. *Herman Melville: A Biography.* Baltimore: Johns Hopkins University Press, 1996.

Parry, Albert. *Tattoo: Secrets of a Strange Art Practiced by the Natives of the United States.* 1933. New York: Collier, 1971.

Pattee, Fred Lewis. *The Feminine Fifties.* New York: D. Appleton-Century, 1940.

Patterson, Mark. "Racial Sacrifice and Citizenship: The Construction of Masculinity in Louisa May Alcott's 'The Brothers.' " *Studies in American Fiction* 25 (1997): 147–66.

Patterson, Orlando. *Slavery and Social Death: A Comparative Study*. Cambridge, Mass.: Harvard University Press, 1982.

Patton, Venetria. *Women in Chains: The Legacy of Slavery in Black Women's Fiction*. Albany: State University of New York Press, 2000.

Perry, Phyllis Alesia. *Stigmata*. New York: Hyperion, 1998.

Peterson, Carla. *"Doers of the Word": African-American Women Speakers and Writers in the North (1830–1880)*. New York: Oxford University Press, 1995.

Pettid, Edward J. "Olive Ann Oatman's Lecture Notes and the Oatman Bibliography." *San Bernardino Museum Association Quarterly* 16 (Winter 1968): 1–39.

Piepmeier, Alison. *Out in Public: Configurations of Women's Bodies in Nineteenth-Century America*. Chapel Hill: University of North Carolina Press, 2004.

Pitts, Victoria. *In the Flesh: The Cultural Politics of Body Modification*. New York: Palgrave Macmillan, 2003.

Putzi, Jennifer. "Harriet Prescott Spofford." *American Women Prose Writers, 1870–1920*. Detroit: Gale Group, 2000. 322–31.

Reynolds, David S. *Beneath the American Renaissance: The Subversive Imagination in the Age of Emerson and Melville*. Cambridge, Mass.: Harvard University Press, 1988.

Reynolds, David S., and Kimberly R. Gladman. Introduction. *Venus in Boston and Other Tales of Nineteenth-Century City Life*. By George Thompson. Amherst: University of Massachusetts Press, 2002. ix–liv.

Rice, William B. "The Captivity of Olive Oatman: A Newspaper Account." *California Historical Society Quarterly* 21 (1942): 97–106.

Riley, Glenda. *Inventing the American Woman: An Inclusive History*. Vol. 1. 2nd ed. Wheeling, Ill.: Harlan Davidson, 1995.

Roediger, David R. *Colored White: Transcending the Racial Past*. Berkeley: University of California Press, 2002.

———. *The Wages of Whiteness: Race and the Making of the American Working Class*. New York: Verso, 1991.

Root, Virginia. "Following the Pot of Gold at the Rainbow's End in the Days of 1859. The Life of Mrs. Susan Thompson Lewis Parrish of El Monte, California." 8 pp. typescript. Henry E. Huntington Library, San Marino, California.

Roper, Moses. *A Narrative of the Adventures and Escape of Moses Roper, from American Slavery*. 1838. Y. Taylor 489–521.

Ruland, Richard. "Melville and the Fortunate Fall: Typee as Eden." *Critical Essays on Herman Melville's Typee*. Boston: G. K. Hall, 1982. 183–92.

Russo, Mary. *The Female Grotesque: Risk, Excess, and Modernity*. New York: Routledge, 1995.

Ryan, Susanna. " 'Perversions of Volition': Self-Starvation and Self-Possession in Dickinson and Stoddard." *American Culture, Canons, and the Case of Elizabeth Stoddard*. Ed. Robert McClure Smith and Ellen Weinauer. Tuscaloosa: University of Alabama Press, 2003. 128–48.

Samson, John. *White Lies: Melville's Narration of Facts*. Ithaca, N.Y.: Cornell University Press, 1989.

Samuels, Shirley, ed. *The Culture of Sentiment: Race, Gender, and Sentimentality in Nineteenth-Century America.* New York: Oxford University Press, 1992.

———. "The Identity of Slavery." Samuels, *Culture of Sentiment* 157–71.

Sanchez-Eppler, Karen. *Touching Liberty: Abolition, Feminism, and the Politics of the Body.* Berkeley: University of California Press, 1997.

Sanders, Clinton R. *Customizing the Body: The Art and Culture of Tattooing.* Philadelphia: Temple University Press, 1989.

Savage, Kirk. *Standing Soldiers, Kneeling Slaves: Race, War, and Monument in Nineteenth-Century America.* Princeton, N.J.: Princeton University Press, 1997.

Sayre, Gordon M. *Les Sauvages Americains: Representations of Native Americans in French and English Colonial Literature.* Chapel Hill: University of North Carolina Press, 1997.

Scarry, Elaine. *The Body in Pain: The Making and Unmaking of the World.* New York: Oxford University Press, 1985.

Sedgwick, Catharine Maria. *Hope Leslie.* 1827. New Brunswick, N.J.: Rutgers University Press, 1987.

Shakinovsky, Lynn. "The Return of the Repressed: Illiteracy and the Death of the Narrative in Hawthorne's 'The Birthmark.' " *ATQ* 9.4 (Dec. 1995): 269–81.

"Six Years' Captivity among the Indians—Narrative of Miss Olive Oatman." *New York Times* 4 May 1858: 5.

Slotkin, Richard. *Regeneration through Violence: The Mythology of the American Frontier, 1600–1860.* Middleton, Conn.: Wesleyan University Press, 1973.

Smith, Robert McClure, and Ellen Weinauer. "Introduction: Crossing Can(n)on Street." *American Culture, Canons, and the Case of Elizabeth Stoddard.* Ed. Robert McClure Smith and Ellen Weinauer. Tuscaloosa: University of Alabama Press, 2003. 1–20.

Sofer, Naomi Z. *Making the "America of Art": Cultural Nationalism and Nineteenth-Century Women Writers.* Columbus: Ohio State University Press, 2005.

Sontag, Susan. *Regarding the Pain of Others.* New York: Picador, 2003.

Sorisio, Carolyn. *Fleshing Out America: Race, Gender, and the Politics of the Body in American Literature, 1833–1879.* Athens; University of Georgia Press, 2002.

Spillers, Hortense. "Mama's Baby, Papa's Maybe: An American Grammar Book." *diacritics* 17.2 (Summer 1987): 65–81.

Spofford, Harriet Prescott. "The Strathsays." *Atlantic Monthly* 11 (Jan. 1863): 99–118.

Stallybrass, Peter, and Allon White. *The Politics and Poetics of Transgression.* Ithaca, N.Y.: Cornell University Press, 1986.

Sterling, Dorothy, ed. *We Are Your Sisters: Black Women in the Nineteenth Century.* New York: W. W. Norton, 1984.

Stern, Julia. " 'I Am Cruel Hungry': Dramas of Twisted Appetite and Rejected Identification in Elizabeth Stoddard's *The Morgesons.*" *American Culture, Canons, and the Case of Elizabeth Stoddard.* Ed. Robert McClure Smith and Ellen Weinauer. Tuscaloosa: University of Alabama Press, 2003. 107–27.

Stevenson, Brenda E. *Life in Black and White: Family and Community in the Slave South.* New York: Oxford University Press, 1996.

Steward, Austin. *Twenty-Two Years a Slave and Forty Years a Freeman.* Rochester: William Alling, 1857. Syracuse: Syracuse University Press, 2002.

Stoddard, Elizabeth. "Letters to Edmund Clarence Stedman." *The Morgesons and Other Writings, Published and Unpublished.* Ed. Lawrence Buell and Sandra A. Zagarell. Philadelphia: University of Pennsylvania Press, 1984. 335–38.

———. *The Morgesons.* 1862. *The Morgesons and Other Writings, Published and Unpublished.* Ed. Lawrence Buell and Sandra A. Zagarell. Philadelphia: University of Pennsylvania Press, 1984.

———. *Two Men.* 1865. New York: Johnson Reprint, 1971.

Stone, Deborah A. *The Disabled State.* Philadelphia: Temple University Press, 1984.

Stowe, Harriet Beecher. *A Key to Uncle Tom's Cabin.* 1853. Bedford, Mass.: Applewood, 1998.

———. *Uncle Tom's Cabin.* 1852. Ed. Elizabeth Ammons. New York: W. W. Norton, 1994.

Stratton, Royal B. *Captivity of the Oatman Girls.* 2nd ed. San Francisco: Whitton, Towne, 1857.

———. *Captivity of the Oatman Girls.* 1858. 3rd ed. Lincoln: University of Nebraska Press, 1983.

———. *Life among the Indians: Being an Interesting Narrative of the Captivity of the Oatman Girls.* 1st ed. San Francisco: Whitton, Towne, 1857.

Tate, Claudia. *Domestic Allegories of Political Desire: The Black Heroine's Text at the Turn of the Century.* New York: Oxford University Press, 1992.

Taylor, Edith S., and William J. Wallace. "Mohave Tattooing and Face-Painting." *Southwest Museum Leaflets* 20 (1947): 1–13.

Taylor, Louise, and Greg Kocher. "Doctor Is Sued over Branding of Uterus." *Lexington Herald-Leader* 25 Jan. 2003: A1.

Taylor, Yuval, ed. *I Was Born a Slave: An Anthology of Classic Slave Narratives.* Chicago: Lawrence Hill, 1999.

Thompson, George. *City Crimes; or Life in New York and Boston.* 1849. *Venus in Boston and Other Tales of Nineteenth-Century City Life.* Ed. David S. Reynolds and Kimberly R. Gladman. Amherst: University of Massachusetts Press, 2002. 105–310.

Thomson, Rosemarie Garland. "Crippled Girls and Lame Old Women: Sentimental Spectacles of Sympathy in Nineteenth-Century American Women's Writing." *Nineteenth-Century American Women Writers: A Critical Reader.* Ed. Karen L. Kilcup. Malden, Mass.: Blackwell, 1998. 128–45.

———. *Extraordinary Bodies: Figuring Physical Disability in American Culture and Literature.* New York: Columbia University Press, 1997.

———, ed. *Freakery: Cultural Spectacles of the Extraordinary Body.* New York: New York University Press, 1996.

Tolnay, Stewart E., and E. M. Beck. *A Festival of Violence: An Analysis of Southern Lynchings, 1882–1930.* Urbana: University of Illinois Press, 1995.

Tompkins, Jane. *Sensational Designs: The Cultural Work of American Fiction, 1790–1860.*
    New York: Oxford University Press, 1985.
"A Tour through Arizona." *Harper's New Monthly Magazine* Nov. 1864: 689–711.
Truth, Sojourner. *Narrative of Sojourner Truth, a Northern Slave. Classic African
    American Women's Narratives.* Ed. William L. Andrews. New York: Oxford
    University Press, 2003. 42–126.
———. "Speech Delivered to the Women's Rights Convention, Akron, Ohio (1851)
    [Campbell Version]." Logan 26–27.
Turner, Arlin. *Nathaniel Hawthorne: A Biography.* New York: Oxford University Press,
    1980.
"A Typical Negro." *Harper's Weekly* 4 July 1863: 429–30.
Washburn, Wilcomb E. Foreword. *Captivity of the Oatman Girls.* By R. B. Stratton.
    Lincoln: University of Nebraska Press, 1983. v–xv.
Webster, J. Carson. *Erastus D. Palmer.* Cranbury, N.J.: Associated University Presses,
    1983.
Weir, Sybil. "*The Morgesons*: A Neglected Bildungsroman." *New England Quarterly* 49
    (1976): 427–39.
———. "Our Lady Correspondent: The Achievement of Elizabeth Drew Stoddard."
    San Jose Studies 10.2 (Spring 1984): 73–91.
Weld, Theodore Dwight, ed. *American Slavery as It Is: Testimony of a Thousand
    Witnesses.* 1839. New York: Arno, 1968.
Wendell, Susan. *The Rejected Body: Feminist Philosophical Reflections on Disability.*
    New York: Routledge, 1996.
Wexler, Laura. "Tender Violence: Literary Eavesdropping, Domestic Fiction, and
    Educational Reform." Samuels, *Culture of Sentiment* 9–38.
Wiegman, Robyn. *American Anatomies: Theorizing Race and Gender.* Durham, N.C.:
    Duke University Press, 1995.
Williams, Andreá N. Introduction. *Narrative of the Life of Moses Grandy.* Andrews
    133–51.
Williams, Sherley Anne. *Dessa Rose.* New York: William Morrow, 1986.
Wolff, Cynthia. " 'Masculinity' in *Uncle Tom's Cabin.*" *American Quarterly* 47 (1995):
    595–618.
Yellin, Jean Fagan. *Women and Sisters: The Antislavery Feminists in American Culture.*
    New Haven, Conn.: Yale University Press, 1989.
Young, Elizabeth. *Disarming the Nation: Women's Writing and the American Civil War.*
    Chicago: University of Chicago Press, 1999.
Zagarell, Sandra A. "The Repossession of a Heritage: Elizabeth Stoddard's *The
    Morgesons.*" *Studies in American Fiction* 13.1 (Spring 1985): 45–56.
Zanjani, Sally. *Sarah Winnemucca.* Lincoln: University of Nebraska Press, 2001.
Zitkala-Ša. "The School Days of an Indian Girl." *Classic American Autobiographies.* Ed.
    William L. Andrews. New York: Penguin Books, 1992.

INDEX